fP

ALSO BY LEE EISENBERG

Breaking Eighty: A Journey Through the Nine Fairways of Hell

THE NUMBER

WHAT DO YOU NEED FOR THE REST OF YOUR LIFE, AND WHAT WILL IT COST?

LEE EISENBERG

FREE PRESS
New York London Toronto Sydney

This book contains the opinions and ideas of its author. Neither the author nor the publisher is engaged in rendering investment, financial, accounting, legal, tax, insurance or other professional advice or services. If the reader requires such advice or services, a competent professional should be consulted. Both the author and publisher specifically disclaim any responsibility for any liability, loss or risk, personal or otherwise, which is incurred as a consequence, directly or indirectly, of the use and application of any of the contents of this book.

*f*P
FREE PRESS
A Division of Simon & Schuster, Inc.
1230 Avenue of the Americas
New York, NY 10020

Copyright © 2006 by Lee Eisenberg
All rights reserved,
including the right of reproduction
in whole or in part in any form.

First Free Press trade paperback edition 2007

FREE PRESS and colophon are trademarks of Simon & Schuster, Inc.

For information regarding special discounts for bulk purchases,
please contact Simon & Schuster Special Sales at 1-800-456-6798
or business@simonandschuster.com.

Designed by Helene Berinsky

Manufactured in the United States of America

1   3   5   7   9   10   8   6   4   2

The Library of Congress has cataloged the hardcover edition as follows:
Eisenberg, Lee, 1946–
The number : a completely different way to think about the rest of your life / Lee Eisenberg.
p. cm.
Includes index.
ISBN 0-7432-7031-2
1. Finance, Personal.   2. Retirement—Planning.   3. Quality of work life.
4. Quality of life.   5. Lifestyles—Economic aspects.   I. Title.

HG179.E387 2006
332.024'0145—dc22   2005051870

ISBN-13: 978-0-7432-7031-1
ISBN-10:   0-7432-7031-2
ISBN-13: 978-0-7432-7032-8 (Pbk)
ISBN-10:   0-7432-7032-0 (Pbk)

For Linda, Ned, and Katherine—
the perfect investment

CONTENTS

PART THREE

FINDING IT

PROLOGUE

MAKING HAY

In the early spring of 2004, I ended a five-year stint at a job I never could have imagined, in a part of the world that was never part of the plan. The unexpected detour started with a phone call on a cold winter afternoon. At that moment I was half in, half out of the workplace—downshifting, as it's called these days. My wife, Linda, our two young kids, and I were living a comfortable life in a pleasant New York suburb. A few days a week I worked on articles and a book. On the other days I hopped the Metro North line to Manhattan, where I had a consulting arrangement at Time Inc. My job there was to think up blue-sky projects for *Time* magazine. I spent my hours brainstorming ideas for special issues and new projects such as a newsweekly for grade school kids. But during those morning and evening commutes I secretly agonized over whether I had enough money socked away to be so casually employed.

I was worried about the Number.

The man on the phone was the vice chairman of Lands' End, at the time a public company with revenues approaching two billion dollars. Lands' End meant very little to me. Like many occasional customers, I viewed it as interchangeable with its archrival, L.L.Bean. Both sold sturdy preppy clothing, canvas tote bags, and goose-down everything else. But I did know that Lands' End was admired for its folksy phone operators, who dispensed friendly service from a little town in the Midwest.

The vice chairman told me that Lands' End had recently appointed a new CEO whose mandate was to bring new energy to the company. The Lands' End catalogs, he said, needed more surprise and sizzle. The company wanted to revitalize the brand. He said the company was looking for a publishing type who could generate covers and features you'd be more likely to find in national magazines than in clothing catalogs. Lands' End wanted some fresh juice in its national advertising and someone to help advance its fledgling online business. All this would fall into my area, the vice chairman said, trying his best to set my chinos on fire. He wondered whether I'd have even a remote interest in flying to Madison, Wisconsin, then trekking out to company headquarters in Dodgeville, a tiny hamlet some forty miles west of the capital.

Was he smoking prairie weed? The idea of me in the pajama game was surreal. The closest I'd ever come to the garment trade was back when I edited *Esquire*. I was obliged to take regular trips to Paris and Milan, where I schmoozed menswear designers from Armani to Zegna. *Esquire* depended on the men's clothing industry for much of its advertising. Fashion pages were its commercial lifeblood. Nonetheless, I regarded these trips as delightful boondoggles, days of wine and risotto. Once back at the office, and until I longed again for a steamy bowl of brodetto, the menswear pages dropped to the bottom of my priority list. I didn't know a placket from a mitered yoke.

As for Wisconsin, had you shown me a map, put a pistol to my head, and asked me to identify the state, I would have straightaway pointed to Minnesota. To my astonishment, though, I found myself listening to the vice chairman's pitch with wary curiosity. He was an interesting guy who'd once been a mover and shaker in the advertising business. I vaguely knew that in the 1980s he'd left Madison Avenue to serve at the right hand of Lands' End's founder. Under his watch the company grew into a direct-marketing juggernaut. Lands' End was solidly profitable. Thanks to an IPO and a consistently healthy balance sheet, the firm bestowed some big numbers on a handful of people, including the man on the phone. But it wasn't his net worth that mattered. It was how he chose to use the outsize Number he'd acquired. He enjoyed a golden-age lifestyle most of us would die for, details of which I was to glean from others who knew the company from the inside.

The vice chairman grew up a working-class kid in Chicago. When he retired from active duty at Lands' End, he and his wife restored a splendid farmhouse on a spectacular Vermont hillside. A chocolate Lab at his side, he was the picture-perfect gentleman farmer, favoring Lobb custom-made boots, French silk socks, and moleskin trousers. He lorded over a prizewinning herd of Belted Galloways, 1,300-pound bovines that are as close to designer cattle as cows may reasonably aspire to. He also had a passion for thoroughbreds, so he acquired a stake in a top-tier Kentucky racing stable. What did it take to pull all this off? Forty, sixty, a hundred million dollars? One can speculate. But it was plain that this man had more than enough acorns squirreled away up there in New England to indulge his luxurious enthusiasms for the rest of his days.

The same could hardly be said for my own long-term prospects, which is why, to my own surprise, I was already halfway hooked. Even as I put down the phone, I braced for the reaction of friends and family: *Are you out of your mind?* I thought about how I might possibly explain it. I could say that I was genetically encoded to go into the clothing business, citing an uncle who back in the fifties worked for a Seventh Avenue dress company and traveled the South with a trunkful of samples. But even a dumb-ass Wisconsin dairy cow was smart enough to figure out that any move to the heartland had nothing to do with a latent chromosome—and everything to do with money.

When I told my wife about the Lands' End call, she put on her L.L.Bean barn coat and, without saying a word, took the dog for a walk. She was gone for so long I began to wonder if she'd left me. Wisconsin?

Why not Uzbekistan? Iceland? At the time we believed we had just settled down for the long term. And the reasons to stay put were overwhelming.

We were, first of all, well into the middle of middle age. I was fifty-two, my wife a few years younger. We had kids who were just seven and nine; we felt strongly that they should grow up rooted to a place. We had chosen the place after much torturous thought and planning.

Second, all of our friends, as well as my wife's family, lived in and around New York. The only person in Wisconsin whose name I could immediately recall was Brett Favre, and my wife had never heard of him.

Third, we'd pretty much come to accept that our professional years were winding down. Why fight the clock? The graceful thing to do was exactly what we were doing—surrender to part-time, then no-time, careers.

Fourth, we had just renovated a house barely thirty minutes from midtown, turning its ample garden into just one of the many things we loved about the place.

Fifth, like everyone else we knew, we had aging parents who'd doubtless need more care in the years ahead. Wisconsin would take us very far away. Why even think about turning our lives inside out at this stage?

Well, here's why:

We often talked about how ten years down the road our kids' combined college tuition would amount to half a million dollars, this according to the online calculators I'd peck at glumly in the hush of night. Although we cherished the house and garden, that freshly minted property happened to be located in one of America's most expensive real estate markets. The giant sucking sound we heard from our newly laid stone patio was a $25,000 property tax bill. Gross that up and you're talking $50,000 in retirement income just to cover it. Those taxes would only go up. And there was always the prospect of a catastrophic illness, years of nursing care, assisted living, should things come to a not-so-pretty pass in the decades that remained. Anyone in the mood for a big nut?

On the plus side, we were fortunate to have a decent reserve stashed away. By most standards we were certainly comfortable—not Bill Gates comfortable, but sufficiently flush that we'd never have to worry about setting up house in an empty Sub-Zero carton. But the question of whether we had achieved a sufficient Number, whether we had enough to shelter us from life's jolts, nagged at me more days than not. *Did* we have enough? How much *is* enough? And if we didn't have enough, what compromises, and sacrifices, were we prepared to make?

With these anxieties swirling, I boarded the Lands' End company plane and headed west on a clear, starry night. Within days I'd accepted an offer. Just like that, I was working in Dodgeville (pop. 3,022), bedding down in the town's Best Western while icy winds rattled the windows. (Imagine *The Shining,* only this time in a motel.) When the school-term ended that spring, my wife, kids, and faithful if bewildered dog—hopelessly strung out on canine Valium—stepped off the plane just in time to see the prairie flowers bloom in our new backyard.

To the hoots of family and friends, I gamely tried to explain our departure in terms that were anything but financial. I said I wanted to experience at least one more intense chapter in my curiously erratic career. I said Lands' End was appealing because it was a company with a powerful culture dedicated to treating its employees and customers with uncompromised integrity. I said I wanted to take part in the Web frenzy, help the company seize an evident opportunity in the flashy New Economy. I said that having been the "creative guy" all my life, I wanted a chance to play in the grownups' sandbox. As a member of the executive committee of a public corporation I'd have dealings with Wall Street analysts and investment bankers—a dubious attraction but for some reason intriguing at the time. Although each of these reasons was true, what I didn't get into was the Number. I never came right out and said it, but our move was a swing for the financial fences. Which, of course, everybody already knew.

That first summer we took frequent evening drives through rolling farm country and tried to convince ourselves that we'd done the right thing. The fact was, the Number was leading us around by our noses. The landscape was bucolic, and the sky bright and boundless, yet every road looked alike and we didn't have a damn clue as to where we were. I'll spare you the details of the rest of the epic detour. Except for this: two and a half years into the tour of duty, Sears, Roebuck and Company lumbered into the picture and made a drop-dead offer for Lands' End. Sears hoped that by adding Lands' End merchandise to its stores it could induce more people to shop there. (Searing strategic insight: 192-piece Craftsman lug wrench sets and Kenmore dryers don't generate impromptu visits to a mall-bound Sears.) For the Lands' End crew, the change of control meant that stock options automatically vested and employees could cash in their chits.

Shortly after this, I began to think it was time to put the world of casual bottoms (trade term for chinos, jeans, sport-knit pants) behind me. My wife and I sat down with a financial adviser. We bared our assets and asked him what it would take to be confident about a second-half life that met expectations. No fancy Scottish cows or fractional jets; just a house we liked; decent standard of travel and leisure; education and health costs covered. We were in good shape, he said. And we were. The kids had adjusted well to the move. I'd gotten a chance to work at a terrific company with the most extraordinary and committed workforce. We were beyond fortunate at a time when so many others in the country were fighting job loss and health problems. Still, littered across his printouts were a lot of ifs, maybes, and who-the-hell knows?

At Christmastime, a few months before I was to leave Lands' End, we took our kids to Paris. We told ourselves this was an academic investment because they were both studying French and the trip would be instructive. Truth was, my wife and I were in the mood to celebrate, grope at our next chapter, wherever that might lead. One night we arranged to get together with friends, an American couple more or less in our position who had recently packed up their young kids and moved to Paris full-time, leasing an apartment in a lovely part of the city. They had enrolled their kids in a bilingual academy. Dad, a writer, took French lessons every day and worked on smart, well-crafted books. In the afternoon he picked up his kids at school and enjoyed quality time. Très Adam Gopnik. His wife, intelligent and charming, also studied French, delving into the joys of a new place. What could be bad?

Over drinks we talked about where our lives were heading. The short version: full retirement was still a long way off, though it was great not to go to an office every day. To stay busy, useful, and flexible, that was the trick. As for the Number, who could be sure? It was a passport to live here or there. Otherwise, what good was it?

Not long after we returned to Wisconsin, I started to think about this book. I began to ask men and women in their forties and fifties how confident they were about the rest of their lives. They, too, were mainly people on the lucky end of the disparity curve. Do you have a plan? I asked. I discovered right away that almost no one wanted to talk about it, although they would admit that they saw themselves coming to a fork in the road. One fork, a man told me, leads to cranky, self-pitying old age, the other to years of physical and intellectual vigor. He said he was hell-bent on taking the latter fork. Well, you can afford to, I said to him. The man was well fixed. He had a solid consulting deal, worked half the year and traveled the other half. He and his wife, to whom he is devoted, have an understanding. If he wants to mountain-bike through Bhutan, he picks up and goes.

"Yes, money helps," he said. "But in the end it's irrelevant." He talked with fervor about the men and women in their seventies, sometimes eighties, who are his companions on Elderhostel bike trips and other adventures. "Most of them have very little money," he told me. "But they are among the most extraordinary, upbeat, and well-adjusted people I've ever known."

• • •

This book is about money, but ultimately it's about the life you want, the life you don't, and the costs of each.

For tens of millions of middle-aged travelers, this is an odd moment, riddled with paradoxes. We are at once old and young, parents and kids, generally prosperous yet uneasy. For me, this moment evokes a memory—late afternoon, back when I watched the Phillies play in the final years of decrepit Connie Mack Stadium. I remember how the shadows sliced across the diamond, moving closer and closer to home plate until half the field was in bright sunlight, the other in gathering darkness. It was a really weird time of day.

PART ONE

CHASING IT

1

WELCOME TO NUMBERLAND

There's a large crowd gathered at the intersection of Easy Street and Middle Age Boulevard. Financial planners, tax preparers, estate lawyers, assisted living and nursing home developers, urologists, proctologists, cosmetic surgeons, pharmaceutical companies, AARP, the Weather Channel, makers of ocular implants and magnifying glasses, Sunbelt chambers of commerce, politicians, and restaurants with early-bird specials are among the interested parties vying for prime storefront locations on the corner of Easy and Middle Age. Chances are, you're on the way there, too, facing some nasty questions you'd just as soon duck.

What are the chances that you'll live out your days in comfort? Do you have what it takes right now? What happens if you don't make it to your Number? And, assuming you're not fighting for sheer survival, what are you prepared to give up? Are you open-minded about living in a place that's about the size of your family room?

Are you ready for the good news and bad news that's around the bend? That you'll live longer than you ever figured, which is the good news. And that you'll live longer than you ever figured, which is also the bad news. Are you up for the challenge that this extended stay will call for a great deal of planning, and you'll be the sole proprietor of that effort? Do you have a plan for all this?

I've got manila folders full of partial answers and clues, a growing archive dutifully arranged in a file cabinet that's a monument to things we'd rather not think about: the Cabinet of Dread and Denial. Stored inside are folders labeled Debt, Aging, Long-Term Care. The file at hand, Self-Absorption, is stuffed with research reports and newspaper clippings about baby boomers berating themselves for being spoiled and reckless spendthrifts. Boomer bashing is so intense the *New York Times* ran a piece about the trend recently. It quoted Daniel Okrent in *Time* magazine: "As unforgiving as the present has become, our future could be bleaker. It is truly stunning how financially unprepared for retirement boomers are." The paper also interviewed Joe Queenan, author of a "short but self-important history" of the baby boom, who bloviated: "I loathe my generation. We became culturally frozen in time at a very early age and continue to think of ourselves as trailblazers. It's completely pathetic."

There's a growing urgency in this kind of boomer doomsday commentary. It's not just hectoring-as-usual. The clippings say that this is the moment when tens of millions of people should be getting down to business. Retirement is right around the corner. If boomers are ever to become serious about saving, to sign up for a twelve-step Spenders Anonymous program, that time is now. And yet too few are doing so, according to the research papers piled high in front of me. Everyone's still grazing at the trough. All kinds of data bear this out. I could easily extract the facts and figures from these files and turn them into the rest of the book, but the story isn't found in the numbers, it's found between the ears. If it's reams of data you're after, go to the Internet. Go to AARP. Go to the think tanks and academic research sites. Log onto the big financial services. There you'll find all the data you could possibly want about the costs and challenges of second-half life. And you'll also find every imaginable financial product, in such profusion they'll make your head spin.

For my part, I'll try to keep the numbers short and sweet. Just a handful of statistics will confirm that America may be a nation of red states, but decidedly not a nation of Little Red Hens. Forty percent of those asked say they are saving nothing for the future. Americans put aside barely a penny out of every dollar they earn. In 2004 the national savings rate was the lowest since 1959. Instead, these people are spending money like crazy. They're spending on things they need, things they want. Groceries and prescription drugs. Beer and cigarettes. Ralph Lauren Purple Label and Christmas in Cabo.

Of workers fifty-five and older, only one in four has invested assets of more than $100,000; one in three has less than $50,000. One out of every two baby boomers will not have accumulated enough to match their current standard of living. Nearly one of two boomers say they are less than confident they will outlive their money.

If there are sleepless nights associated with these numbers, I don't hear people talking about them. If there's anxiety, I can't detect it with the naked eye. The folks I see on airplanes are confident and relaxed and seem to have their acts together. Just about everybody is happily attached to an iPod. Recently I sat near a woman who had hers tucked away in a little Gucci case trimmed in silver and leather. If she can afford $195 to wrap her music player in a honeycomb of double Gs, can we assume she has a handle on debt, a tidy bundle in her retirement plan? That she isn't losing sleep over the Social Security trust fund?

The numbers in my file suggest that she and many others must be feeling the heat. They indicate that Gucci-toting street-jammers are likely to be carrying five-figure debt loads just on their credit cards, that they have little more than fumes in their 401(k)s, and that they probably know more about the details of Paris Hilton's trust fund than about Social Security's. No, I take that back. Maybe they know more now. Social Security has been in the news quite a lot, almost nudging the Hilton sisters off the front page.

NUMBER ANXIETY

Ask people what their Number is, and what it means, and you get answers that range from bluster to blank stares. When I ask a successful Wall Street broker what the Number signifies to him, he promptly offers the standard Street definition, predictably succinct: "It's fuck-you money," he declaims, jaw jutting. It's how much he feels he needs to walk away on his own terms, never to look back. Note that he doesn't say it's how much he needs so he can take time off to write the play that's always been in him or finance a children's health clinic in Haiti.

I talk with a savvy hedge fund partner. He's exceedingly interested in the fact that I'm writing a book about the Number, and he's more than pleased to share at least three unassailable verities (that is, as unassailable as verities ever are on Wall Street).

The first is that everyone he knows harbors a very specific Number and most require no more than a minimal prod—a mere sip of a martini, two olives, served in a glass that's three times bigger than it should be—to boast about what his Number is, down to the last mil.

The second unassailable verity, the money man says, is that his buddies on the Street are continually retiring one Number and launching a new one. I hear this quite frequently from people who work downtown. For a master of the universe, to ratchet up a self-proclaimed Number is no more momentous than adjusting a necktie. This man says that when he started out as a junior broker twenty-five years ago, he set his personal trigger at a million dollars, which he had pseudo-humbly regarded as a "hugely vast sum." Then his Number quickly ballooned to five million. Then fifteen. As of today, it's north of thirty, although it will probably be higher by the time you get to the end of this paragraph. He says that everybody he knows sets and resets their Number all the time. It doesn't matter if you're inconspicuous in your consumption of houses and toys or are a Dennis Kozlowski. Whatever you thought your Number was at age thirty will strike you as amusing by the time you're forty, a regular laugh riot at fifty.

The third unassailable verity is that even though everybody he knows spends their time recalibrating their Numbers, almost nobody walks away. Rarely does somebody say, "Screw you, I'm gone!" While people on Wall Street harbor the illusion that the Number equals freedom, they rarely cash it in for that. "What could they possibly do with freedom?" my man asks. "Most of these guys are about two things. Money and golf. And even *they* know they'd go nuts playing golf every day."

While money mavens swagger over their Numbers, reasonably affluent people stammer and stutter when the subject comes up. They would sooner offer personal guided tours through their medicine cabinets, provide detailed dossiers on their sessions with psychotherapists and cosmetic surgeons, or describe in graphic detail which particular sex acts they long to perform with this or that man, woman, or farm animal, and with what boot, whip, kitchen appliance, or hand tool. The Number, I have come to understand, is the Last Taboo.

This was an insight I had in my grasp a few years ago, yet hadn't realized how blindingly incisive it was. At the time I just thought I was being obnoxious, which was also true. One day on a golf course I casually teased a friend about how well he and his wife, Manhattan attorneys, seemed to be doing. When I saw how much this gratuitous, inane observation annoyed him, I went further. Just as he was lining up a putt, I asked how much they'd managed to sock away. He missed the putt, never answered, and has pretty much not spoken to me since. Nor do I blame him.

At dinner one night on New York's West Side, I bring up the Number with a couple I've known for years. They are financially secure but not loaded. Because they're among our closest pals I assume I'm on safe ground, so I ask them whether they think much about saving for their golden years. When the husband shows some inclination to divulge details of their holdings (this time I don't ask for particulars), his wife, likewise a good friend of mine, cuts him off with a brusque Don't Go

There. It's as if I've been transformed into an Oreck salesman who has weaseled his way into the apartment. "Some things are not meant to be shared," she says with bone-chilling finality.

Undeterred, a few days later I'm at it again, this time with a person whose Number isn't boundless but it's more than plenty. So let's call this person Plenty. I give Plenty the Bracket Quiz. "Tell me what you consider 'rich,' " I say.

"A hundred million," Plenty answers promptly. "Rich is having all the houses and a plane, with no need for a job. You owe nothing. That's rich."

"Okay, if 'rich' is a hundred million, what do you consider, say, 'well-off'?" Plenty needs a moment here.

" 'Well-off' is fifteen million," Plenty says. But judging from the way Plenty says it, I gather fifteen million is borderline. Plenty then adds a qualifier: "It's fifteen million without debt and with no further expenses on kids, or old parents, or friends who might run into trouble."

"What's below that?" I ask.

"I guess 'comfortable' is below that," Plenty says. "Six million. That's with a little bit of housing debt but no other major obligations. Or three million with no debt at all. I'd say that's 'comfortable.' But three million isn't enough to withstand a big hit, like loss of a job, a big health problem."

Based on Plenty's lifestyle I'd guess Plenty is somewhere between comfortable and well-off. This person is certainly not fighting for survival. Plenty shops on Madison Avenue, thinks nothing about hopping on a plane, spur of the moment, for long weekends in Florida or the Caribbean. Plenty indulges in frequent rejuvenation at the best spas, and gives upwards of $30,000 a year to charity.

"What if, God forbid, something happens? The stock market crashes? You suffer a stroke?" I ask Plenty. "What do you give up?"

This is a stumper. Madison Avenue? No! The pink sand at Harbour Island? No! Hot stone massages? No! Charity? No!

"I guess I could give up some apartment space," Plenty eventually concedes. "I could give up a bedroom. Anything more and I'd rather swallow a bottle of Ambien."

Even with plenty, we have anxieties. When I bring up the Number with a prominent media executive—his job is to stay abreast of what's important in the world of politics and global business—he tells me emphatically that it's his Number that he thinks about when he goes to bed, and it's his Number that pops into his mind when the alarm goes off. An influential PR man in Chicago, a man who is adept at thinking actions through to their consequences, informs me he has decided to do a U-turn and go back to work exactly three weeks after he announced to clients that he was retiring for good. The turnabout goes unexplained.

Why is the Number so hard to talk about?

One reason is that most of us were told at an early age that it isn't nice to talk about money, period. It isn't nice to brag about having money, and it's wrong to envy those who have more than we do. The Number is also hard to talk about because it holds a different value for each of us. What's a big Number to me is not to you, and vice versa. The Number can be a hundred thousand. A million. Ten million. Or infinity, if you're an investment banker.

The Number means different things to different people, which is another reason it's hard to talk about. The Number is about net worth, and most people think of it that way. But the Number is also about *self-worth*, which many people don't like to admit. Because I have so little money, I'm a failure. Or, because my house is small, even if it's on the preferred shore of Long Island, I'm a failure.

The Number offers assurance that we won't starve. The Number signifies that loved ones will be taken care of, more or less, after the Numbered passes on. The Number is a validation of career success, the ultimate performance bonus for all those years of dragging tired bones to and from the office. The Number can be the ticket to flashy toys and a bounty of goodies: cruises, spa treatments, tummy tucks. The Number can also be the ticket to a spiritual journey, but those who so invest in it will tell you it has no intrinsic meaning unto itself.

Seeking answers to why so many people are reluctant to talk Numbers, I start hanging out with financial planners. Some of them have clients with stratospheric Numbers, while others minister to average Joes. Most people think financial planners and accountants are the most boring people on earth, but they're not. They hold backstage passes to our psyches. Some of what planners hear is heartbreakingly sad, some of it is ridiculous and delusive. If you ever think it would be fun to be a shrink but you can't hack medical school, let alone being awakened in the middle of the night by a frantic patient, you might consider a career in financial planning.

Financial planners are in on all the juicy intrigue that goes on between people and their money. Planners are also big-time talkers. They are quick to tell tales out of school—discreetly, without names—about husbands and wives who confess that they maintain slush funds to underwrite top-secret indulgences. Hidden bank accounts, money-market funds, and safe-deposit boxes are occasionally tapped to pay for everything from serious indiscretions (mistress cozily tucked away in downtown love nest) to merely expensive guilty pleasures (false panel in closet conceals colossal collection of furtively acquired Jimmy Choos). Almost every planner I meet likes to tell the same story about husbands and wives discovering things about each other when they come in for an initial sit-down. It's the *I didn't know that about you!* moment. Another frequent episode is when a spouse makes a hushed follow-up call to divulge an asset or two that wasn't noted when the wife or husband was in the room. Many spouses prefer that their better halves remain at least partially ignorant of their overall financial picture lest one day a judge does a King Solomon on their joint holdings.

When it comes to the Number, every financial planner says, divorce is a kick in the balls.

LIFESTYLE RELAPSE

Financial planners will tell you that their clients are terrified of Lifestyle Relapse: the universal nightmare that one day you'll find yourself penniless, a geriatric ward of the state imprisoned in a nursing home, nobody to swab your drool, your bodily functions in disarray. One would think that fear of Lifestyle Relapse would provide a powerful incentive for people in their forties and fifties to plan for the future. Incredibly, it doesn't work that way.

I sit down with an investment adviser in Chicago's Loop to shoot the breeze about Lifestyle Relapse. We are fifty-seven stories up, in an office with breathtaking views of the city's skyline. He is chairman of a management firm with over $3 billion under its wing, including the investment portfolios of major foundations, corporations, and extremely wealthy individuals. He notes that although people are acutely concerned about Lifestyle Relapse, they almost always underestimate what it takes to escape its clammy grip. He cites the person who sells a business, then seeks a portfolio designed to yield the same living standard enjoyed while he was still in the saddle. The investment portfolio he seeks must replace not only his salary but also many justifiable and perfectly legal expenses partly or entirely written off by the firm, including, for example, a chunk of travel and entertainment and certain tax prep and financial planning fees. The adviser does a quick mental calculation on this question. "Think of it this way. Say a person has $50,000 worth of business-covered expenses every year, which is conservative for many business owners. And say that after he sells his business he wants to live his life exactly as before, which is only reasonable. Well, using very conservative investment assumptions, he'll need to add a million dollars of liquid assets to his Number just to generate the fifty thousand needed to keep his lifestyle at the level it was."

And so it goes with the Number: one man's million-dollar fortune is another man's club dues.

A different money manager tells about a potential client who's on the brink of retirement. The client comes to see him about setting up a postcareer investment portfolio. He says he wants a plan he can count on so he doesn't have to worry about Lifestyle Relapse. The man's Number has reached $2 million, which should be enough, you'd think, assuming a reasonable level of prudence. The man seems intelligent, possessed of good judgment. Then he lays out his conditions. He tells the money manager his $2 million has to be orchestrated to yield $125,000 a year to support his current lifestyle. The adviser says it will be impossible to assure this kind of return for any length of time. "But it's what I *need,*" he persists. Then he adds that no investment plan can be initiated until an additional $200,000 is pulled off the table. Incredulous, the financial adviser asks why. "I need eighty thousand for a new Mercedes, another eighty for a small boat. The rest I need so that I can pay the rent on my girlfriend's apartment."

Lifestyle Relapse is again the topic of the day when I have lunch in Madison with the CEO of a regional financial services firm. Over Cobb salads at his hushed downtown club, he echoes how executives don't fully appreciate the degree to which legitimate expense-account living adds to the perceived quality of their lifestyle. But there's another aspect of Lifestyle Relapse he thinks about a great deal, and that's community standing. "Money buys relevance," he says. "If you hold down an important position you're in demand. You're invited to parties, sit on the boards of local associations, and get tickets to sold-out basketball games. Once you leave the job, you'll still get some of that stuff, assuming you have the bucks and give some to the people throwing the parties. But if you don't think invitations matter, if you don't think feeling relevant matters, you're kidding yourself."

2

A FIELD GUIDE

Number chasers fall into four basic personality types:

Most people are Procrastinators. These are men and women who have reached their forties, even fifties, without any sort of financial plan in hand. Avoidance is the name of their game, fear of Lifestyle Relapse notwithstanding. Why the sloth? Well, some people don't want to think about old age. Others don't understand how they should invest. All are in limbo, concerned lest they discover they don't have enough to see them through their dotage, or because they can't discuss it with their spouses for fear of starting World War III.

Next come the Pluckers, people who carry very specific Numbers in their heads. Trouble is, they've simply plucked these Numbers out of thin air. A Plucker (like that guy who claims to need a new Mercedes and the boat) will say things like, "I need a million live, end of story." Pluckers are generally less fearful than Procrastinators. But they are too lazy, frugal, or arrogant—sometimes all three—to devote adequate time and resources to creating a coherent plan for the future. A Plucker's Number is ephemeral. This is the Wall Street syndrome. The second a Plucker achieves his Number he drops into shot-put mode and grunts it farther downfield.

Then come the Plotters. In sharp contrast to Procrastinators and

Pluckers, Plotters are those who roll up their sleeves, put on the old green eyeshade, sharpen their pencils, and go to town crunching every financial data point they can get their hands on. Plotters are eager middle-aged beavers with powerful left-side lobes, forever tapping alternative scenarios into their Quicken software. Plotters are well versed in the vicissitudes of the stock market, Monte Carlo simulations, the importance of inflation adjustments, the need for long-term-care insurance, estate planning designed to keep the tax man from snatching hard-earned assets out of the mouths of grandchildren as yet unborn. Plotters are, by and large, conscientious souls who are determined not to be a burden on their offspring and who are equally committed to leaving behind at least a few crumbs. These are people for whom traditional financial planning is well suited.

Finally, there are the Probers, highly developed right-brainers whose minds are alive with interests and passions. Probers see the Number not as an end but as a means, a highly versatile tool with which to finance inner journeys and fulfillment. Probers like to travel and wear sensible clothes from catalogs. "When I retire I'm going to travel to interesting places" is a classic Prober aspiration.

The quartet is represented in the table below. Take a moment and see where you fit:

Number Type	Characteristics	M.O.	Planning Profile
Procrastinator	You are in denial about the need for any kind of post-career plan; or you are lazy, confused, scared, or so woefully impoverished that it doesn't matter if you have a plan or not. You hope for the best, dread the worst.	You totally ignore warnings and entreaties from family, friends, employers, the media, and marketers of financial services. You have no time for fables like "The Hare and the Tortoise."	You have no plan, no real sense of the Number, no nothing. Hiding under the comforter often seems like the best solution.

Number Type	Characteristics	M.O.	Planning Profile
Plucker	You pick what seems like a good Number out of the ozone. "Hmm, that sounds about right for an adequate nest egg."	You base your plans on a series of best guesses and blind stabs.	You have sort of a vague plan and an arbitrary Number. The plan, however, may turn out to be filled with helium or bricks.
Plotter	You possess well-developed left-brain capacity. You harvest, then crunch, a ton of available data to arrive at a rational, if incomplete, second-half Number.	You dutifully study life-expectancy charts, projected rates of return, inflation forecasts, projected health care costs.	You have a plan and a Number that is cogent and conscientious. But one key question is conspicuously absent: *What the hell am I living for?*
Prober	You relentlessly pursue quests, journeys, and explorations into your inner being. Your goal: to figure out who you are, what you really want, and how much fulfillment actually costs.	You hungrily consume some or all of the following: meditation, psychoanalysis, self-help books, spa vacations, massive doses of *Oprah* and *Dr. Phil*.	You have a plan and a Number centered on what would really make a difference in your second-half life. Chances are, this plan calls for simplification and downsizing. Your one big fear: *What if it turns out I really* like *wretched excess?*

Or, looking at these four classes with a brain scan:

Procrastinators	Pluckers	Plotters	Probers
Brainless	Scatterbrained	Left-brained	Right-brained

Procrastinators, you'll note, try not to tax their brains at all. Life's easier if you spend it working on your short game or watching *The Apprentice* on a 42-inch plasma. A Procrastinator is under no obligation to know the difference between a stock and a bond.

Next along the spectrum, Pluckers are usually very good at knowing the difference between a stock and a bond but they are more likely to bet the farm on stocks and leave bond buying to girlie-men. Attention spans are not their thing.

Plotters are, literally, numbers people. Cranking hard, they labor under the belief that anything worth doing is worth doing on an Excel spreadsheet. Then one day they wake up at age sixty-five and realize that they have never figured out how to have fun.

Probers hit from the other side of the brain. Dreamers and seekers, they almost never have a great deal of money.

There are other ways to divide the world. One afternoon I ask a money manager to provide thumbnail sketches of clients he deems typical of the Number chasers he counsels in his practice. He answers with a litany of observations, the way an entomologist might catalog bugs.

There are *The Guys Who Once Were*. He says he is very good at a game called Spot the Million-Dollar-a-Year Guys. Million-dollar-a-year guys are clients who, when they first visit his office, reveal very little, won't divulge their net worth, remain guarded and uptight through the first meeting. What they will always tell him, and tell him within the first few minutes, is that they used to make a million dollars a year. "I can predict who will tell me that in about five seconds," he says.

There are *Differences Based on Religion*. "Jewish people are much more inclined than Catholics to leave a lot of money to their kids," he says. "And it's incomprehensible for Catholics to give much to their kids while still alive." He himself is Catholic.

There are *Those People Who Can't Have Enough Housing*. He says many high-net-worth clients have one house too many, perhaps as a function of years of low interest rates. He says that a couple with less than $5 million or $6 million should think twice about owning more than one house, given the costs associated with maintaining a home. These costs are often underestimated, he says. Ideally, a couple should have around $10 million if they want to own two luxury properties and

not house themselves into a corner. If you want three houses—a pied-
à-terre in the city, a place in Florida, a flat in London—you should have
a $20 million Number or greater.

Another adviser I meet assigns his clients to a bestiary of his own
making. He says he sees a lot of "little fish" who think there's some kind
of silver mullet out there, a real estate investment, say, or a series of
stock plays, that will get them to the Number in one quick leap. More
formidable are "the sharks," he says. Number sharks, according to the
bestiary, are continuously in money motion, hungry to accumulate
more, confident there's another meal coming up, always feeding, taking
bites. People who approach the Number the way a shark would, he
says, never look inward. Other clients are akin to "tree-swinging pri-
mates," he observes. Each tree is a career stop where they land in order
to accumulate some ripe bananas—a signing bonus, stock incentives—
before jumping to another tree for a few years. Tree-swingers are adept
at juggling severance deals so they're munching on bananas from the
old tree even as they're settling in on the branches of the next.

RAMPING UP

I don't know where I stand. That's what people say no matter where they
fall in the field guide. The reason they don't know where they stand is
because nobody's talking. Keeping your Number to yourself is a throw-
back to a time when people held themselves to minimal standards of
gentility. Today, except for the Number, everything is out in the open.
Paris Hilton. *Jackass,* the motion picture. (If you haven't seen *Jackass,*
do. On second thought, don't. It's funny, but it's gross.) The other night
my wife and I were innocently channel-surfing when we ran into this
movie, in which, among other picaresque vignettes, a member of the
ensemble inserts a small blue toy car into his most private anatomical
cavity, then goes to have it X-rayed just to freak out the radiologist. My
hunch is that the same guy would demur blushingly if asked how much
money he had in the bank.

And it would be fruitless to guess how much he might have. Appearances are deceiving. We all know people who are loaded and don't live like it, and those who aren't who live large. The former were dissected some years ago in the best-seller *The Millionaire Next Door*. The book was dedicated to the idea that any Tom, Dick, and Harry can reach a seven-figure Number if only he can grasp a little-known law of financial physics: what comes in doesn't have to go out again. This is not one of those jaw-dropping discoveries of the twentieth century. It held true long before Mr. Micawber told David Copperfield (the original one, not the Vegas headliner): "Annual income twenty pounds, annual expenditure nineteen nineteen six, result happiness. Annual income twenty pounds, annual expenditure twenty pounds ought and six, result misery."

The road to riches is indeed as straight as it says in *The Millionaire Next Door*. BMWs, Rolexes, and weekends at the Auberge du Soleil are swell, but—admit it—they're not basic necessities. Your unprepossessing millionaire next door understands this, and accepts the premise that saving money comes before spending it. These are people who are perfectly content to live in split-levels sheathed in aluminum siding, drive ordinary American-made cars, and wear indestructible suits and dresses as fashioned by Kevlar of Paris.

Then there are the evil twins of the millionaires next door: the faux millionaires next door who look, dress, and act the part of the very rich but who have little or nothing salted away, save for a hunk of home equity, if that. They are house-rich and cash-poor, a circumstance carried to the level of art form all across the country and to a level of genius in California. Faux millionaires take comfort in the fact that at least their real estate gains have kept them in the game. Housing prices just keep going up and up, a thumb in the eye of all known natural laws. One night a New Yorker mentions that the value of her two-bedroom West Side apartment has more than tripled over the past fifteen years, from $300,000 to over $1 million. Selling it would yield a nice chunk of change. But then what? Live in a dump?

Who's got the Number? Who's flaunting it? It's really hard to know. The best Number sniffers, at least the ones I've run across, are people who have honed their instincts in the Northeast corridor. They can tell the difference between wealth and pretend-wealth the way a sow can root out a truffle in a forest of mushrooms. One day I'm talking to a man who owns a summer home on Martha's Vineyard. He exudes confidence over how well he can tell those who've truly attained big Numbers from those who are still chasing the difference between big money and a big year. He says he acquired his skills by observing subtle dynamics at cocktail parties. "It's the little things they say around the pool," the man tells me. "After a glass or two of Chardonnay, a guy or his wife might make a passing reference to last year's bonus. You know at once they're probably the poorest people in the neighborhood."

Heartlanders are not that astute when it comes to discerning who's got it and who's faking because they have fewer opportunities to observe this phenomenon. There just aren't as many fakers in the real world as there are in the Northeast. But make no mistake: heartlanders are as nosy as anyone when the topic turns to people and money. Just mention the Number and they lean in a little closer.

The best way to give people a sense of where they stand is to lay out some data. Every three years the Federal Reserve Board conducts a national survey that tracks the financial health of American households. The Fed slices and dices this stuff with the vigor of an Iron Chef; the result is a rich, if dry, array of offerings on household net worth, pension and income levels, plus other demographic side dishes. Whenever I slip these tidbits into cocktail-party chatter, people are surprised to realize how little money it takes to win a gold star from the Fed. If you and yours are bringing in $40,000 a year, you're doing better than half the households in America. Or, as a Washington think tank recently pointed out: if you're a teacher married to a policeman, your combined household income puts you in the top 25 percent of all households in the nation.

Below you'll find the average income picture sliced into income lev-

els. Think of this chart as a parking ramp. If your household income is
$170,000, you're among the nation's top 10 percent wage earners and
get to park on the top floor. Anything in six figures means you're in the
top 20 percent and get to park on the floor right below.

ANNUAL INCOME PARKING RAMP

Income Level (percentile)	Median Income (rounded)
Level VI (90–100)	$170,000
Level V (80–89.9)	$99,000
Level IV (60–79.9)	$65,000
Level III (40–59.9)	$40,000
Level II (20–39.9)	$24,000
Level I (< 20)	$10,000

Before-Tax Family Income, 2001 Federal Reserve Board Survey

So does making $170,000 a year make a person "rich"? Last year a
plurality of respondents in a *New York Times* survey (29 percent) said
that "rich" was making between $100,000 and $200,000 a year. Unfortunately, the survey didn't break out how many people in that salary
range considered *themselves* rich. If the people I talk to are any indication, very few do.

Of course, income is only one part of the equation defining where
you stand. Net worth is more telling. Net worth, as every financially
precocious schoolchild knows, is the sum of one's assets—home equity,
investments, savings accounts, retirement funds, cars, furnishings, and
such things as jewelry, furs, wine collection, old baseball cards—minus
all outstanding liabilities such as mortgage balance, revolving and
credit card debt, college loans, and so on. Across all households, the national median net worth is $86,000. Half of your fellow citizens have
more than that, half less. As you see opposite, there's a massive disparity between the haves and have-nots.

NET WORTH PARKING RAMP

Net Worth (percentile)	Median Net Worth (rounded)
Level VI (90–100)	$833,600
Level V (80–89.9)	$263,100
Level IV (60–79.9)	$141,500
Level III (40–59.9)	$62,500
Level II (20–39.9)	$37,200
Level I (< 20)	$7,900

Family Net Worth, 2001 Federal Reserve Board Survey

We live in a country that once celebrated itself as egalitarian, yet 1 percent of the population—nearly three million people—currently has as much money as the hundred million people at the bottom of the ramp.

Yet when I ask those at the top of the ramp how they feel about the future, whether their fortunate place on the ramp gives them a measure of confidence about it, they shake their heads. They give me a look that says What planet do *you* park on? Indeed, a 2005 survey by the Spectrem Group, a wealth-research company in Chicago, indicated that the richest Americans were among the most pessimistic when asked about the future of the economy, keeping a good hunk of their money in cash and safely away from the market.

HOW YOUR BROKER SEES YOU

If you're not parked near the top of the ramp, you're of little or no interest to financial services firms and financial advisers. There's no money to be made at these levels. Last year a handful of Wall Street firms told their brokers they would no longer receive commissions on accounts holding less than $50,000. This effectively tells people with nano-Numbers to get lost. But for the Wall Street firms there's gold on the floors above. The greater the household assets, the more fees and transaction costs can be extracted from an account. The result is a flood of advertising that captures a lifestyle so gloriously affluent it's enough to make *everybody* feel poor.

Those who manage Numbers break customers down into innumerable segments, the better to target them through their marketing efforts. These segments take into consideration all the usual demographic characteristics such as age, income, and net worth. Other segmentation models define you according to psychographic qualities: personal interests, leisure-time activities, whether you are active or passive when it comes to managing your affairs—including, for instance, how comfortable you are using a computer. Once a financial services company figures it has your Number, it will use what it thinks are the most effective channels to get its hands on it. It will place advertising in the magazines and newspapers you read and the television shows and Web sites you browse. And it will probe you incessantly through the mailbox, testing or selling financial products and services.

The Number industry divides people on the top floors of the garage into three broad segments of wealth, each of which is nicely profitable.

The biggest and broadest affluent segment consists of people with investable assets of between $200,000 and $1 million to $2 million. This group is sometimes referred to as "mass affluent," and it would be fair to think of it as the meat and potatoes of the financial services business. If you're at the lower end of that range—if you have, say, $300,000 in your accounts—you're definitely of prime interest to the brokers and customer reps at Merrill Lynch, Smith Barney, Vanguard, and the rest. But they need to be careful lest you cost *them* money. To assign a real live broker (oops, financial consultant) to a client who keeps too low a Number is tantamount to Safeway assigning a personal shopper to anyone who comes in to buy a quart of milk. Still, there are profitable ways for financial services firms to serve smaller customers: the telephone, assuming they can keep the calls short and to the point and, better still, the online channel, where self-service is highly cost-effective. This is

not to say that firms aren't happy to see you walk into their investment
centers for a quick hello and a fill-out-the-papers session. They'll shake
your hand, put an arm around your shoulder, even pour you a cup of
coffee. After that, the more you manage your own modest Number, the
better for them and the more cost-effective for you.

The next segment up from mass affluent is where the action gets
white hot. This parking level belongs to those designated as High Net
Worth Individuals. There are no universal criteria here. Generally,
HNWIs have invested assets of at least a million dollars, although some
companies also target younger households with healthy six-figure in-
comes, knowing that their net worth is likely to reach target levels in the
near future. Right now there are well over seven million high-net-worth
households in the United States, with a forecasted growth rate of 16
percent a year and projected assets of $32 trillion. Yum.

If their marketing efforts are any indication, Wall Street firms see
HNWIs as the happiest people in the world, no matter that so many of
them are, rightly or wrongly, distressed over their long-term prospects.
Distress is not what's pictured in the ads. The ads are filled with images
of zippy seniors who flash large white teeth and incredibly healthy gums.
They dance. They jog. They bike. They fish. They golf. They snuggle. According to the ads, life is a theme park expressly designed for the middle-
aged. Graying boomers waltz across their living rooms, raise glasses to
one another on the decks of ocean liners, and exchange smiles secure in
the knowledge that a surefire blue-steel erection is just a pill away.
These ads remind us that we are living in the Golden Age of Aging. Not
only are we younger and healthier than middle-aged people used to be,
many of us would probably have been blind, disabled, or dead by now
had we had the bad luck to have been born just a tiny bit sooner.

One of my favorite HNWI ads is the Morgan Stanley commercial in
which a handsome woman of a certain age and her "husband" (we're
supposed to think it's her husband but it's really her broker; the "real"
husband is snoozing off-camera) are sitting by the water on a lazy afternoon. The "husband" says to the handsome woman in a gentle and

soothing voice, "You know that summer house you've always wanted to build here? Well, I think that with a little portfolio shuffling here and there we just might be able to pull it off sooner than we thought!"

What a many-splendored message! One, life at the top of the ramp is good and can only get better. Two, your broker can make all of your High Net Worth Dreams come true, even if your flabby husband is napping at the switch. Three, your financial adviser is a companion so faithful he deserves to be dragged along even on idyllic lakeside weekends, as if he were some financially astute golden retriever.

The bottom line is that the Number industry has affluent baby boomers in its teeth and will be shaking them like rag dolls for the next couple of decades. Thirty years ago boomers were coveted for their youth; today the world loves them for their assets. There is so much money at stake that no one can agree on exactly how much. I've seen estimates that say that between $40 trillion and $130 trillion will change hands in the coming decades. Whatever it is, the figure is immense, since it includes everything boomers' parents will bequeath in the form of houses, stocks, bonds, and collectibles. That's an estimated $10 trillion right there. And it includes the accounts seventy-seven million boomers will be looking to roll over, distribute, and reinvest as they leave their jobs in the years immediately ahead. The big financial services firms, banks, and insurance companies are licking their chops in anticipation of the greatest asset free-for-all their professions have ever imagined. As one senior executive at a financial services firm says: "We are about to witness the largest transfer of wealth in the history of the world."

VALET PARKING

If you've made it onto the top levels of the ramp—say you have at least $5 million in investments—you are deemed to be an *Ultra* High Net Worth Individual. This is a very nice position to hold in life, all the sweeter thanks to recent federal tax cuts. People earning $10 million a year hand over a smaller percentage of their income to the government than those earning a tenth of that and—to a great degree—escape the gotcha snare of the alternative minimum tax, according to the *New York Times*. Today there's an all-out war going on over UHNWIs. Last year the Swiss-based UBS group hired a management team away from Merrill Lynch and announced plans to create a hundred wealth-advisory hit squads around the country. Smith Barney countered by deploying a number of nationwide "wealth planning centers" where UHNWIs can go to set up trusts and philanthropic programs. In making its announcement, a company spokesman noted that assets held by the top 1 percent of the population are growing three times faster than the rate of those anywhere else in our parking garage.

The treatment extended to a UHNWI approaches that accorded to royalty. As a UHNWI, you aren't offered a cardboard cup of day-old sludge from a Mr. Coffee machine. Now you qualify for a china cup of freshly brewed java from a gleaming French press. They'd better get another grinder or two. The Boston Consulting Group reports that three thousand new households a year lay claim to $20 million or more in invested assets. Should you be among them, put your feet up and just whistle for service. If getting yourself to a firm's teak-paneled office is too much of a schlep, the investment advisers will hightail it to you. They'll be more than delighted to take you to dinner at the best place in town and toast your success with the finest vintages on the menu. They go to this expense because they obviously respect your business prowess and find you personally charming. Mostly, though, they admire you for your assets. They will ply you with leather binders filled with laser-printed pie charts, bar graphs, and three-dimensional wave diagrams. Over dessert, they will produce PowerPoint slides that show how your nest egg will incubate and eventually burgeon into a soaring phoenix that will carry your Number higher and higher, all thanks to their nurturing and personal attention.

They will also start talking to you in funny, stilted language. While financial services firms switch on the sunsets to capture the attention of

the merely mass affluent, they become superdignified when making
pitches to the megawealthy. They use grandiloquent terms that are to
the ear what a marble bank lobby is to the eye—reassurance that, as an
UHNWI, you have come to just the right place. The higher you are in
the net-worth parking ramp, the more twisted and self-congratulatory
the lexicon. Take, for example, *The 2004 World Wealth Report,* published by Merrill Lynch and Cap Gemini, a consulting firm. The
report's purpose is to underscore just how well Merrill understands the
sensitive financial temperament of the UHNWI. It takes proper note of
the fact that the wealthier you are, the more you demand of your financial servants. The less affluent, it observes, can be served through what
the report politely refers to as "leveraging of technology" and "cost-
efficient distributions channels." Meaning, if you're rich but not that
rich, give us a buzz, go to the Web, but stay out of our face. But you, you
gorgeous hunk of net worth, you deserve something much more *je ne
sais quoi* from an institutional custodian. Plain-vanilla financial and retirement planning for the merely mass affluent can be delivered by a
back-office clerk and a computer program. But you, idling up there on
the UHNWI ramp, require access to "alternative investments" (hedge
funds), as well as assistance with "multigenerational wealth planning"
(Byzantine trust and estate strategies). When you get to be this rich, the
report implies, you stop thinking of yourself as a mere mortal and begin
to fancy yourself an *institution.* You deserve not just an accountant or a
tax man but "advisors who can serve in a CFO-type function," who
"offer an integrated mix of tax-sensitive solutions, legal counsel, and accounting advice on top of financial planning and investment management." It isn't enough to have the right investment mix; you deserve an
allocation that "balances risk, reward, and liquidity." It isn't sufficient to
fill your portfolio with solid, low-cost index funds; you must "base your
investment selections on fundamental analysis and due diligence." Finally, you "need professional advice and ideas garnered from multiple
specialists, and thorough analysis of investment products and goals."
Pretentious? *Oui!*

There is yet one more place to park, higher up and more exclusive still. This spot is for people for whom even discreet, private banking is déclassé. On this level of the ramp you forgo the wealth managers at even the toniest trust companies and rely instead on your own "family office," complete with its own in-house investment manager and staff. Typically, families with family offices have a hundred million, five hundred million, a billion, enough to blow off even the Lehmans, the Goldmans, and the Northern Trusts of the world. At present, there are now approximately five thousand family offices around the country. Family offices are not for strivers—at least not yet. But family offices may be going the way of fractional jets, shared yachts, and high-end vacation-home clubs. People with only twenty million Numbers have begun to band together to create, in effect, multifamily offices to oversee their investments and estate planning.

Back down on the street, though, it's another world. Most people have to circle the block, just looking for a way to get into the damn garage.

3

THE EISENBERG
UNCERTAINTY PRINCIPLES

I t was just five years ago that culturally attuned, affluent boomers saw their own happy reflections in books such as David Brooks' *Bobos in Paradise*. *Bobos* depicted a generation soothingly afloat in Frappuccino, facing daily challenges no greater than finding the right cabinet pulls at Restoration Hardware. Today these people are diving for comfort under their fraying Frette Hotel Collection sheets. A dicey job market, a jumpy stock market, an imploding bond market, soaring health care costs, and a looted Social Security lockbox threaten the putative paradise observed in the late 1990s. The result is a forecast that calls for highly unsettled weather. People feel discontented about tomorrow. It isn't so much future shock as future denial. There are a half dozen good explanations for why people aren't planning for the next few decades. Call these the Eisenberg Uncertainty Principles, which will guide the twists of the story to come.

A disclaimer before the curtain goes up on the Uncertainty Principles: Deliberately excluded from the list are a couple of the truly big hairy reasons why people close their eyes to the future. These are the obvious über-dreads that are indisputably beyond anyone's day-to-day control:

Fear of death. Woody Allen has no monopoly on this one. Fear of dying certainly ranks high among disincentives to plan. It weighs heavily on the mind of a psychiatrist I meet at a resort in Florida. We have ten minutes of friendly conversation, then he asks about the book I'm working on. After listening to the details, he says with a smile that he's so obsessed with death he has never been inclined to sweat the details of something as mundane as retirement planning. I tell him I'd rather not discuss this on my vacation.

Fear of global annihilation. Skittishness over the possibility of a cataclysmic event (terrorist, environmental) also renders people disinclined to plan. In other words, let's just get through the week, and then we can get cracking on that cash-flow analysis.

The Eisenberg Uncertainty Principles have to do with things we could change if we had the will, or knew how:

1. *The uncertainty that results from living in a society and culture so steeped in the moment, and awash in debt, that there's little social or peer pressure to get one's financial house in order.*

Easy credit makes it easier to spend than to save, more pleasant to shop than to plan. We throw money around. We piss it away. We treat ourselves to new shoes or a smart phone when we're feeling blue. The *Wall Street Journal* recently reported that since 1990, median household income has risen 11 percent, adjusted for inflation; median household debt, on the other hand, has risen 80 percent. Consuming is all-consuming, a full-time job unto itself. Who has time to gather expenses onto a budget worksheet, even if the budget is designed to restrain us?

2. *The uncertainty and lack of motivation that come from not knowing how money works.* Doing money right is not a core competency for most people. This is either a baffling irony or a natural consequence of a materialistic culture. People feel stupid about money, so they keep it at arm's length, sometimes for decades (call these the Lost Years, which we'll get to). People may be OK when it comes to earning money and quite adept at spending it, but a great many of them confess to feeling

clumsy, myopic, and highly inept when it comes to managing it. Surveys bear this out. Many of them indicate that even educated and professionally successful people don't know the basics, e.g., that a money-market fund isn't made up of stocks; or that the value of a bond goes down when interest rates go up. Not knowing the fundamentals is definitely a roadblock to proactive planning.

3. *The uncertainty caused by knowing that the old retirement support systems are withering away.* Until recently it was fairly simple to live and pay for a lifetime on the planet. You worked, you retired, and you died shortly thereafter, in more or less dutiful compliance with accepted timetables of the day. There were reliable systems in place to finance your retirement. Most people knew exactly how much money would arrive in their mailboxes every month, and it always arrived as promised. For a host of reasons (we'll get to these, too) it doesn't work that way anymore.

4. *The uncertainty caused by the immense cloud that hangs over future retirement benefits: bankrupt corporate pension plans; what an angry stock market god might do to smite private retirement savings plans.* This uncertainty thrives like mold in the brave new petri dish of financial self-determination. Just as we scratch our heads over where yesterday's security went, we have too little faith in tomorrow's. Companies implode and take our benefits with them; others try to chisel their way out of old commitments or simply find they can't fulfill them. United Airlines recently won a court ruling in the largest pension-default case ever. Its pension fund was short nearly $10 billion, only half of which was insured by a government agency. The government agency *itself* is going broke. Then there's that little matter of Social Security.

5. *The uncertainty that comes from failure to see the larger picture in all of the above.* It would be helpful to have trustworthy teachers, mentors, and financial counselors who are accessible to everyone, no matter how rich or poor. Financial life is wildly confusing, fraught with subjectivity and arbitrary calls. There are too many decisions and choices to be made, lots of arcane minutiae to juggle. There is endless fine print and

gobbledygook about estate planning, tax codes, disbursement strategies. Not to mention the fact that those damn politicians down in Washington are always changing everything around in bizarre ways. It's like a bad stand-up routine. Sunset provisions! Are they nuts, folks, or what? Taxes recede, expire, then come back as if they'd never gone away—unless, of course, they get changed in the meantime, which they probably will be, but who knows where or when? How can anybody plan amid all the confusion and static?

6. *Finally, the profound uncertainty over what truly matters at the end of the day.* Let's assume that you're lucky or smart enough to navigate the foregoing uncertainties. Having gone to so much trouble, do you really want to wake up one morning, throw open the shutters on a glorious day, gaze at the dewy rose garden below, and watch the sun rise on the rest of your life, screaming, "I'm so wrinkled, miserable, and bored I wish I was dead"? The greatest uncertainty of all may be the uncertainty over what money is good for. We bury this uncertainty under a million clichés. Money can't buy happiness. Oh, no? Money can buy time and opportunity to do the things we most love. It can help us fulfill our obligations as parents to our kids and as kids to our parents. It buys quality health care. But somehow or other, we get our knickers all twisted up when it comes to figuring out the real value of money. Could it be that in the end the reason we don't plan is because we don't have anything meaningful to plan for?

MILLIONAIRE SHMILLIONAIRE

Here's another uncertainty: just as millions don't know what it means to be poor, they also don't know what it means to be a millionaire—if that means anything anymore. A lot of people who belong to the millionaires club feel they don't have remotely enough money to get through life. Many of these people are millionaires on paper, millionaires under house arrest. A millionaire under house arrest is someone whose net worth runs to seven figures but for whom a significant portion of those assets—20, 30, 40 percent or more—is tied up in the value of their homes. That so many people fall into this category has to do with the extraordinary run-up in housing prices over the past decades. As far as net worth goes, home equity counts, but to get themselves out of house arrest and have real money in their clutches, people would have to trade their McMansions for more modest dwellings. This transition is hard if you've grown accustomed to a great room, a hearth room, an office for him, an office for her, a media room, a billiards room, an indoor driving range, a workout room, a swimming pool, a spa, a wine cellar, and a four-car garage, even if they're all crammed onto a third of an acre. To give these up is to court the heartbreak of Lifestyle Relapse. A lot of financial planners will tell you the obvious, as one told the *Wall Street Journal* recently: people who want to feel millionaire-ish have an "ego thing" about holding on to the trappings of wealth, no matter that the road ahead is paved with risk.

Paper millionaires have good reason to feel financially uncertain, but so do even true millionaires. A million dollars conservatively invested yields $50,000 a year in income, which is hardly what it takes to feel like a million bucks. And there are a lot of people feeling such disillusionment right now. While one of every 125 Americans is today a true millionaire, many haven't been millionaires for very long. Many aren't particularly money-smart or experienced at remaining millionaires. Roughly 80 percent of those millionaires became millionaires in the stock market boom of the 1990s and are now coping with what happens when the market decides to fall or move sideways for a prolonged period. Only one in three of these true millionaires say they have anything like a formal investment or retirement plan in place.

Even though being a millionaire isn't what it used to be, you can't turn around without somebody telling you how to become one. You can do it! You can do it! Just go to the bookstore and choose from the dozen varieties within arm's reach: the automatic millionaire, the armchair millionaire, the one-minute millionaire, the weekend millionaire, the instant millionaire, the spiritual millionaire, and, of course, that millionaire next door.

WHEN TWO MILLION ISN'T ENOUGH

Many Americans can have a million dollars, even two, and still feel as if they're scraping bottom. The message is delivered this very morning by no less an authority than the daily diary of the American Dream, the *Wall Street Journal*. The paper quotes Yale economist Robert Shiller, who, in less than irrationally exuberant language, points out that "people might be deceived and think $1 million is a lot of money." Shiller's nervous-making observation runs under a story with the headline "When $1 Million Isn't Enough for a Comfortable Retirement." It's precisely the kind of article that's guaranteed, even calculated, to provoke a response. For some, the headline elicits tremors of fear; for others, it tees up the charge, yet again, that we are a nation of overfed wastrels. The tragic hero of the article is a doctor who, because of ill health, retires from his practice. Still in his fifties, he is under the impression that with $2 million in invested assets he'll be "home free." Within seven years, however, all manner of bad things happen to this good person.

Shmillionaires of America, this can happen to you:

1. Stock prices tank, and along with them about a third of the doctor's retirement savings.
2. The doctor realizes *after* retiring that his preretirement calculations were all wrong. They were based on the assumption that he would not be obliged to pay income tax on money withdrawn from tax-deferred accounts.
3. His health insurance premiums go up about $100 a month. Not only that, he begins to pay premiums on long-term-care policies he and his wife decide they need.
4. The property taxes on the tranquil retirement home he and his

wife have purchased—a modest enough place, but on twenty-two acres—turn out to be considerably more than they paid when they lived in their suburban home.

Depressing conclusion: what seemed like a super-safe, $2 million cushiony life now feels like a bed of nails. While there's no danger the doctor and his wife will relocate to the poorhouse any time soon, he reports that he feels little security about what might happen five years down the road.

The *Journal* story triggers a hail of reader comments. A few years ago a couple of letters to the editor would have answered a piece such as this, and then all trace of it would disappear into the recycling bin of yesterday's news. Now, online message boards keep debates going indefinitely. The *Journal* story touches all the bases: social, moral, cultural, and financial. Everybody has something to gripe about. One post is from someone who's mad as hell and won't take it anymore: "It is absurd! These millionaires can reduce their expectations, live more modestly and still enjoy material comforts far exceeding the average American, not to mention the average world citizen. . . . A person who is at retirement age and has not yet learned that they don't need to impress others with their material wealth has not even begun to grow up." Another is from a really nice person who has apparently been watching too much Suze Orman: "$1 million does, indeed, work. We get by on ¾ of that thanks to zero debt, avoidance of bubbles, hobbies that cost zero and free lodging at our favorite travel destination (granddaughter's house ;-)."

My office is now piled even higher with newspapers, magazines, and books filled with handy-dandy guides meant to help you figure out what your Number is. Sadly, they usually wind up adding even more uncertainty. Or they're just wrong. Experts, in the form of self-help authors, lull their readers into thinking it's a snap to acquire sufficient dosh to last a long lifetime. Personal finance magazines also do this, which is why they are so full of pics these days. Last year a money magazine showed a baker taking some luscious pies out of the oven to illustrate how "hands-off" investors should rely on so-called target funds, mutual funds whose allocations turn more conservative over time. Many self-appointed financial journalists try to stuff the Number into convenient, one-pie-fits-all formulas. Consider the oft-repeated generalization that you can arrive at your Number simply by calculating a percentage of your current preretirement income. What could be simpler, Simon? All that's required are a few taps on the keys of a pocket calculator.

The assumption here is that it costs less to live in retirement than it does to live while you're still working. The kids are out of the house (or should be). Your commuting costs are history. You're content to wear musty old clothes. Consequently, some experts contend, you may need only 70 percent of what you lately earned, though others will tell you that's too low given the soaring costs of health care, for example. For the sake of illustration, let's stick with 70 percent, though. Assuming you're currently living an acceptable existence on an income of $150,000 a year, all you need to do to come up with your annual Number is:

$$150000 \qquad \times .7 \quad = \quad 105000$$

(6 taps)   (3 taps) (1 tap)

Bingo! Your Instant Target Annual Retirement Income Number is $105,000, in only ten taps!

The method is flawed. You need quite a few more taps to be able to tap annual income into the reliable overall Number you need to generate that much annual income. These missing taps require you to do some thinking. How old are you when you're tapping these taps? Are you a quivering blob of Jell-O when it comes to investment risk, which will determine presumed investment returns? How long do you and your spouse expect to live? How healthy are you right now? How many dependents do you have and what are their ages? How important is it to you to leave money to them or to a good cause? How safe is your company pension, assuming you have one, and is it indexed to inflation (most aren't)? How and where exactly do you most want to spend your retirement? And how much have you even thought about what would make you happy and fulfilled?

As important as these questions are, many financial writers are content to ignore them and continue to crank out simple but useless rules of thumb. Feel free to ignore them. A solid, reliable Number will not fall out of the pages of a magazine or newspaper. If you're looking for certainty in a Number, a large factor of *you* must be added into the equation.

The same goes for pieces that are so detailed with specifics—somebody else's specifics—that they have no real bearing on your situation. I come across a piece in the Sunday business section of the *New York Times*. The writer, I'm convinced, is really Freddy Krueger, cleverly concealed under the byline of Ben Stein. The details are too gory to get into. Let's just leave it that Freddy comes out slashing, wielding a calculator instead of his customary butcher knife. He offers a couple of bloodcurdling case studies—a woman who needs a Number of over $4 million to replicate how she was accustomed to living when she made a salary of $185,000; a lawyer who needs over $12 million to keep up the life he'd gotten used to. Freddy moves in for the kill, saying there is "the bore of a gun pointed right between the eyes of baby boomers. [What] on earth are we going to do about retirement?"

Although Freddy's math might check out, he leaves too many puncture wounds in his victim's stories. That woman who needed over $4 million? How was her health (before Freddy got through with her)? How many dependents did she have? Did she own her apartment outright, and if so, what if she drew down its equity? Wouldn't that make a huge difference? More important, just who *is* this woman? As a human being, I mean? What exactly will make her happy, and what would that cost? Freddy paints his victim by numbers, ignoring dreams and emotions. Nevertheless, all innocent readers remember from his horror flick is that people like them need $4.6 million to live sort of OK in Manhattan. That could be true. It could also be a gross exaggeration. Or hopelessly underestimated.

4

DEBT WARP

The first Eisenberg Uncertainty Principle says that a key reason people remain suspended in an uncertain state about their long-term prospects is because there is no positive social reinforcement to do otherwise. In fact, there's more social pressure to avoid thinking about the Number than there is to wrestle with it.

Where's the peer pressure to live small today so that we might live comfortably tomorrow? Where's the celebrity spokesperson to tell us how way cool it is to eschew the little luxuries of the moment in order to afford a long-term-care policy? Where's the slick marketing campaign that can convince us to forgo a year's worth of hair, makeup, and Botox injections to the forehead in order to pay an accountant to tell us we spend too much money and we'd be advised to downsize? And besides, none of our friends or neighbors are doing any of these things. Without a comparative yardstick, or the peer pressure to keep up with the Joneses' retirement planning, we are not motivated to save. So we keep up with the Joneses in the usual way: consumption. An iPod for an iPod.

This leads to Debt Warp.

Psychologists might say Debt Warp is a casebook example of adaptation, the phenomenon whereby we grow accustomed to a circumstance—good or otherwise—until one day, well, we just take it for granted. Any misgivings that may exist prior to adaptation, such as reluctance to go into debt, gradually fade as peer pressure mounts. Beclouded by Debt Warp, gusseted by glossy magazines that revel in "wealth porn," people live in houses bigger than they can afford and make more or less timely payments on monster vehicles that chugalug premium fuel. They dine with impunity at pricey restaurants; they fill their clutch purses and belt holsters with sleek electronic gear, all made possible by generous grants from Visa and MasterCard.

Total consumer debt ($6.5 trillion) in the United States is now reckoned to exceed the much-fretted-over national debt, although it gets a fraction of the attention. Personal debt in the United States in 2002 was equal to the gross national products of Great Britain and Russia combined. Revolving credit card debt is, for millions of households, the financial lifeline that connects them to the biggest-ticket items in their lives, such as medical bills, tuition costs, and car payments. It comes as no news, of course, but plastic, once a convenience, is now society's everyday financing tool. It's a financing tool, however, that levies typical interest rates of 18 percent APR, maybe more, maybe less, with the more running to upwards of 40 percent *per month* in extreme cases—i.e., in the cases of those who are least creditworthy.

DEBTORS IN PARADISE

Debt Warp holds that our whip-it-out credit card culture makes it so easy to buy stuff that people delude themselves into thinking they're more affluent, better set for the future, than they are. Debt Warp reshapes reality and turns age-old precepts about frugality upside down. We are so accustomed to buying things we really don't need, or can't afford, that indebtedness starts to feel like a normal state of being, not an affliction. Debt Warp works its will in boom times and busts, and it's most intense during a protracted period of low interest rates. Debt Warp and interest rates inversely correlate: the lower the interest rate,

the more indebted we become, and the greater we succumb to Debt
Warp. We have benefited from very low interest rates for a long time. As
a result, over the past five to ten years—precisely the period when
seventy-seven million baby boomers should have been thinking about
their futures—Debt Warp has intensified exponentially. Starting in
2000, two of Debt Warp's principal components, automobile loans and
credit card debt, rose a full 33 percent. Also in this time, U.S. consumers showered themselves (hosed themselves is more like it, using
German-made, multiple-head, full-body shower sprays) with $2.3 tril-
lion of new mortgage debt, an increase of 50 percent.

The lending industry considers 80 percent of U.S. households cred-
itworthy, which gives new meaning to the phrase "benefit of the doubt."
Accordingly, there are well over a billion credit cards currently in circulation on the North American Plastisphere. On average, a person gets a
solicitation for a new one seven times a year. (At our house we get them
seven times a week, either because of, more likely in spite of, the fact
that we try to pay our balances in their entirety every month.) According
to the *Wall Street Journal,* households with at least one credit card carry
a debt load of over $9,000, up 23 percent over a five-year period, ad-
justed for inflation. That's quite a nosebleed. An American declares
bankruptcy every fifteen seconds, says the *New York Times.*

It is exceedingly difficult to escape Debt Warp's grip; there are hold-
outs, but not many. One evening I run into a young professional. Likeable, just out of business school, newly married with no kids, making
$85,000 a year at a Fortune 500 company, he has just relocated to Min-
neapolis. He is to a Debt Warped society what Keanu Reeves is to the
Matrix, a man fighting against an alternative reality. He is at once re-
solved to keep his balance sheet healthy yet deeply annoyed that having
to do so is just not fair. Everybody he knows is "living better than I am,"
he says. Everybody he knows is also highly leveraged. Nevertheless, this
young careerist has decided to fight Debt Warp by renting an apartment
instead of buying a house. Although he knows he's "doing the right
thing," he's down on himself for being such a financial wimp. But com-

ing up with the down payment would clean him out, he says, and he's leery about getting himself in too deep this soon in a new place and a new job.

If you believe this thoughtful young man is fighting the good fight, holding out against the forces of Debt Warp and keeping his powder dry, you're wrong. When carried at a proper level, mortgage debt is a *good* thing. Uncle Sam subsidizes home purchases through the deductibility of mortgage interest. Home ownership builds equity, which in turn becomes a principal source of retirement funds later on. At what point, though, does wise get Warped? When I was his age, there was a rule of thumb, in this case a useful one. It said that a person should devote no more than one-quarter of his monthly income to housing. Everybody seemed to know that rule; I kept it in mind as I searched for my first little apartment. Today, almost nobody can tell you how much debt, relative to income, is too much, and that's a big part of this young man's problem. I search my pile of folders looking for an up-to-date rule of thumb. It takes thirty minutes before I find one, an eternity in this age of information on demand. The current rule of thumb hasn't changed much: it's 28 percent. A mortgage should consume no more than twenty-eight cents out of every gross dollar a person makes. (Credit cards, car payments, student loans should add no more than another eight cents.) I ask the young man if he has ever heard of these guidelines, or any others. He says no.

Shortly after I meet this person I open the *New York Times* and come face-to-face with his alter ego, a veritable poster boy of Debt Warp. He's a twenty-eight-year-old living in Denver, making a good if not spectacular living. Debt Warped to the max, he decides to purchase a $500,000 suburban town house even though he can't afford to put a penny down. But low interest rates allow him to neatly execute a Debt Warp two-step. Step one is to apply for, and receive, a mortgage to cover 80 percent of the purchase price. Knowing that he'll be pinched to make these monthly payments, he opts for an adjustable-rate, interest-only loan, meaning that he'll be building zero equity in his new pad, but who's counting? Step two is to pony up the remaining 20 percent with a home-equity loan.

When the reporter asks him—I now picture the Debt Warpian sitting in an empty great room or an equally barren den—if he's worried that rising rates will sooner or later (it's getting sooner all the time) make it impossible for him to meet his monthly payments, he replies, "I'm too young to be scared." Then he adds, carrying Debt Warp logic to the breaking point, "There is a difference between being poor and being broke. Being broke is more of a temporary condition."

Is this what the Ownership Society is all about? Is this the sort of person who will ever enjoy a healthy relationship with money? Why do I think our man won't be a good boy when it comes to faithfully making deposits into his personal retirement account? And if he doesn't, then what happens? Whose taxes will bail him out? Yours? Mine? Our kids'?

Chances are, our deeply mortgaged hero became Debt Warped not all that long after he reached puberty. Like tobacco companies, wireless phone companies, credit card companies, and lots of other companies are well aware that if you can get them while they're young, they're yours for life. You mean text messaging isn't *free*?! At a few cents a one-liner, high school kids routinely run up monthly text-messaging bills of hundreds of dollars. You'd think their parents would object. Well, not if Debt Warp has already taken control of their parental faculties. "It's hard to be critical, because of the way we use e-mail and BlackBerries and Palm Pilots," a suburban mother told the *New York Times*.

The national lobbying association for profit sharing and 401(k) plans last year reported that nearly three-quarters of young careerists just out of college have at least one credit card. One out of three such Banana Republicans has at least three cards. A decided majority of them fail to take advantage of the 401(k) plans where they work. Granted, easy credit isn't the only reason young careerists overwhelmingly shun tax-deferred retirement plans. Many are paying off student loans, and many are hopping from job to job so quickly they don't meet tenure requirements for company matches in 401(k) plans. Company match is a key reason people sign up for these plans, notwithstanding the fact that a tax-advantaged savings program is in and of itself worthwhile. A typical twenty-two-year-old who deposits 6.9 percent of her annual salary in a tax-deferred plan will have close to $1.5 million by the time she reaches retirement age.

My wife and I are transformed into head-shaking bluenoses when we walk into Best Buy and see so many people—teenagers and young adults, blue collar, white collar, no collar—filling their carts with truly forgettable DVDs (*Battlefield Earth, Lucky Numbers, Domestic Disturbance, The Punisher,* and those are just the John Travolta titles) selling at $29 a pop. Or they carry off the entire treasury of *Sex and the City* for a mere $300, which, I suppose, is still cheaper than a pair of Blahniks. This spectacle puts us into a cranky fuddy-duddy fever. We skulk through the aisles tsking over how much disposable income is wasted on *Shrek* and *dreck* alike, not that it's any of our business.

KILLER BRANDS

Debt Warp is a silent Number killer that afflicts young and old, rich and poor. It works at the high end of the marketplace, it thrives at the low. According to Federal Reserve studies, the richest 1 percent of all Americans carry just 6 percent of the nation's debt; the poorest 90 percent carry 70 percent.

Debt Warp affords the illusion of equality and has been misguidedly heralded as the "democratization of luxury." A couple years ago a book titled *Trading Up* offered an account of how once out-of-reach and numbingly expensive designer brands have devolved into opiates of the people. The book introduces us to an ordinary Joe named Jake, a thirty-four-year-old construction worker who makes $50,000 a year but carries $3,000 worth of Callaway golf clubs in his trunk. Jake bought the sticks not just because he loves to play golf but also, he admits, because "they make me feel rich." I'd wager dollars to duck hooks that Jake bought his Big Humongous Elephantine Berthas with a credit card, although his method of payment goes unmentioned by the authors. Also unmentioned is what Jake holds in his retirement plan, assuming he has a retirement plan. Debt Warp.

Trading Up is an interesting piece of social commentary. We learn about the rise of so-called accessible superpremium brands. The authors don't say so, but I think this trend also owes much to Debt Warp, which encourages middle-class tipplers not to think twice about feeding their Debt Warped schnauzers Eukanuba Premium Performance dog food ($32.99) instead of Alpo Grrravy kibble ($18.49). Similarly, Debt Warp has helped spread the widespread acceptance of so-called masstige brands. Consumers are quick to spend 275 percent more for a tube of Bath & Body Works skin moisturizer while Vaseline Intensive Care lotion languishes on the shelf at La Maison Walgreen.

Trading Up also does a fine job chronicling the emergence of "Old Luxury brand extensions." Mercedes C-class sedans are now within reach of people who once bought Toyota Corollas—just a few hundred more Debt Warp dollars a month does the trick. Or, as suggested typographically in a recent ad for the Volkswagen Phaeton V-8:

Turn your garage into a *garage*

There's one problem with the book. *Trading Up*'s index is devoid of such entries as "Bankruptcy, personal"; "Credit card, incidence of default"; or "Saving, rate of." Debt Warp has befogged the authors' ability, and our own, to see the true connection.

TAXING SOLUTIONS

Robert H. Frank, a noted economics professor at Cornell, has a slightly different take on how social pressures help drive the middle and lower classes to financial distress. He blames the growing disparity of wealth for setting lifestyle standards too tempting for the less fortunate to resist. Frank's argument is that wealthy people driving around in 6,000-pound, $60,000 Lincoln Navigators make families driving Honda Civics feel not just physically at risk but unnervingly poor, and that the existence of 8,000-square-foot mega-homes challenges the less wealthy to upsize into homes they can't afford. One of the more blatant paradoxes of the past twenty years is how the average size of a new American home has increased 25 percent while the size of the nuclear American family has diminished (we're not talking weight here).

Robert Frank thinks he knows how to break the grip of Debt Warp: tax it into submission. Almost everybody wants the tax code to be simpler. That's understandable given that the current version runs to over 60,000 pages and consumes 6.6 billion hours and $140 billion in prep time a year, according to estimates published in the *Atlantic Monthly*. A smaller subset of reformers wants the tax system to be fairer. The devil, as always, is in the deductions. Professor Frank's antidote would be to scrap our current income tax code in favor of a progressive consumption tax, which, like it or not, would represent a stealthy strike against the evils of Debt Warp. Frank's idea is different from Europe's value-added tax, which adds a surcharge to the price of goods and services at each level of production, paid by the consumer. VAT is a tax that punishes the poor more than it restrains the buying habits of the rich. Frank's proposed fix would amount more to a luxury tax, a levy on big spenders rather than a tariff levied on every lightbulb or pair of shoelaces. Without getting into the minutiae, it basically grants every family a standard spending deduction plus a deduction for putting money away in a retirement account. If that takes care of the family's balance sheet for the year, the family's off the hook for further taxes. However, any family that exceeds its allowance would pay an increasing amount of tax on the goods and services it consumes. In this scheme, people who live high and spend conspicuously, especially on things like Gucci iPod cases, would pay a price for screwing up everybody else's material values.

Fat chance of any of this happening. Such a tax runs headlong into the fact that consumer spending makes the economy's wheels go round. It will be seen as a disincentive to work hard. It will be denounced as an environmental disaster in the making, because America would become one giant landfill, with mountains of discarded plastic cards as far as the eye can see.

5

THE LOST YEARS

There are people who confess that they've been thinking about the Number for as long as they can remember, setting goals, keeping score. It's why they picked the college majors they did, why they chose Wharton over Grinnell. They aren't, however, most people. Most people say that as young and not so young adults they never gave the Number a second thought, which is why they read Amy Tan, not Andrew Tobias. These are the members of the Lost Years Club. In the Lost Years Club you can go for decades without a serious glance at the financial pages. Money comes and goes, with a little put by—a pity, as these are the years when we could be digging a solid financial foundation, smugly aware that compounding dollars multiply over time as merrily as bunnies.

When people talk about their experiences in the Lost Years Club, they tell pretty much the same story: it's a time marked by equal measures of insouciance and ignorance. These are the people most afflicted with Uncertainty Principle 2: they never get around to learning how money works, how it grows, how others make money off it, how it can be spread around various types of assets to optimize returns and minimize risk. They have other things on their minds. They get out of col lege and start working—if they're lucky enough to land a job—then decide they've made the wrong career choice and spend a few years retooling their qualifications. Then big changes kick in. Marriage. Domestic partnership. Civil union. He works. She works. Kids wander into the picture. Nobody has any time. No time to plan. No time to save. A little time to shop. It's hard. It's complicated. Everybody needs stuff. Everybody wants stuff. Food. Clothes. Toys. John Travolta movies.

Some people stay in the Lost Years Club forever. Some just accept it, others develop a chip on their shoulder when it comes to money. I know quite a few people who carry these chips. They believe that if there was any justice in the world there would be a direct correlation between the size of one's Number and one's ability to be funny, original, and charming at dinner parties. It drives them crazy that the people with big Numbers—the Wall Street crowd, the guy who owns a string of car dealerships, trust fund babies—are boring or arrogant at parties. They ask each other the overarching existential question of the Lost Years: *How come it's always the jerks who have all the money?*

ROACH MOTEL

My own membership in the Lost Years Club lasted two decades, through which time I kept an undernourished Number languishing at one of the big brokerage houses. The account, or at least my management of it, was devoid of any strategic time line or investment philosophy. I came to think of the vast, impersonal brokerage as a capitalist roach motel. I'd checked in one year on the advice of a tax preparer who suggested I consolidate my modest holdings; then, through all the Lost Years, I failed to check out. I was, over that time, financially comatose—a key symptom of the Lost Years—possessed of no good idea about what to do with my nest egg. I also had no clue as to how the roach motel made any money off my account, no idea of what slice of that modest pie was feeding my broker's Number, not my own. There wasn't much action in that account; few commissions were ever paid out. I did no stock trading via the firm, preferring instead to make the occasional impulsive bet through a discount broker. My stagnant little investment pot was filled with safe, low-yielding government bonds, plus a few exotic hybrid products I never understood.

From time to time it occurred to me that it might be a good idea to bust out of the roach motel and find an avuncular money adviser who'd take active guardianship of my financial destiny, but I never did much about it. You probably didn't either. In the Lost Years there are always better things to do than worry about moving too little money around. But there was also a human dimension at work: some misguided allegiance to my broker held me back—that is, the man who was my broker until the day, as reported on my quarterly statement, he was elevated to financial adviser, or investment consultant, or asset consigliere, or something equally daunting, I don't precisely remember.

The freshly titled financial adviser was a nice enough guy, an occupational prerequisite. Genial, responsive, somewhat hyper, a fast talker, he commuted to Manhattan from New Jersey. He sent me Christmas cards every year, remembered my birthday, and was unfailingly friendly and enthusiastic whenever he got me on the phone. The phone calls bugged me. He had a knack for ambushing me at the office as I was trying to close an issue of the magazine. The calls caught me off guard. I found it hard to shift gears, to make a snap decision about a bond coming due just as I was haggling with a Hollywood press agent who was demanding photo and writer approval on behalf of a no-name ingénue. The broker's calls were erratic. Sometimes he'd phone up a couple of times a month, then six months would go by without contact. Often he called when he had something new to pitch, a product that, he predictably noted, was "in limited supply." These opportunities sounded fishy even to an investment ignoramus like me. My account, as I said, was microscopic, so I questioned his motive for letting me in on the action. Was he looking to unload investment dog meat, a scoop of hash the big boys had already sniffed at before moving on to filet mignon?

His descriptions of these offerings made my head hurt. He talked so incredibly fast that I didn't have a clue as to what he was selling. The products seemed immensely complicated—mixed-breed, inflation-hedged, shock-resistant and waterproof derivatives, which, he said without taking a breath, could only go up, never down. These products usually had collars, or floors, or wing nuts attached to them. Best of all, he added, these opportunities carried "no sales fee," which didn't prevent me from assuming that there was something cleverly embedded in them that would cost me money. Was he deploying notorious broker tricks such as carpet-bombing the unsuspecting with arcane facts till the customer cried uncle and said yes? Was he relying on marketing, not financial, prowess to exploit my weaknesses? Nah, I told myself. He was too nice a guy to play these games. I generally gave him the benefit of the doubt.

Even so, for those twenty years I kept my guard up. Nine calls out of ten I said I was in a meeting and would get back to him, which I almost never did. For a while I felt guilty, but such remorse was short-lived as I came to realize that he never held my failure of etiquette against me. Brokers, er, financial advisers, like all good salespeople (and unlike normal people like you and me), learn not to take things personally. Sure enough, in due time he was right back on the horn.

So it went, year after year. I reached age thirty, thirty-five, forty. I rarely met my broker face-to-face; whenever I did, I saw the passage of time all too clearly. We were both getting old, with graying hair and deepening creases. These were the years, I realize now, when I should have been sketching out a plan. But nobody had a plan back then. And nobody was telling us to have one—certainly not the newspaper ads, whose messages shifted with the state of the stock market. When the market was going up and up, the ads featured stampeding bulls. When times were tough, they turned earnest, squishy, reassuring; they were shot in black and white, oozing sincerity. The brokerage wasn't a faceless capitalist maw intent on hoovering as many assets as possible, but a close trusted friend, that kindly and astute uncle I sometimes wished I'd had to help me find my financial way.

LOST NO MORE

The mysteries that marked the Lost Years begin to reveal themselves one day as I'm Googling financial terms, including the word *wirehouse*. While wirehouse has fallen into disuse among civilians, it's still tossed around in Wall Street circles. The term dates back to the days when Merrill Lynch established a national network of branch offices tied together by Teletype wires. Today, because everyone—Merrill, Smith Barney, UBS, you, me—has access to real-time data, the wirehouses have had to adapt to changing times and technologies. But they've adapted well, after some fitful ambivalence about the potential of the Internet, and have remade their business models. Wirehouses survive as financial behemoths: Merrill Lynch holds $1.5 trillion in client assets; Smith Barney, nearly a trillion.

Anyway, there I am, Googling *wirehouse* when my gaze lands on an intriguing link: "Secrets of the Wirehouse." It turns out to be an exposé, a rant written by a former wirehouse employee who worked there in the mid-1990s, a few years before Eliot Spitzer took some mutual funds and wirehouses to his Albany woodshed. Reading it, I find the mist lifting from my Lost Years confusion. The author is Scott Dauenhauer, a thirty-one-year-old investment adviser who now has his own private planning practice in Laguna Hills, California. His screed doesn't charge that brokers do anything blatantly illegal, or there's much risk that one will take your hard-earned portfolio and invest it in the daily double at Monmouth Park. What mainly bothers Dauenhauer are the invisible fees and your broker's questionable competency.

Dauenhauer comes across as a straight shooter, a middlebrow guy with all the right values. He is, by his own description, a dedicated churchgoer, an avid sports fan, a couch potato, and a fan of all things

Star Wars. His Web site carries a quote from Yoda—"Impossible to predict, the future is"—an appropriate disclaimer for any person or institution in the business of managing investments. (It is certainly less fatuous and more original than the headline I saw in the *Washington Post* the other day: "Risks Cloud Sunny Forecast." Really, guys.)

Dauenhauer tells me he served time at several of the big roach motels, including my old address. He's one of the many thousands of brokers who exited them over the past five or six years, casualties of the wirehouses' evolving business model. More than a few of these former brokers have tried Dauenhauer's path: they got themselves certified and set up independent shops to serve investors who are more comfortable taking advice from someone who charges by the hour and doesn't try to sell dog meat on commission. Although most of the former brokers went quietly, Scott Dauenhauer did not. With "Secrets of the Wirehouse" he broke a lot of dishes on the way out. As a result, he says, he received a variety of absurd online threats (vague warnings about his family's safety) and slurs (he's *gay*—pass it on!) from fellow brokers he left behind.

During our phone conversation, I tell him about my Lost Years and my ignorance about how anyone could make money off my plain-vanilla holdings. It was easy, says Dauenhauer. Those bond issues I bought were quarried out of the firm's own inventory, which probably meant that wiser, grown-up investors had already passed on them. The firm made money on the "spread," meaning it tacked a few invisible basis points onto the price. This enabled my broker to say, half truthfully, that the bonds carried "no commission." Dauenhauer then cites a case from his own wirehouse days when a wealthy client bought $3 million worth of munis that netted the brokerage a cool $100,000—all without a transparent sales charge.

Even though years have passed since he posted "Secrets of the Wirehouse," and despite Eliot Spitzer, Dauenhauer generally stands by his indictment. He is still worked up over how some wirehouses pretend to be producing comprehensive and custom financial plans when, in fact, the plans are cranked out assembly-line style. Your friendly wirehouse financial consultant has little or nothing to do with it, Dauenhauer notes. He says the big firms sell financial plans as loss leaders, adding with more than a little disdain that your plan is executed in the firm's back office "by some guy in New York" who plugs in numbers and sends a slickly printed kit back to your broker in Omaha, who proudly hands it over to you. Not enough time is spent, he says, drawing you out on what you truly want from the plan. It's all numbers, no values.

We also talk about how wirehouses play footsie with mutual fund companies. There's a pay-to-play system at work, by which a mutual fund company will pay a fee to rent "shelf space" on the wirehouse's "platform" of available funds. This is an area where there's been at least partial reform as a result of Spitzer's cage rattling: Dauenhauer says brokerages are now required to disclose "pay-to-play" arrangements on their Web sites and other channels. So here's a suggestion for a rainy Sunday. Go to big brokerage Web site and play a game of Where's Waldo? Only instead of Waldo, look for the pay-to-play disclosure. When I played the game I didn't find it, but maybe my middle-aged eyes are failing.

BOOK LEARNING

The Lost Years live on. There's a woman I've known for years. Perceptive, funny, a quick learner, she's got polished opinions on a great many topics: show business, psychotherapy, the quirks of New York society. Yet here she is, berating herself over how illiterate she is when it comes to money. She asks me whether I think I have a good understanding of how money works. I have a decent understanding of money, I say.

How did I acquire even a decent understanding? From books mostly, I tell her. Learning about money from a book is like learning about sex from a book: it's not the most thrilling way but sometimes it's the best you can do. Thinking back on the Lost Years, I remember a few books that, for me at least, afforded rudimentary lessons in how to get a grip on the mechanics of money.

The first money book I remember reading with any interest was Andrew Tobias' *The Only Investment Guide You'll Ever Need*. It was originally published in 1978, around the dawn of the Great Inflation, when the oldest baby boomer was thirty-two and had plenty of time left to shuck off the lethargy and confusion of the Lost Years. Looking back at that time, as Tobias does in subsequent editions of the book, it's striking to consider how much has changed. In 1978 there were no index funds, no 401(k)s, and no online brokers. The top federal income tax bracket was 70 percent.

Until Tobias came along, books about personal finance were dry and insufferably earnest. Remember Sylvia Porter? Tobias was a wisecracking New Yorker clever enough to understand that dry and earnest wasn't how you talked money management to a generation that (a) had never known financial adversity, and (b) didn't take managing it very seriously. Tobias recognized that many boomers were hopelessly innocent about money. In the years following the book's publication, this innocence was hijacked by unbridled hubris fueled by a roaring stock market. How are these for annual returns? In 1980 the S&P 500 rose 32 percent; in '82, 21 percent; in '83, 22 percent; in '85, 31 percent. I don't know about you and your friends, but my circle of pals had a blast. We forgot those chips on our shoulders and played the market with a zeal hitherto reserved for the Rotisserie League. The daily drill was to go out to lunch, trade stock tips over tuna sandwiches, then race back to the office to phone in our bets. For a while, almost every bet we made turned out to be a winner. At the end of each workday I bought the late edition of the *New York Post* and pored over the stock tables as I walked down lower Park Avenue, oblivious to oncoming pedestrians and traffic, daring buses, taxis, and bicycle messengers to flatten my newfound enthusiasm for the equities market.

The hubris that hijacked the Lost Years was chronicled in a book called *A Fool and His Money* by John Rothchild. It was a blow-by-blow account of what happens when a man decides to spend his waking hours in pursuit of a common fantasy: what if you quit your day job and played the market full-time? Or, as Rothchild observed, "As the waist expands and the arteries contract, sex seems to take a merciful back seat in the libido, supplanted by an obsession with where to eat and how to increase one's net worth." Rereading *A Fool and His Money* today, I am comforted to know that my own Lost Years were not unique. Rothchild, too, is a confessed weenie when it comes to confronting a broker. He wonders how it can possibly be that a rational, intelligent person has no difficulty dressing down a clerk for overcharging a couple of bucks, then devolves into a jelly doughnut in the face of a broker whose dumb advice results in the loss of thousands.

The Lost Years took a turn for the worse on Black Monday, October 19, 1987. The oldest baby boomer was now forty-one and counting. Retirement was just around the corner. Millions of creaky boomers were all at once clinging to Numbers that were mere shadows of their former selves. It was now a new world of self-preservation, self-reliance, detailed with fine precision in the last book we'll take down from the Lost Years bookshelf: Joseph Nocera's *A Piece of the Action*. This book was about the big picture: how personal finance in America had profoundly changed through the latter half of the twentieth century; how the financial markets, once the province of the wealthiest few, sucked in the middle class. It was about how money market funds, with trading accounts attached, replaced the passbook as our savings' principal refuge; how portfolio management went the way of self-service. It was about how we transformed ourselves from savers to fledgling investors. And about how banks, once local, became global powerhouses, and how a majority of American families became stakeholders in public companies. It was about how IRAs, Keoghs, and 401(k)s became the lifelines to the future; how the out-of-control inflation of the 1970s redirected the tone and course of American politics. It was about how all of a sudden there were books and magazines and newsletters and cable channels all screaming urgent tips. And finally it was about how the blanketing of our lives with credit cards utterly changed how we saved (or didn't).

Nocera's forty-year history is a tale of emancipation and empowerment. Freed from the darkness of the self-imposed Lost Years, we had now gained the freedom and the tools with which to take our financial destinies into our own trembling hands.

6

ALONE AT SEA

Once upon a time, the drill was to hit sixty-five and retire. People owned their homes outright, paid for things in cash, bit into apples knowing that their Polident would hold. Not long afterward, they kicked the bucket. In the *old* Rest of Your Life, retirement was underwritten by old-fashioned company pensions and Social Security. The checks were as good as gold. Nobody worried about accounting frauds that could pull the rug out from under the Rest of Your Life. Nobody was expected to know how to manage an elegantly diversified portfolio.

Since it's the *new* Rest of Your Life that we're concerned with here, I won't spend much time on an obituary for the old one. Yet there's a measure of understanding to be gained in briefly looking back at it. In the great sweep of things, the old Rest of Your Life was a historical blip destined to be swept aside by mighty tidal forces—political, economic, and demographic. It is gone but not forgotten. The old Rest of Your Life still reverberates in the form of Uncertainty Principle 3: once-familiar support systems are fading fast, which understandably makes everybody nervous. Where did it come from, this strange idea that a person worked till he or she was sixty-five, at which point a paternalistic employer and/or government agency would offer sufficient subsistence to get them through what relatively little time remained?

The answer plays out in, more or less, three acts.

THE BLIP: ACT I

Americans born in 1900 had an average life expectancy of just over forty-nine years. Retirement wasn't a given. It was common for those who lived into their seventies to keep on working. Through the early part of the century, the percentage of workers still on the job at age sixty-five exceeded 60 percent, not including farmers, who almost never retired.

Retirement as we came to know it didn't happen because the masses were clamoring to hitch trailers to their old Fords and head for the Sunbelt. It came about because early-century capitalism, which was undergoing dramatic transformation, saw bottom-line opportunity in shortening the careers of older workers. More and more Americans had left the farm and gone off to toil in the offices and on the factory floors of increasingly large corporations. As these workers grew old, managers began to view them as unproductive. According to William Graebner's definitive A *History of Retirement,* management and labor leaders alike warmed to the idea of mandatory furloughs. There was nothing altruistic about this. To replace old guys with young bucks augured a more stable and less expensive workforce. Management could better control labor turnover. In no time at all a host of industries, also religious denominations and universities, mounted initiatives to trade hidebound old-timers for cheaper replacement parts, employees they believed were more malleable and, the watchword of the era, more "efficient."

At the same time, work was increasingly becoming identified with a six-letter word with which it is today all but synonymous: stress. According to Graebner, "work [came to be] associated with nervous strain, tension, anxiety . . ." Aging workers were judged to be "burned out," "used up," "exhausted." Mandatory retirement was deemed to be in the best interest of the employee's emotional health. Some things never change.

The question was, though, what exactly would society do with these people? Old, stressed-out employees couldn't just be left out on the street. Many of the displaced old-timers no longer had family farms to return to. Without adequate means they faced an uncertain existence in the crowded cities where they'd come to stake their claim in a newly industrialized nation. There was nothing remotely like Social Security, which was not yet a gleam in the eye of young Franklin Roosevelt, who at the start of the last century was still a stripling at Harvard.

In the 1910s and '20s some old-timers had pensions to fall back on, sort of. Military pensions had been around since colonial days, according to Augustana College historian Joanna Short. And a fair number of corporations and labor unions also offered them, albeit on terms that today would make a job-hopping employee blanch. To qualify for a pension back then, you usually had to put in a minimum of thirty years' service *and* reach a retirement age of seventy.

During the Blip there were no active adult communities for retired people, no clubhouses, game rooms, fitness centers. According to Short, in the early decades of the last century, more than half of all "retired" Americans bunked with their children or other relatives. They lived in small family homes where it was common to find three generations peeling potatoes in the kitchen, trying to scrape by. Lest we romanticize this quaint, if cramped, domestic tableau into a fantasy that families were beneficent to the older generation, consider this: many codgers felt compelled to draw up wills that stipulated that their worldly goods were to be bequeathed *only* if their kids made good on agreed-on sustenance, right down to specific amounts of vittles and firewood. Ample legal documentation suggests that this enforced largesse amounted to the early twentieth century's answer to retirement planning.

THE BLIP: ACT II

The next phase of the old Rest of Your Life began with the Jazz Age and ended at the soup kitchen. Through the 1920s and '30s considerable national schizophrenia arose over the issue of mandatory retirement. Hard-liners continued to insist that older workers were suboptimal, if not subhuman. Graebner's retirement history cites a Metropolitan Life Insurance Company report that characterized the older employee as "a very touchy individual." According to Graebner, the view was shared by a Harvard professor, who asserted that when a worker approached middle age he developed a host of unfortunate personality traits including, but not limited to, the inability to adapt, rigid insistence on routine, and impatience with newfangled ways of doing things.

Others, more enlightened, saw forced expulsion from the workplace as just plain wrongheaded *and* bad for business. This counterview regained some ground lost in the 1920s. From around this point forward, studies began to cite evidence that older workers were *more* reliable, and displayed better work habits, than their greenhorn colleagues. Older workers, data suggested, had a keener grasp of the problems facing management. Their presence in an office or factory was a source of stability and provided invaluable mentoring for younger counterparts. Cruel, cold efficiency wasn't the only yardstick with which to measure the value of middle-aged human chattel.

August 14, 1935, 3:30 P.M. As the debate over how-old-is-too-old continued, America underwent a major change in social climate. When FDR signed into law the Social Security Act, the sun rose on the then new but now old Rest of Your Life. The idea that the government should be in the business of taking care of the disadvantaged was outrageous to many people then, just as it is to many people today. In something of a prescient political call, presidential candidate Alf Landon condemned the funding method embodied in the bizarrely complicated Social Security trust fund as a "cruel hoax" on the American people. It took a while to get the kinks out, but in time the Social Security Act came to be regarded by nearly all as one of the most significant pieces of legislation of the century. It amounted to an unofficial new plank in the Bill of Rights: the right to a decent Rest of Your Life. With senior Americans now nestled in the arms of a kindly and protective Uncle Sam, Eleanor Roosevelt was pleased as punch, as she told Social Security supporters in a speech in 1934:

> Old people love their own things even more than young people do. It means so much to sit in the same old chair you sat in for a great many years, to see the same picture that you always looked at!
> And that is what an old age security law will do. It will allow the old people to end their days in happiness, and it will take the burden from the younger people. . . . It will end a bitter situation— bitter for the old people because they hate to be a burden on the young, and bitter for the young because they would like to give gladly but find themselves giving grudgingly and bitterly.

Now, stop for a second and compare Eleanor Roosevelt's tone of voice with the way Social Security is debated today. Think about how today's Rest of Your Life political debate is framed around dollars, not human values. Even if your political taste in women favors Ann Coulter over Eleanor Roosevelt, at least give Eleanor credit for this: she kept Grandma and Grandpa warm and cozy in their own house, not yours.

THE BLIP: ACT III

The old Rest of Your Life came into its own following World War II. Company pension plans were on the rise because, as Joanna Short explains, wartime wage freezes forced employers to attract workers with the promise of retirement payouts. Between the war years and 1960, the growth in corporate pensions was explosive: nearly a third of the American workforce received monthly checks from their former employers.

At the same time, Social Security was growing into the eggplant that ate America. In 1950 Congress passed a law that provided for annual cost-of-living adjustments, and benefits jumped 77 percent that first year. Coverage was extended to farmers and domestic workers, and disability benefits were broadened. In 1961 a bill passed that lowered the age at which men may receive retirement benefits: sixty-two, just as it was for women. The Rest of Your Life could now start even earlier.

Then, on July 30, 1965, at a ceremony in Independence, Missouri, with Lady Bird Johnson in a robin's-egg-blue dress behind him and Harry and Bess Truman seated to his left, LBJ signed into law HR 6675. It provided basic health insurance for everyone over age sixty-five. Medicare had arrived. With a safety net below and doctors and nurses standing by, the old Rest of Your Life looked like the Real Deal. Business and government had really stepped up. What was missing, though, was an add-on benefit that a new generation would view as essential: the lifestyle entitlement.

SHOCK OF THE NEW

The old Rest of Your Life was about others taking some responsibility for you. The new one is about you taking care of yourself. (Yes, there's still Medicare, which is not insignificant, but which of course has its own problems.) Today, *personal* retirement plans are the rule, which is all well and good except that they rest shakily on whether you have enough self-discipline and know-how to make them work. Self-discipline? Know-how? Honchos in the financial services field tell me that it's difficult to get anyone much younger than fifty to gather more than a popsicle stick or two with which to build a life raft for the new Rest of Your Life. But as fifty approaches people start to pay attention. Why the awakening? The impulse is most often triggered by the daydream of an early retirement. This reverie, however, is frequently disturbed by all those nasty questions about how much is enough. So here you are, pushing fifty, your doubles partner is dead, and nobody makes eye contact with you anymore. Yep—time to plan for the new Rest of Your Life.

That life raft analogy invites a squall of nautical metaphors. Retirement account shipwrecked or pirated by scandalous accounting? Does the Rest of Your Life look like a beached minnow? This is where Uncertainty Principle 3—the demise of the old "defined benefits" system—meets Uncertainty Principle 4—questions over the viability of what replaced it. These uncertainties leave you wringing wet. When you pry open the treasure chest ten or twenty or thirty years from now, will there be anything in it but old clamshells? You've played by the rules. You've trusted the system. So what?

The shift from defined benefits (pensions, a secure Social Security system) to defined contributions (personal retirement plans) is regarded as "one of the most dramatic transformations in the economy over the last two decades," says Edward N. Wolff of New York University, who studies the impact defined contribution plans have had on the economy and the lives of seniors. For reasons we'll get to in a second, Wolff rues the day DBs turned into DCs. For now, just ask yourself: once embarked on the Rest of Your Life, which would provide you with more peace of mind? A retirement plan funded by a guaranteed income stream, monthly checks you could count on, or a retirement managed by little old you? The question is moot. Nobody is about to let you return to the promised land of guaranteed benefits. Pensions are expensive propositions, especially now that so many boomer employees are marching toward the Rest of Your Life. This is why the news in the papers isn't pretty. Just as editors don't assign stories about safe landings, they don't commission pieces about pension funds that are robust enough to meet present and future obligations. It takes only one crash to make every flier nervous as hell, and the papers report a pension crash almost every day. For older companies in mainline industries, pension obligations and the health plans welded to them present immense fiscal challenges. General Motors, for example, provides health care coverage for 450,000 retired workers, the result of decades of negotiations with its unions. In 2004 GM paid out over $3 billion into its retirement health trust fund, or nearly three times its earnings. Airlines, carmakers, energy companies, big retailers, cities and states, just to mention a few, are looking for ways out of existing obligations. But when I ask executives in the financial services field how serious the pension fund shortfalls are, they're inclined to wave the question off, saying that things look bad only because the stock market has been in the dumps over the past few years, and just wait till the next bull market. Easy for them to say. It's the Rest of *Your* Life we're talking about, not theirs.

For forty-two million people, the defined contribution plan of choice is the 401(k) (teachers and government employees use different terms for the same idea). At present there are about two trillion dollars invested in 401(k)s. Under such plans, employees and employers each contribute a set amount. The individual bears all the risk as to how, or whether, these investments grow—employers bear zip. Personal retirement plans have worked very well for many people and have certain advantages over old-style pensions, portability being the greatest. Unlike health care coverage, we retain our accumulated assets as we move from one employment stop to the next, no matter how many calculated, serendipitous, or calamitous turns we take in a career.

Roughly 80 percent of those eligible do indeed put some money into a 401(k)-type plan—typically 5 to 6 percent of their pay. Those who don't contribute say they can't afford to, or find it too confusing, or would rather buy a Porsche Cayenne. Of those who are enrolled, many fail to apportion their assets properly. Some people are too risk averse, putting their nest eggs in fixed income funds with modest dividend payouts; others are way too aggressive, whether purposely or not. There's a consensus among the managers of these plans that most people don't make the right investment decisions. An oft-quoted survey of 401(k) account holders several years ago reported that half of those asked believed that money-market funds were made up of stocks and bonds. Forty percent weren't aware that a balanced fund is a blend of stocks and bonds. A 2003 survey revealed that 38 percent of workers in their twenties held no equities in their retirement portfolios. At the same time, 13 percent of workers in their sixties owned portfolios containing 90 percent stocks, which for most of them is a bit aggressive.

Are people too lazy to figure things out? Too busy? Too stupid? The director of Boston College's Center for Retirement Research takes a diplomatic middle ground, according to the *Wall Street Journal*: "[401(k)s] are simply too complicated for people to handle. It's not that people are dumb. It's just that . . . becoming a financial expert is low on their priority list." Others say that people screw up their 401(k)s because companies offer too many choices, a dizzying array of mutual fund options—dozens, sometimes hundreds of them—that they don't understand. These vast menus lead people either to make bad allocation decisions or become so paralyzed by indecision that it's easier to pass on participation. The hard fact is that people must learn to live with direct contribution plans. They're here to stay. Political conservatives and the financial services industry love them, of course. Professor Wolff, on the other hand, proposes that we look carefully at whether defined contribution plans have really been good for people:

- Over time as pensions began to give way to direct contribution programs, the average net worth of older households has indeed shown substantial growth. That's the good news.

- The bad news is that the above good news is highly misleading. Wolff discovered on closer analysis that these "average" net worths were highly skewed by the immense gains enjoyed by the richest households, those with holdings of over $1 million. Less affluent older households had marginal, if any, gains.

- Furthermore, Wolff points out, the old pension system kept a lot of seniors out of poverty, a trend I presume he doesn't feel nearly as confident going forward, given the risks and vagaries of the stock market.

SOCIAL INSECURITY

Social Security is not just the third rail of politics. It is—after pensions and private retirement plans—a third stream of uncertainty, a hardly insignificant worry for the two out of three American seniors who regard it as their major source of retirement income. In 2004 all hell broke loose. Social Security, swept under the rug for years, suddenly was the nation's most pressing domestic issue. The White House, Congress, AARP, financial lobbies, think tanks, editorial writers, pundits, and cable news went into mass hysteria over whether there's in fact a crisis destined to leave everyone penniless, whether we're sentencing our children and grandchildren to a real-life reenactment of *Oliver!*, or whether this whole brouhaha is at bottom just a Bushworld conspiracy to undo the social welfare programs of the past seventy-five years, and a sop to the stock market at that.

Given all the publicity the issue has received, there's no need here to go into the sordid details. But to remind you of the two dark dates everyone's talking about: by 2019, the so-called dependency ratio—the number of taxpaying workers relative to those collecting benefits—will be so out of whack that unless the system changes (higher taxes, lower benefits, older eligibility ages, or all of the above) it will be hemorrhaging (not dripping, not oozing, but hemorrhaging) red ink. Then, says the Social Security Administration, look out for 2042 or 2052 (if you prefer the Congressional Budget Office's more optimistic projection). At this point the trust fund will be able to deliver only 70 percent of current-level benefits.

Where will you be in 2052? If you're my age, you'll be a spry, wiry, 106-year-old. And you'll be one angry, hungry, and poorly dressed old coot, or so the alarmists would have us believe. As for politicians, most of them wish George Bush had put a sock in it. In the ringing words of Congressman Rob Simmons of Connecticut: "2042? I will be dead by then."

Now that we have heard from the politicians, what do normal people think? I bring up the subject of Social Security with a friend of mine in New York, a professor in his sixties, a political liberal, still working, and pretty well fixed. I ask if Social Security is important to his retirement. "Hell, yes!" he fires back. "I paid into it, and I think I should get something in return. Do I need it to put food on the table? No. But who couldn't use another eighteen thousand dollars a year to spend in your dotage?" Then he adds, "It could pay for the wine we drink."

That brief exchange speaks volumes about what's wrong with Social Security, and why it will be so vexing to fix it. For millions of people parked high on the ramp, Social Security is not needed for what it was meant to be: an insurance policy, a safety net, a payment of last resort. For people like my friend it's a bonus, a cushion, a bottle of wine on top of other, more significant sources of retirement funding.

There are also people—all of them young—who are stunningly blasé about the whole thing. One day I'm on the phone with a financial planner from California. He's all of thirty years old, engaging and outspoken. I ask if many of his clients are worried lest future Social Security shortfalls slice holes in their Rest of Your Life safety net. He answers without a beat, with sunny, West Coast nonchalance, "The clients who are my age, the ones in their twenties and thirties, are not counting on ever seeing a check." So there you have it: Social Security has devolved into the biggest distrust fund ever conceived.

Peering into the future, one out of every two people questions whether his or her lifestyle will be as comfy as it is now. Still, many aren't doing much about it or they can't afford to. For the past fourteen years, the Employee Benefit Research Institute has conducted a Retirement Confidence Survey that measures how Americans regard a host of midlife issues surrounding retirement. In its most recent survey, the EBRI presents a ton of data indicating that few people are gearing up. The number of Americans saving for retirement has not increased in the last three years, for example, and four out of ten workers say they're saving nothing whatsoever for the future. EBRI reports that no more than four out of every ten people admit they have ever taken steps to calculate the actual cost of a comfortable Rest of Your Life. Of those who have spent a few minutes with paper and pencil, one in three doesn't remember what those calculations revealed. As for what respondents say they have put aside, assuming they have put anything aside, 45 percent say less than $25,000. Only 18 percent have more than $100,000 in Rest of Your Life reserves. None of these numbers bode well. There's denial in the air.

And here's the punch line: more than half of Americans today feel the government or their employers, rather than they, should take on greater responsibility for the new Rest of Your Life. Nonetheless, they'd better get cracking. The new Rest of Your Life is different from the old not just because their funding streams are different. It also lasts much longer. We are a population of geriatric Energizer bunnies, powered by pacemakers and fortified with implants of every description, from drug-eluting stents to titanium femoral components. Yes, we keep on ticking. Beginning forty years ago, developers stopped building retirement communities and started to market "active adult communities" replete with so many hobby centers and assorted amenities they might more properly be called hyperactive adult communities.

All kinds of businesses and organizations are retooling themselves. In January 2000, at the tender age of forty-two (it seems much older, doesn't it?), the American Association of Retired Persons opted for a dramatic nip-and-tuck job on its own identity, excising the obsolete and offending R-word from its name and announcing that henceforth it would be known only by its yelping dog of an acronym: AARP. That's the new name: AARP. What was going on here? The AARP people knew they'd have a recruiting problem unless they got rid of the R-word. AARP's then executive director, now r*tired, noted that the change was driven by the recognition that more than a third of AARP's thirty-three million members were not retired at all.

AARP also had an image problem. To lifestyle-entitled fifty-somethings, who shop at Urban Outfitters and Diesel, not just Wal-Mart and Sears, the old AARP was about as cool as Bermudas worn with black socks. AARP knew it had to adjust. It knew that today's fifty-year-old looks like yesterday's thirty-five-year-old. She drives a sporty Cadillac SUV, wears a jeans jacket, and tones her body every morning by draping herself over a giant plastic roly ball. He gets his eyelids lifted and struts around with a perpetual, pharmacologically induced man-hood. AARP might have been dowdy, but it was neither blind nor hard of hearing. It was aware that its membership card in the mailbox was occasionally the butt of ridicule on the late-night talk circuit. The card no longer held out merely a welcome invitation to discount movie tick-ets. Its arrival in the mailbox had become a grim foreshadowing of memory loss and arthritis. Remember all the guffawing when Bill Clin-ton got his? (His card, that is.)

Before the name change, if AARP was having trouble sleeping through the night, it had nothing to do with a shrinking bladder. Survey after survey pointed to the reality that the old Rest of Your Life had been turned inside out. In response, AARP rejuvenated its old chestnut of a magazine with covers featuring such midlife hunks and you-should-look-so-good-at-her-age chicks as Harrison Ford and Jane Seymour. And they crammed in so many pieces about financial planning you'd think you were leafing through *Money*.

The old Rest of Your Life used to be about doing nothing or as little as possible. Good-bye to that, according to current AARP research:

- Nearly 70 percent of preretirees say they plan to work at least part-time in their "retirement" years, or plan never to retire at all.

- More than two-thirds say that the reason they want to continue to work is because that's how a person stays active, remains useful, and has fun.

- And oh, yes. They also say they plan to work because they know their Numbers may not be robust enough to foot the bill for the longer and more complicated Rest of Your Life that lies ahead.

THE RETIREMENT OF RETIREMENT

As regards the new Rest of Your Life, nobody thinks *retirement,* the word, does the trick anymore. People relate to neither the style nor the substance of traditional retirement. For many, it invokes a drab, pointless existence in which everything happens too early in the day— waking, eating, bedtime—and the hours in between are spent hosing out the garage, knitting booties, and walking around the mall in squeaky-clean Rockports.

The concept of "retirement," like the old AT&T, is judged to be rather too monolithic for these dynamic times. To fit a changed world, the old retirement needs to be broken up into multiple baby retirements. Larry Cohen is paid to try to figure out what to call these baby retirements. As a vice-president of SRI Consulting Business Intelligence, in Princeton, New Jersey, his task is to crank out proprietary research about the new retirement stages. In a report called "Redefining Retirement" (its epigraph quotes Jethro Tull: "Too old to rock and roll, too young to die!") Cohen explains why retirement would be better understood if busted up into four baby stages:

- Preretirement, when we attempt to accumulate assets specifically for retirement.

- Revolving retirement, when we perhaps try a new field for a while; take a short-term position if only for health benefits; otherwise go in and out of the workforce to (a) keep busy and (b) delay drawing down a fragile Number.

- Middle retirement, a lukewarm version of revolving retirement, when we're pretty much living off our invested assets, with a dollar or two picked up greeting customers at Wal-Mart.

- Late retirement, or what we once knew as retirement, when we're not working at all.

What do all these baby retirements add up to? Let's just say that in the new Rest of Your Life, a person needs to be captain and crew of his own ship. You and you alone must take the helm and point your vessel toward the sunset on the far horizon. With a steady hand through the next several decades, you must guide your leaky tub across what will be turbulent and occasionally angry seas. Job loss, illness, dirty bombs, falling dollars, mounting debt (yours and Uncle Sam's), rising interest rates, environmental crises, economic and political calamities—it's enough to make even the pluckiest helmsperson green around the gills. It isn't fair, mate. They plopped you into a battered boat without teaching you how to trim the sails. You can no more tell a reverse mortgage from a home equity loan than you can distinguish the leech from the luff. So there you drift, rudderless and off course, the sunset sometimes to the port, then to the starboard.

Dramamine, anyone?

7

THE FOREST FOR THE TREES

If sailing metaphors don't do it for you, let's try hiking. To make it through the new Rest of Your Life, you need to know how to get from point A, perhaps up a creek, to point B, out of the woods. What you need is a big map with lots of detailed information. Once you've got the map in hand, you're obliged to faithfully follow the trail, not wander off thinking there's plenty of time to get back on before sundown. Unfortunately, not everyone knows how to draw the big map or even where to look for a cartographer. This is what Uncertainty Principle 5 is about: who's out there to help if we can't see the forest for the trees?

A lot of people don't have maps because they're not sure where they want to wind up. Out of the woods, while nice, is a rather big place. A show of hands, please: how many of you are ready to devote next weekend and many thereafter to arriving at the conclusion that your Number may be inadequate and that you're fundamentally clueless as to how to spend your next thirty years in a meaningful way?

Thank you, sir, you may put your hand down. Now, how many of you would rather treat yourself to a facial than go through that agony?

Figuring out the Number for the new Rest of Your Life does not rank high on people's list of favorite hobbies. The thought of pre-

retirement planning jangles the nerves. A pandemic of cognitive dissonance sweeps the baby boomers. Cognitive dissonance refers to the
fact that even intelligent human beings would just as soon avoid information that causes distress. There is at present no vaccine for this condition.

It's not as if there aren't numerous interested parties telling people
to get a better lock on the Number, or at least to pry their fingers from
their ears: investment managers, brokerages, banks, insurance companies are, as we've seen, all out in force. We are exhorted dusk to dawn to
get on with that big map. However easy it is to deflect those messages
with a click of the remote, there's one place we can't escape them, and
that place is at work, where the custodians of 401(k), profit sharing, and
pension plans have us in their sights, up close and personal. This could
be, indeed should be, a convenient place to draw your map. Your retirement plan is already on file; your employer might still have a solvent
pension plan; the companies managing those funds are potentially
valuable partners.

Except few companies go to the trouble. Yes, company benefit managers are persistent in reminding workers that saving money paycheck
to paycheck is the way to go, thanks to the miracle of compounding returns. And they're diligent about telling employees that anyone who
fails to take advantage of a tax-deferred retirement account, with the
added bonus of a company match, is the dimmest of bulbs. A study
commissioned by the accounting firm KPMG reveals that companies
that offer even perfunctory planning seminars will have 401(k) enrollment rates that average more than 70 percent of eligible workers. Companies that ignore employee education altogether have a sorry 33
percent enrollment. Rarely, however, does a company venture into the
deepest dark muck of retirement planning. Few bother to ask whether
you are ready, really ready, to face down the emotional heebie-jeebies
that come with retirement planning.

PREP SCHOOL

Yet some companies are making a real difference in the lives of prere-tirees. One such firm has an employee workshop coming up, and I ask for the chance to sit in. Arrangements are made without much fuss and not long after, I find myself outside the Crowne Plaza hotel in Atlanta, about a mile from the airport. A continuous racket assaults the senses. The noise comes in dual, brain-rattling forms: one is the thunderous roar of takeoffs and landings at Hartsfield-Jackson; the other is the steady drone of traffic on I-85. The challenge here is to get inside the lobby with your senses intact, then summon every ounce of self-discipline to stay inside till it's time to brave the trip home. The next trick is to be able to live without daylight for forty-eight hours.

The session I'm here to attend is part of an ongoing program offered by the Weyerhaeuser (not to be confused with wirehouse) Corporation, the Seattle-based forestry company. Some sixty employees and their spouses have signed up. Most are in their early fifties. Everyone is courteous and friendly, folks of good North American paper stock. The couples have come to Atlanta on the company's nickel, which covers air tickets, rooms, and meals for all attending employees and their spouses.

The Weyerhaeuser human resources team has supplied each couple with a three-ring binder as thick as an NFL playbook. A good stand of hardwoods must have gone into its making. The binder includes comprehensive summaries of Weyerhaeuser's retirement benefits and a tabbed anthology of articles about how to think about the bugaboos that haunt the first months and years of the postcareer experience. Extensive planning materials on investment strategies and asset allocation are also included. All this represents an admirable gesture toward men and women who are counting the days to the time when they can flip a farewell bird to the company. Most corporations don't come close. On the very day I received a copy of the retirement playbook from Weyer-haeuser, I got a notice from Lands' End, the company I'd recently left. The Lands' End notice was in the form of a one-page flyer informing me that a rep from American Express, the custodian of the company's ben efit plans, would be in town for a day should anybody have a question or two about the 401(k) plan.

That Weyerhaeuser chooses to dive into this morass of preretirement planning is especially commendable given that it is an old-line company in an old-line industry. It would be reasonable to suppose that a macho corporation like this would just as soon tell exiting middle-agers to vacuum the crumbs out of their desk drawers and go roll a log. Weyerhaeuser is not perceived to be touchy-feely; it's a big, brawny Fortune 200 firm with annual sales of $20 billion. It manages vast tracts of timberland and dozens of paper mills from Kingsport, Tennessee, to Kamloops, British Columbia. It has a ton of people to keep track of—65,000 in North America. And it has plenty of other potential uses for spending its discretionary dollars, for instance big-time public relations and marketing campaigns. A giant paper company is ever in the crosshairs of hikers, bird-watchers, climatologists, and environmentalists, all of whom need reassurance that Weyerhaeuser won't desecrate the planet.

If you want to appreciate fully the extent of Weyerhaeuser's efforts, put yourself in the place of one of the employees who've come here. Take a seat, along with your spouse, at one of the twenty round tables in the room. You're a manager, say, in the Enterprise Group, a Weyerhaeuser division located in, say, Beaverton, Oregon, where you turn out interminable reams of perforated paper for those annoying continuous computer feeds; the little rolls of receipt paper found at the cash register; the tissue paper specifically made for hangers at the dry cleaner's, the paper sheets used to cover the instrument trays in your dentist's office.

Assume that you're fifty-something years old, in good health, and itching to get your act together so you and your spouse can retire within the next few years. You have twenty-three years of service at Weyerhaeuser. Your kids are out of college and—at least for the moment—out of the house. You live in a nice 4,500-square-foot, transitional-style manse in, let's call it, the highly desirable Beaver Toothe subdivision. Life is super. But it would be better still if you could figure out how to begin your final approach into rest and relaxation. Maybe you want to buy a farmette in the rolling hills outside Nashville, where you could keep a couple of horses, play golf three or four times a week, and travel frequently to visit your three kids and grandkids scattered hither and yon. This happy prospect is why you and your spouse made tracks to Atlanta, looking sharp in fresh new business casual threads with polo ponies all over them, lugging the three-ring binder that landed with a thud last week.

Like the good, eager Beavertonian you are, you've done your assigned homework. You've downloaded a pension estimate from Vanguard.com, which provides abundant data on when and how you might choose to receive your retirement income once you decide to pull the trigger. And you've perused the required reading in the binder. One is an article entitled "Retire Happy," a recent reprint from *Money* magazine. "Retire Happy"? A better title would be "Keep Working." As you read through it, you're assailed by second thoughts about your decision to retire in the first place. The piece features a cast of characters who threaten to turn your every wishful thought upside down.

"It's not in my personality to sit on my butt," says a former sales rep at Procter & Gamble.

"This arrangement is good for me and it's good for the company," says a former assistant VP at CIGNA who returned to the big insurer two days a week after a drive-by retirement.

"Retirement has turned out to be a boring wasteland," says Ken Dychtwald, author of *Age Power*.

"I used to be able to afford just one good trip a year. Now I can go wherever I want," notes a former bank manager turned part-time travel agent.

The point of the *Money* story is that a little work goes a long way in keeping the fizz in your mind, spirit, and net worth. At the end of the piece there's a chart that shows how, if you retire at age sixty-three and work for seven years at 40 percent of your old salary, you'll increase your annual income by 21 percent a year should you live to be ninety-five.

You put that article back into your binder and pull out other material. This one's a monograph produced by a Seattle life-planning outfit, Money Quotient, Inc. It, too, underscores how important work will be in the new Rest of Your Life. It says how important it will be to fine-tune the day-to-day art of time management. "Most of your life someone else has structured your day. . . . Now [it] is all up to you."

Gulp.

OUT ON A LIMB

The person in charge of the workshop is Sally Celeste Hass. A slight woman in her midfifties, she presents herself with an easy smile and a wry delivery. It takes about two seconds to realize that beneath these pleasantries is a woman of unshakable determination, tenacity, and a hardwood will. Her mission is to jar busy people into cutting through layers of sloth and diffidence so they can get on with the business of figuring out their lives. Hass' title is Benefits Education Manager at Weyerhaeuser, where she has worked for twenty-three years. These scant details may evoke an image of a drab bureaucrat who has managed to keep her head down and survive in the manly world of lumberjacks, but this is decidedly not who Hass is.

Credit for launching the preretirement program at Weyerhaeuser belongs to another woman, Pat Goelzer, an indomitable pension manager who twenty years ago recognized that many of the company's workers would easily live a quarter of their lifetimes after leaving the company. Goelzer spurred the firm to accept that it had both a business and a moral obligation to help prepare them for that perilous passage. She maintained that traditional financial planning wasn't the only prerequisite of a good retirement education. Retirement prep, she argued, needed to address emotional challenges as resolutely as it tackled pension calculations. Goelzer and her team worked up a curriculum and began offering seminars to Weyerhaeuser executives over sixty. But it's been Hass who has kept the program alive for this long, through a dozen years of corporate downsizing and budget cuts, through an era in which "nonessential" services and benefits at most companies have been eviscerated or eliminated outright. She has kept it going even though the Weyerhaeuser human resources department is stocked with fewer and fewer humans and resources.

Behind the ever-present smile, Hass is a shrewd cookie. When her program is recognized with a national award, she doesn't wave it in the face of senior management. To do so, she allows, would invite blowback. Hass knows that the key to keeping senior management from plowing the program under is to position it as good business strategy, not just limp-wristed altruism. She keeps files of testimonials from employees thanking the company for opening their eyes to how retirement planning is a 360-degree process; how appreciative they are for the insight that it's best to plan early for the transition and not go into it cold turkey; and how the sessions Hass organizes are a beacon throwing light into the tunnel of middle age. If you carry nothing else away from this workshop, they attest, you leave with the comfort of knowing that You Are Not Alone, that everyone in the room is similarly apprehensive about health, money, and fear of boredom.

Having facilitated enough of these workshops, Hass has the drill down pat. People walk in "obsessed with their Number," she tells me. "And until we give them some assurance that we will address their financial concerns, we really can't get their attention about anything else. This has been the case from the beginning." But a "wild card" is now emerging, she observes. More and more attendees are alarmed about the cost and availability of health care. Another concern she has is that the financial services folks are increasingly "brokering fear" in an effort to gain management accounts and push high-profit products. Although she's no Pollyanna about the risks on the baby boomers' horizon, she doesn't want the program's participants leaving with more dread than they walked in with: "People just won't focus on what's important about

their futures, that is, meaning and purpose, if they are worrying themselves sick running financial scenarios."

In any case, here you are, raring to get started, surrounded by fellow
tree people. Hass announces that the first item on the agenda is to go
around the room so that everyone, employees and spouses alike, can introduce themselves and share what they most look forward to in retirement—and also what they're most worried about. The request is so
disarmingly friendly that no one seems reluctant to comply. As the confessions begin, it's clear that everyone in the room puts concerns about
health and money at the top of the fear chart, with more than a few
adding the double-whammy fear of not having enough money for health
care. The next biggest worries are likewise intertwined: how to produc-
tively fill the hours in a day and—this from many women in the room—
whether an otherwise good marriage can survive a restless husband
hanging around the house all day. "I do worry about twice as much husband, half as much space," says a stay-at-home spouse, patting the back
of her sheepish-looking hubby.

A few courageous souls admit to not having enough hobbies. One
notes sardonically that "if I had some I'd be retired already." A woman
mentions that she loves jazz but her husband hates it. She is more than a
little vexed that now she won't be able to listen to her favorite music.
Several couples are concerned about "boomerang kids" moving back in.
These existential issues get tossed off with an easy laugh, sometimes a
wisecrack. Not to judge, but I get the sense that some people here don't
appreciate the idea that hobbies aren't just hobbies, they can be pas-
sions. In his farewell column last year, William Safire of the *New York
Times* wrote, "By laying the basis for future activities in the midst of current careers, we reject stultifying retirement and seize the opportunity
for an exhilarating second wind." Enough already with all this talk about
asset diversification. Isn't *passion diversification* just as important?

As for the hopes and dreams, it would be nice to report a
groundswell in the room on behalf of intellectual self-improvement or a
desire to give back to the community. And to be fair, a number of peo-

ple, mostly women, mention these kinds of things. Most of the men, however, say they just want to play golf—two, three, five, seven days a week. Hass knows this is coming and also knows that if she doesn't do something to stop it, the workshop will be dominated by "the G-word," as she calls it. This is her cue to unveil the large sign she posted on the wall before the meeting began: the word GOLF with a red strike through it. Golf, she decrees, will be an unutterable four-letter word for the remainder of the session.

Professed hopes and dreams continue to float through the air like happy and colorful balloons. Quite a few people say they want to pursue a part-time or full-time second career. One man says he wants to learn how to cook. In fact, he says, when he goes to Barnes & Noble he now finds himself heading for the cookbook shelves instead of the business section. So far, so good, but this part of the agenda doesn't last very long. One of Hass' co-presenters steps up to assure the group that it is highly typical, citing a recent national AARP survey on what preretirees say they are most concerned about. At the top of the list: health and money. Then, in order of ranking, fear of having nothing to do; anxiety over loss of relationships with people at work (hmm, no one has mentioned this at all); worry over feeling worthless; concern about screwing up a marriage; the specter of loneliness; the prospect of death or bereavement; confusion over where and how to put down roots; and a nagging anxiety that financial documents are outdated or inadequate. Banana slices off the tee and yips on the putting green fail to crack the list.

Weyerhaeuser's compensation and benefit packages are comparatively generous. If yours have remained this solid, you should feel good. Weyerhaeuser offers a 401(k) retirement plan with a company match, although in this case the match comes in the form of Weyerhaeuser stock. It has been amply demonstrated that too much company stock, or the wrong company stock, can destroy a life faster than you can say "Ken Lay." The company also provides an annual bonus (in the form of deferred stock options) and regular stock options according to employee wage and managerial levels. Ditto the Ken Lay point. Traditional at its core, Weyerhaeuser maintains a pension plan of the sort that's fast vanishing from the scene. On top of this, it provides employees with a profit-sharing opportunity known as the Performance Share Plan (PSP). This could provide a nice annual bump to your Number, especially if you (a) look at these payouts as distributions to be socked away in your long-term Number bank; and (b) your company has profit to share in the first place. At Weyerhaeuser, as elsewhere, less than stellar business results over the prior three years have prompted employees to call the PSP the "Pretend Share Plan"; that is, there have been no PSP payouts in recent years.

The room begins to sag under the weight of bar graphs and pie charts. Especially bewildering are the choices an employee has when it comes to payout schedules and other distribution strategies. The presenters make it clear, or try to, that much rides on how you take your money *out*, not simply how much you have *in*. The whole business is overwhelmingly complex. Every plan, every pot of money, every payout, comes with strings attached and trade-offs. Are you better off taking a lump-sum pension payment or choosing an installment or annuity-type distribution? Do you elect to begin drawing Social Security when you're first eligible, at age sixty-two, or do you put it off a few years? Should you leave resources in your company's retirement plan or roll them over into an IRA? How do estate and tax planning figure in? Should you set up a trust, and if so, what kind? What sort of health insurance can tide you over between the time you leave your company's health plan and the time you get your Medicare card? And have you thought about the need for long-term care? Hey, what time does the bar open?

THE BOAT

At the end of the day, Sally Hass likes to unwind with a glass of wine and some easy conversation. I'm curious about how she came to run this sort of humanitarian relief program at a company like Weyerhaeuser. Well, there's a methodical and disciplined side to her, which you'd expect from a manager of human resources. Nearly thirty years ago, she says, when she was in her twenties, she reserved a place at the Seattle assisted-living residence of choice. But there's another side to her that's quirky, independent, thoroughly original. In her younger days she was an avid and accomplished downhill skier. Although she never married, she talks with effervescent delight about a lifelong circle of terrific friends. Nevertheless, a few years ago, she says with a laugh, she came to the realization that "maybe I had to start eating my own dog food. I asked myself what I might regret as I approach this time in my own life. And I thought about how important it was that I come to know what a deeply loving relationship is about."

As if on cue, that relationship showed up one day in the person of a gold miner, a man named Dan who has spent the past two decades going back and forth from Seattle to the Arctic, where he prospects with a fleet of backhoes, ATVs, and what Hass describes as the largest Caterpillar tractor in the world. He was forty-eight, and materialized just as Hass was approaching her fiftieth birthday and planning a celebratory ski trip to the Alps.

"I'm going with you," Dan told her.

"I don't think so," Sally said, adding that she had no intention of being slowed down by a nonskier.

"Give me till February," Dan replied. Three months later Sally and Dan were skiing the Matterhorn together. At one point Dan passed her on a slope. Traveling forty-five miles an hour, he called out, "Get the lead out, mama!"

At the moment they're building a boat together, and not a small retirement canoe, either. It's a steel-hulled, full-displacement trawler that looks like a deep-bellied tugboat. When finished, the boat will sleep six, measure fifty-two feet long, weigh 120,000 pounds, and have a range of 3,000 miles. They're building it with their own hands.

"What's it like, building a boat that big?" I ask her.

"It's like trying to build a six-thousand-square-foot house on a high cliff, hauling all of the materials up yourself. It's extremely hard, physically, mentally, and financially."

"And what will happen once you finish it?"

"Well, as Dan says, that boat ain't going to be sitting on the dock," she tells me. "Our plan is to get it in the water and let the adventure begin."

For Hass, the nautical metaphor promises happy sailing, not turbulent seas. Other women may fret over how to adjust to round-the-clock living with husbands who don't like the same music; Hass seeks even closer quarters with a soul mate. So yes, let the adventure begin.

PART TWO

FIGURING IT

8

CRASH DUMMIES

Sooner or later you'll come to that fork in the road. A long life, comfort, and security lie in one direction. Everything you'd rather not think about lies in the other. If you're anything like the good people at Weyerhaeuser, the two things you'd rather not think about the most are getting sick and outliving your money. That people are living longer only ratchets the stakes higher: what if you get sick, what if you outlive your money, and what if you still have twenty or thirty years to go?

"Everybody wants to live long, but no one wants to grow old," says David Wolfe, a wise counselor to companies who wish to communicate effectively with customers of a certain age. Among noninstitutionalized Americans over the age of sixty-five, 41 percent have one form of disability or another. About one of every two people who are now sixty-five will spend time in a nursing home. One out of ten will spend more than three years in one. Nursing home rates vary widely, but in the Northeast the annual cost can easily exceed $100,000. The rest of the country is rapidly catching up.

More and more you hear the cries of boomers who want to live long but would prefer to do so without getting old. Says Daphne Merkin, writing in the *New York Times Magazine* last year:

Why the big rush, may I ask? What's to get hepped up and festive about when all I can see in front of me is a decades-long campaign of vigilantly keeping the forces of decrepitude at bay as I totter forward over the next 15 years into first the demographic embrace of the "young old" . . . then into the trembling clutches of the "old old" . . . and then, if the fates and my genes are so inclined, finally into the frail company of the "oldest old."

Translation: we may be adding years to life, but not life to years, to invert the motto of the Gerontological Society of America. Adding years to life adds expense. Adding expense demands a bigger Number. A bigger Number requires a financial plan and, long before that, a determination to save diligently and buy selectively. You'd think dread of years in a nursing home would be motivation enough. Not.

CASES IN POINT

The fork in the road calls for some case studies to cast some light on what lies ahead. So put yourself in their place:

You're closing in on sixty. You're starting a new life in a new location. Arizona! Perfect climate, great golf, and a reasonable cost of living. Your kids are out of the house, you're free as a bird. You've lined up a consulting job to supplement your savings, which is a good way to make new friends and start a fresh chapter. You've saved a decent amount of money. You're faced with a clean slate: you can adjust work and play in nicely balanced proportion. How much do you need to make it work?

Or: You're a divorced woman living in a cozy apartment in a big city. You're surrounded by cultural attractions—poetry readings, art exhibits, theater. You have a secure job, although the pay is modest. At this point in your life—you're in your fifties—you value companionship but don't wish to give up independence. Marriage is not in the cards. You stare at a solo future without a financial cushion. It's daunting when you consider that you could easily live another forty years. How much do you need to make it work?

Or: You're a successful professional in your early forties. You have a strong desire to use your skills and training in a meaningful way. You don't want to be a wage slave the rest of your life—other things matter more. But you've got a family to support, kids to send to college. How much do you need to make it work?

Or: Hard as it is to believe, you're now eighty-five. Even though your assets are depleting each year, you still get by on your own. Your health, all things considered, is OK. The last thing you want is to be dependent on anyone. How much do you need to make it work?

Until these four strangers showed up, everyone in this book has been real, their names withheld to protect the anxious and uncertain. But these four case studies, and a few others to follow, are members of a fictional family. Think of them as crash dummies. Used as case studies, crash dummies have advantages over real people. A real person's financial picture is sui generis, rarely a good stand-in for your own. When it comes to the Number, many of us don't easily identify with the people we meet in money magazines and self-help books. Too many variables and intangibles: differences in lifestyle, family composition, genetic disposition toward fatal disease. Sometimes we just don't like the house they live in, their sofas or lamps. It's easy to keep a real person at arm's length; with a crash dummy, you just play along. Another problem with real people: they threaten to turn a story into a reality show. Reality shows are for the birds. You never know who's been secretly rigged for effect; you never know who's mugging for the camera. Crash dummies hold one other advantage over real people, which is that they're fun to mess around with. You can tweak their lives without causing offense or inviting lawsuits. You can kill them off, break up their marriages, rewrite their wills. You can make unauthorized deposits and withdrawals from their accounts. In short, you can play Number God. And it's good to be the Number God.

Creating an imaginary family of crash dummies and running them headfirst into financial collisions, that anyone can do. But to put their finances through a complex Number mill, to run cash flow analyses and calculate things like compound interest, to bring advanced computing power and expertise to the party, all that requires professional assistance. So I line up a squad of expert recruits. One is a seventy-five-year-old financial planner in the Detroit area with decades of experience, first in the insurance business, then as a registered investment adviser. Before that he spent twenty years in the trumpet section of the Detroit Symphony. His name is Donald Ray Haas (not to be confused with Sally Hass), and although he doesn't blow his own trumpet that much, he certainly isn't shy about telling you what he thinks is wrong with how clients deal with the Number. Haas tells younger clients that they need to save more. With no less conviction, he tells older people with means that they ought to loosen up and make their lives more pleasurable. Just the other day, he tells me, he tried to get an octogenarian from Florida to fly first class to see her grandchildren in Detroit. (She refused.) Haas is a character. He recently married a woman he'd been living with for thirty years, ever since he was forty-five. When I ask him why he waited so long, he says he wasn't mature enough for marriage until now. But you're mature enough to advise people on how they can get their money to outlive them? I ask. "That's different," he says.

My other recruits belong to a small SWAT team of analysts from Fidelity Investments. As we will see later, companies like Fidelity have a vested interest in getting us to think about the things we'd rather not think about, to understand the crashes that can potentially wreck a person's Number. Acting on the belief that an educated investor is their best customer, a band of Fidelity's premier number crunchers agrees to run some of the crash dummies' finances through advanced software. Call it an exercise in accident prevention.

MEET THE CASES

Our crash dummy family is named Case. They, too, come from Michigan. There's Tom Case Sr. (now dead). There's his widow, Gert Case, still living. And there are three Case children, all of whom are grown up and have crash dummy families of their own. Given that crash dummies all look alike, here's a cheat sheet with cues to help keep everybody straight:

CRASH DUMMY CHEAT SHEET

Name/Age	Key Trait	Key Number-Related Question
Father **Thomas Case Sr.**	Deceased	N/A
Mother **Gert Case (85)**	Self-reliant	Can I remain self-sufficient?
Eldest Child **Tom Case Jr. (60)**	Prodigal	Will I have enough toys?
Tom's Ex-Wife **Jerri (58)**	Indomitable	Can I make it on my own?
Middle Child **Dick Case (53)**	Timid	Can I sleep at night?
Spouse **Jane (48)**	Plucky	Must I wear the pants?
Youngest Child **Harriet Case, MD (44)**	Altruistic	Whither purpose?
Spouse **Ozzie (41)**	Dependent	Whither patronage?

Tom Sr. was born in 1910 on a farm near Ann Arbor and went to U of M. He spent his entire career as an engineer at General Motors—a lifer, no hopping from job to job as people do today. Not to digress, but he worked at GM during the heyday of Alfred Sloan, whose bold ideas about organization created the blueprint for the modern American corporation. Sloan's enlightened tenure, however, did not spare Tom Case from mandatory retirement when Tom turned sixty-five. He was rewarded for his lifetime service with a gold-plated wristwatch and a company pension. The pension would help make life comfortable for Tom and beloved wife Gert. In 1975, they bought a small retirement home in the desert west of Phoenix. Three years later, Tom Sr. doubled over and died of a heart attack. Gert said it was "retirement that killed him, as Tom never had a knack for hobbies."

Gert is alive and more or less kicking at age eighty-five. She is proud of having raised three intelligent crash dummy kids, at least two of whom have turned out swell. Gert never worked outside the home, although she did plenty of volunteer work at the Belle Isle Conservatory. She really loved that place, with its spectacular glass greenhouses and surrounding gardens. It broke her heart a few years ago when a friend called to say that a hundred-year-old date palm in the conservatory was about to be cut down because it had reached the top of the building's dome. Even though Gert lives on a tight budget she was all set to write a big check to spare the palm, even pay to have it moved to Arizona. It was an offer the botanical society declined, much to the relief of the kids.

Five years ago, at age eighty, Gert sold the little retirement house in Arizona and moved her doilies to Siesta D'Oro, an assisted-living home on the outskirts of Phoenix. Here she continues to do quite well on Social Security and the checks from GM. Gert is grateful she never went through what other folks have faced, when collapsing companies pulled their pensions right out from under retirees' feet. Every time she sees stories on the evening news about companies like WorldCom her blood pressure hits 200/120.

Recently Gert amended her will, although she didn't tell the kids. She replaced the name Tom Case Jr. with that of his long-suffering wife. **Invested assets: $300,000**

• • •

Tom and Gert's eldest child, Tom Jr., just turned sixty. He's the one they had the problem with, especially over matters of money. From the start Tom Jr. lacked an appreciation for prudence and frugality, qualities highly praised around the Case dinner table yet somehow omitted from Tom Jr.'s DNA.

After four lackluster years at Michigan State, Tom Jr. took a job at a big Chicago ad agency. Tom Sr. and Gert watched with dismay as he progressively succumbed to indulgences afforded by all those little plastic cards in his back pocket. Tom carried so many of them he had to set his billfold on the dashboard whenever he got behind the wheel of one of his three cars. An auto buff, he owned a gas-guzzling SUV, a mint-condition Austin Healy, and a zippy BMW M-series sedan that resided under wraps in a heated parking garage. Tom Jr. also fancied himself a wine connoisseur and maintained a well-stocked closet in his Lincoln Park apartment. From time to time over the years, and always against her better judgment, Gert broke down and advanced Tom Jr. a few thousand dollars when the card companies and the auto insurance firms threatened to cut him off. Jerri Case, Tom's wife, was as selfless as her husband was self-centered. Each day, after Jerri packed the kids off to school, she worked as a receptionist to help put milk in the fridge. Had it been up to Tom, the family would have subsisted on Chardonnay and Gunk-Out. Once the kids were out of college, Tom announced to Jerri that their marriage was over. Just like that. Jerri got the proceeds from the sale of their apartment, Tom Jr. kept his retirement accounts, the lawyers took the rest. It was at this point that Gert thought to reach into the top desk drawer and pull out the will.

Tom is semiretiring to Arizona. Jerri continues to work and live in Chicago.

Invested assets (Tom): $455,000
Invested assets (Jerri): $386,000

• • •

The Cases' middle child, Dick, never gave Tom Sr. or Gert a lick of trouble. As a kid he was studious and shy, and he never outgrew those qualities. He won a full four-year scholarship to St. Olaf College, went on to graduate school. At fifty-three he's a tenured professor teaching human ecology at UW-Madison. He has never once been to class dressed in anything other than a button-down blue shirt and chinos, which he buys online, replacing each worn-out pair with its exact duplicate.

In grad school Dick met Jane, a coed from Oconomowoc. Compared to Dick, Jane is a boiling cauldron. She majored in European literature—intellectual chick lit: Virginia Woolf, Jean Rhys, Simone de Beauvoir. Today she works as a freelance copy editor, mostly for university presses. She's partial to Birkenstocks, peasant blouses, and when she undoes her tortoiseshell barrette a thick auburn mane cascades down to her lumbar region. Dick and Jane get along perfectly well even though their investment styles would suggest irreconcilable differences. They have one child, a lovely, superintelligent adopted Korean daughter named Caroline, a brilliant flutist who's about to go off to Stanford.

Invested assets (joint): $714,000

• • •

Harriet is Tom Sr. and Gert's little baby, born in 1960, fourteen years after Tom Jr., seven years after Dick. Harriet was reading *Goodnight Moon* by the age of two. She was always self-assured, well organized, and highly focused, qualities that propelled her through four perfect years at Carleton College, then medical school at Northwestern, where she trained in high-risk pediatrics. At forty-four she is regarded as one of the leading specialists in the field. She lectures everywhere, consults for international relief agencies, and makes a good living—around $250,000. Her husband, Ozzie, brings in zero. Ozzie calls himself a graphics designer but is content to play Mr. Mom to Harriet and Ozzie's two boys. They're happily settled in a snug little home in the northern suburbs of Chicago. Harriet and Ozzie's financial situation is in fine fettle: they live below their means and are good savers. With the help of an adviser, they put together a long-range financial plan that they monitor without fail three or four times a year.

So what's wrong with this picture? Nothing whatsoever. But if it were up to Harriet, she'd be working full-time for Doctors Without Borders, doing what she could to make the world a far better place.

Invested assets (joint): $655,000

As the Cases wander in and out of the next several chapters their assignment will be to help reenact the five principal collisions that can dent, sometimes total, a person's Number. In the opinion of Don Haas and the Fidelity team, there are innumerable routes to a sorry outcome. You don't have to be a dummy, crash or human, to skid on life's black ice. Aside from getting sick or living too long, there's the risk that inflation will grind away at your T-bone of a Number until it's hamburger. There's the risk that after you reach retirement you'll spend too much too soon, drawing down assets at too fast a clip. This is a most reliable way to run out of money. And there are myriad risks embedded in a poorly conceived investment plan, if there's even an investment plan to begin with. The Number can be decimated by thoughtless diversification, or alternately by no diversification. Bring on the breakfast-food metaphors: there's risk when you keep all your eggs in one basket. There's risk when you're so benignly neglectful of your portfolio, or scared of risk, that your assets just lie there like a lox.

These are not happy thoughts, which is why it's nice to have an unsuspecting family of crash dummies to take the hits.

THE LONGEVITY CRASH

Tom Case Sr., born in 1910, died when he was sixty-eight. That's young, even for a crash dummy, yet Tom Sr. exceeded his life expectancy at birth by a full fourteen years. Even though he's been dead for decades, he still has a financial pulse. The assets he left behind —his company pension, survivor benefits based on the years he paid into Social Security, and his share of the marital savings—continue to provide Gert with the means to live a dignified, self-sufficient life. Gert, at eighty-five, has beaten her original life expectancy by thirty years. But even at her advanced age, there's enough money coming in, and enough remaining in her investment accounts, to ensure that she probably won't run out of it before she runs out of vital signs.

Tom Jr., by contrast, is a longevity crash victim waiting to happen. He is about to quasi-retire and thinks he has things all figured out. What he doesn't appreciate is that he has a fifty-fifty chance to live to be eighty-five, and a one-in-four chance that he'll make it to ninety or beyond. Tom Jr. has conned himself into believing he has an adequate amount of money if he is—for him, at least—watchful when it comes to spending it. Yet he hasn't fully focused on the length of the road ahead and the potholes and speed bumps that can make the drive perilous, even for an intrepid, freewheeling crash dummy.

Today there are many people like Tom who think, or hope, that they're setting off on a safe, straight highway. They're set to retire or maybe just downshift. They have decent if not spectacular savings. But they're only beginning to understand how many miles there are to travel. Many still carry around the notion that they'll live to be, oh, maybe eighty if they're lucky, which was what they thought when they came of age back when Tom did, in the fifties and sixties. Only *now* is it beginning to dawn on them that eighty might be no more than a rest stop on a much longer ride. They see plenty of evidence of this every time they walk through an airport in Florida or Arizona. They think about it each time they arrange a party to mark a parent's seventy-fifth, eightieth, eighty-fifth, ninetieth birthday.

To assume that you'll die before you're really, really old is risky financial business. Make the wrong assumption and all other assumptions in a financial plan go down like a line of dominoes. When I tell a seasoned researcher I'm writing a book called *The Number*, he asks which number I'm referring to and takes immediate exception to my thesis. "The only number that's really important," he says, "is the number of years you live. Paying your way through life isn't about net worth. It's about cash flow." He's vehement about this but settles down a bit when I suggest that *Cash Flow* is a lousy title for a book.

One day I notice an online post from someone who wonders why there isn't someone out there smart enough to sell a longevity insurance policy, something that pays off when, and if, you reach a certain age— say, eighty or eighty-five. Well, it turns out that there is such a thing, though not nearly so shrewdly named. It's called an immediate annuity and provides monthly income for some specified time, or for the rest of your life. Once purchased, however, it is irrevocable. A hedge against longevity? How strange. But Tom McAdams, a friend of mine who lives in Tennessee, has a handle on it. McAdams is a man of impeccable culinary taste whose bacon-grease-based salad dressing is a killer. An attorney wise in the way of financial matters, McAdams is aware of what the longevity risk can do to a Number yet he also likes to live large. So he wants to have it both ways. His strategy, which he confides in a whisper one night over cocktails, is to hedge the longevity risk by consuming vast amounts of pork products.

Adviser Don Haas gets all charged up over clients failing to understand how the years can do them in. He devours life expectancy tables and the trends that underlie them, and he's a member of the World Future Society, an association of academics, diplomats, and people like Arthur C. Clarke and Alvin Toffler. The WFS examines the world of tomorrow from every imaginable angle; nothing about the future strikes it as unworthy of attention. Globally, there looms a shortage of earthworms. We're moving away from three meals a day to all-day grazing. An aging population means that normal business hours will change, with stores and offices opening at 6:30 A.M. in deference to seniors, who creep out of bed at the crack of dawn.

Haas tells me that he attended an annual meeting of the organization where speakers flatly asserted that a life span of 150 years is closer than we think. By the next century, Haas says, some of us may live to be four hundred (attention, Medicare actuaries!). Humans may thus be joining the ranks of lobsters, sturgeons, sharks, alligators, and tortoises, all of which scientists classify as nonaging creatures. Gerontologist Leonard Hayflick explains that these species just keep growing, albeit more slowly over time. Physiological functions, while reaching a peak, don't demonstrably decline as they age. It's easy to scoff, to write off a four-hundred-year life span as goofball speculation. But to do so overlooks the major leap in life expectancy that has occurred just in the past few generations. The well-known Successful Aging study reminds us that in the 4,500 years between the Bronze Age and 1900, life expectancy rose a scant twenty-seven years. It increased that much again in the last century alone. In the Bronze Age people lived on average to be eighteen (which means that the Olsen twins, Lindsay Lohan, and Ashton Kutcher would have perished of old age before they could have done much damage to pop culture).

Don Haas regards longevity education as one of his most important obligations as a planner. He encourages clients to spend time with a longevity calculator he came across in a book called *Living to 100* by Thomas Perls, M.D., and Margery Silver. He tells clients to take the quiz at the end of the book. It gives positive life-expectancy points for daily flossing and routine consumption of green tea and deducts points for irregular bowel movements and high radon levels in the basement. Haas is especially keen on the dental floss factor, citing the authors' claim that regular flossing minimizes the possibility that toxic substances and bacteria will cause arterial plaque formation that can lead to heart attacks and strokes. He believes that people now in their forties, whether they floss or not, should be setting Number goals that guide them safely to the age of one hundred or beyond.

Flossing or no flossing, the age of the centenarian has arrived, no doubt exceeding Willard Scott's wildest dreams. Today at least fifty thousand Americans are over the age of one hundred. Within forty years, some estimates say, there could be a million centenarians. Raymond Kurzweil, the bold-minded inventor and futurist, believes that the next ten to fifteen years will bring breakthroughs in genetic research that will enable huge jumps in life expectancy. By the late 2020s, he says, developments in nanotechnology will bring about dramatic advances in human rejuvenation. It'll be good riddance to crow's-feet and saggy knees. The cost associated with those treatments, however, will blow your mind.

THE CASE FOR FRUGALITY

If anyone had told Gert Case that she'd make it to eighty-five, approaching the life span of a sponge, she might have scoffed. But a woman today who makes it to sixty-five has a better than 50 percent chance to get to be Gert's age, and a 25 percent chance she can reach ninety-four. Gert's grandkids, of course, will in all likelihood meet or surpass those age targets, even if you think the Ray Kurzweils of the world have flipped their motherboards.

Gert Case didn't have to do all that much to make her Number last as long as she has. She never consumed gallons of green tea, never popped megadoses of Vitamin E and selenium. She didn't keep a dog or cat around to enhance "positive emotionality." She was a reliable if not fanatical flosser. Yet if it's hard to pin down the precise physical and emotional reasons for her longevity, it's a piece of funnel cake to understand why her Number still shows a pulse.

Gert's financial affairs have held up far better than those of millions of other older Americans. One out of every five seniors in America today ends his or her days in near poverty or worse. Many weren't poor before they got old, they became poor after they were old, says Robert N. Butler, gerontologist, psychiatrist, and Pulitzer Prize–winning author on aging. Although a lot of financial planners will tell you that older people spend less because they need less, Butler and others say that's a myth. Old people spend less because they have less.

Gert never felt the need for a leatherette-bound financial plan, nor did too many other old Rest of Your Lifers. She never said to herself, as she plucked numbers out of the air, "I'm going to live to be such and such, so I'm going to need this or that." She certainly never lit up a Cohiba at the Palm, ordered an after-dinner single malt, snapped her Charvet suspenders, and told her sewing circle buds, "I figure we're talking three mil, maybe five, probably ten." But Gert's Number—not that she ever called it a Number, or had the vaguest idea of what a Number is—continues to hang in there. She lives in a style to which she's accustomed and she finds it wholly sufficient. She is, but always was, careful about spending, never got herself Debt Warped, not even a tad. The bottom line on Gert: she's a crash dummy with a bit of time left, but also with scant risk that she'll bang into anything hard and painful, at least not financially. It isn't especially sexy to delve into the particulars of her finances: a case study in wealth porn she's not. But take a moment to consider how Gert's situation plays out. Are you open to a final chapter that reads like this?

You're healthy enough to live on your own, with some daily assistance, save for the flossing (which you can handle yourself). Your assets are dwindling but you still have around $300,000. This is divided between a money market fund and low-risk bonds, plus a small amount in some stock or other—in Gert's case, General Motors, just for old times' sake. A Social Security check ($800) and a pension check ($500) arrive every month, providing a portion of what you need to live on. The rest comes out of your savings. To make this arrangement work, you need to watch the expense side. Will you, can you, be as careful as Gert?

The thing is, when Tom Sr. and Gert retired, they didn't pig out. They didn't opt for Sedona or Santa Barbara. They bought a tiny shoebox of a house way out in the desert. The senior citizen residence that came next was nice, but it was hardly the Ritz-Carlton. If you're like Gert, you'll spend a good bit of the rest of your monthly allowance on health care costs and prescriptions. You'll make tiny but conscientious charitable donations. You'll drop a little money every week when you get on the bus for the trip to Wal-Mart to pick up toothpaste, batteries, birthday and holiday cards, Citracal. Even so, if you're like Gert, you'll face a shortfall. Your monthly income won't cover all of those expenses. That's where your ever-dwindling Number comes in.

When the perfect Harriet flew out for Christmas last year, she sat down at Gert's dinette table and calculated that Gert's savings were going to run out when, and if, Gert hit her midnineties. At this point, Harriet told her siblings, each would have to pony up around $10,000 a year to keep Gert living as she does. Either that, or Gert would be forced into a state-supported nursing home. Dick and Harriet both quickly agreed that prospect was unthinkable, and of course they would pay their share. Tom Jr. blanched but held his tongue.

TOO LITTLE, TOO SOON

Now, slip out of Gert's housecoat and climb into a pair of Tom's Dockers. More than 70 million people right now mirror Tom's longevity risk—men and women between the ages of forty-five and sixty-five, one out of every four Americans. If Tom Jr.'s planning acumen is any indication, they'd better watch their step if they want their money to stretch as far as Gert's. Sitting there in Tom's pants, this is what you see:

Your sixtieth birthday is around the corner, so you decide to head for eternal sunshine. You say it's because you want to be closer to an aging parent, but there isn't a crash dummy alive who really believes you. You're off to the desert because you've got a hankering to play golf year round. Maybe a love interest has entered the picture. In Tom's case, her name is Kelli, a tawny, willowy real-estate agent he met when he flew down to Phoenix to check out The Villas at Gecko Ridge. It was lust at first listing.

As you pack cartons for the move, you're confident your Number is pretty solid. You have close to half a million dollars invested, almost all of it in your retirement account. That you even have that nest egg is because your ex-spouse insisted you take advantage of the company match and not dribble away your dollars on audio speakers the size of a small human. Because, like Tom Jr., you're the kind of person who looks risk straight in the eye, you've invested all your money in equity funds, a risky decision that may or may not come back to haunt you. One day, using an online calculator and eager to justify a conclusion you've already reached, you start plugging in different assumptions till you get the answer you're looking for: an apparent open-and-shut case that you indeed can afford to move to the desert, work part-time for a few years, and never have to worry about reasonably priced Pinot running out. This plan will work, as even Tom Jr. admitted to himself, only if you bring in around $4,000 a month in consulting fees—at least for a while. After this, you tell yourself, early Social Security benefits will kick in to pick up at least part of the tab.

To keep costs down, you settle for that small villa at Gecko Ridge, which costs a fraction of what you'd pay for similar square footage in Chicago. And you tell yourself you'll have to adjust to a single-vehicle lifestyle. So you sell your SUV and your sporty cars and sign a lease—$700 a month—on a new silky smooth Mercedes. You justify it by telling yourself that such cars hold their value. You also join a really fine golf club. This sets you back another $700 a month. Sure, there are daily-fee courses all over the desert but life is short, at least when compared to a sea turtle's.

Then you make tracks to Arizona, where for a time everything comes together, better than you dreamed. Like Tom Jr., you get a kick out of your part-time work at the agency, where you are toasted for your client leads and big-city moves. You and your version of the willowy Kelli spend at least a weekend a month ($500) at a romantic little B&B up in the mountains near Flagstaff. Your monthly nut comes to around $5,000, which seems incredibly reasonable. In fact, you just can't believe how disciplined you're being and still enjoying a sybaritic lifestyle that makes you feel twenty years younger than you did up north. But you're not twenty years younger. You're turning sixty.

I gather up Tom Jr.'s dossier and hand it over to the expert recruits for professional scrubbing. Warning signs flash in yellow neon. Don Haas zeroes in on the consulting gig, noting that he wishes he had a dollar every time a client said he or she was going to build a Rest of Your Life model around part-time consulting. Fact is, Haas says, consulting deals mostly never happen, and if they do, they don't last, especially in a field like Tom's, the advertising business, where revolving doors spin wildly whenever there's client turnover.

The conclusions reached by Fidelity's computer are even less encouraging. They indicate that Tom's chances of having any money when he reaches his mother's ripe old age are only slightly better than a snowflake's chance in the Sonoran Desert. Based on his investment mix, there's about a 5 percent chance that his retirement scenario will work out long-term. Not good odds, even for a risk jockey like Tom Jr. He could run out of money as early as age *sixty-seven,* when a man still has a fifty-fifty chance to live for another twenty years. Can this be? It can easily be. There's no guarantee that your investment portfolio will fire on all cylinders, as you so optimistically projected that snowy night back in Chicago. The projected average annual returns you typed in have not been seen since the tech boom. The likelihood of those returns repeating themselves anytime soon, let alone in your lifetime, range from bad to not even worth discussing. The very richest people in America say they expect a 10 percent annual return on stocks over the next decade. Most financial planners say that's a stretch, especially in light of the view, prominently and recently put forward by the Wharton School's Jeremy Siegel, that rich boomers who now own tons of stock will begin to unload it as they seek to keep their retirement lifestyles up to snuff. Unless Asian investors step up to buy those shares, stock prices will tumble, along with your sunny projected returns.

So what should Tom do? What would you do? Here are your choices: (a) You can stop kidding yourself; (b) You make further cuts in your spending; (c) You go back to full-time work and build a bigger Number; (d) You could, probably should, suck it up and do all of these.

LA NUMBER

Okay, too bad for Tom Jr. But face it, his wounds were self-inflicted. Jerri's wounds were not. For Jerri, indeed for a great many women, and especially for a great many older women, the Number poses special challenges. Alicia Munnell, who directs the Center for Retirement Research at Boston College, has much to say about why women are vulnerable to impoverishment when they reach old age. The biggest determinant, she says, is whether a woman remains married. Gert's is a happy situation compared to that of many of her peers. One out of three single older women is poor or verging on it. That makes for an abundance of them: about 30 percent of American households ages sixty-five to sixty-nine consist of unmarried women, and they make up more than 60 percent of households age eighty-five and up.

Munnell reports that there are many reasons why women, even married women, must fight harder than men to avoid financial hardship. On average they are typically not paid as well, earning around 25 percent less than men over a lifetime. Because of family responsibilities, women are able to spend fewer years in the workforce, not just in their younger years when they are raising children, but later on, when they leave their jobs to care for older parents or ailing spouses. Daughters who take care of elderly parents outnumber care-giving sons by more than two to one. Jerri, who lives two thousand miles away from Gert, calls her ex-mother-in-law several times a week. Tom Jr., who lives just a couple of tee shots away, visits his mother two or three times a month.

Women, of course, also live longer than men, which means that whatever Numbers they have, whether they rest on savings, pensions, or Social Security, must resist the headwinds of inflation far longer. More than five times as many women as men say they worry about their lifestyle being dramatically diminished after the death of a spouse.

Divorce, as in Jerri's case, is particularly harsh on a woman's financial situation, although bucking the material odds can be preferable to suffering through the despair of a sour marriage. AARP tells us that around two out of three over-sixty divorces are initiated by the wife. Even when wives come away with a fair share of marital assets, many must enter or reenter the workforce from a standing start. Most say they have little experience managing personal finances. A recent Prudential survey indicated that 80 percent of women said they needed some level of assistance with money management; over a quarter of them said they needed help with *all* areas of personal finance. But even if a woman is adept, she often has little time to devote to working numbers and projecting future needs because of obligations at work and child care, according to the *Wall Street Journal*. The paper also noted, for good measure, that child-support payments dramatically decline as children of divorced parents move into their late teens. Gert Case wasn't aware of these grim statistics when she decided to cross out Tom's name and write in Jerri's. She didn't need a packet of studies to tell her it was simply the fair and proper thing to do.

9

THE HEALTH AND WELFARE CRASH

Have you had a "senior moment" today? The term drives the geri-atrics lobby up the wall. They hear it as condescending, typical of how a youth-obsessed society disses old people. Call it what you will, short-term memory loss is on the march. It's already knocking on the cortex of a buddy of mine, a compulsively social and intellectually dy-namic middle-aged man whose ability to recall obscure facts ranging from baseball stats to rankings of underrated jazz sidemen to names of horses he bet on thirty years ago at Saratoga, is—was?—the stuff of urban legend. He says he's rattled now by frequent momentary band-width blackouts. In the *Atlantic Monthly* last year, essayist Ian Frazier spoke for many when he confessed that his brain was no longer sharp enough to keep Ashanti, Beyoncé, and Brandy all in focus at the same time, an understandable shortcoming.

Where was I? Oh. None of us are getting any younger.

Like the crash dummies, we all face the prospect of motoring down a very long, very winding, and very expensive toll road that takes us through stretches of health and ill health. Most of the ill health won't kill us; our afflictions will generally be curable or livable-with, but in ei-ther case they will be costly to diagnose and treat. Anthony Smith, in a book called *The Body*, described this stretch of road rather more starkly: "Put at its crudest, the advances in medicine are enabling more of us to achieve senility." Baseball's legendary executive Branch Rickey said the same thing less decorously: "First you forget names; then you forget faces; then you forget to zip up your fly; and then you forget to unzip your fly."

The fact that life used to end quite abruptly but now has us crying out "Are we there yet?" is one reason a discipline known as financial gerontology has emerged. The pioneer in this field is a social scientist named Neal E. Cutler, who believes that financial advisers need to be retrained to have a better grasp on clients' ever-extending life spans. Financial gerontology began to gel some twenty years ago, its mission to analyze what Cutler likes to call a person's, or a family's, "wealth span." Financial gerontologists place you, your aging parents, and your kids under a microscope so they can examine how your collective and individual financial circumstances play out in the new Rest of Your Life. These specialists have desks piled high with actuary tables; population trends; health care costs; Social Security, Medicare, and other insurance payout forecasts; estate-tax tabulations. If you want a detailed view of the mega-trends that swirl around your Number, you've come to the right messy desk.

When not on the road leading seminars for financial planners, bankers, and brokers, Cutler hunkers down near Philadelphia, at Widener University (formerly the Pennsylvania Military Academy). His loftily named American Institute for Financial Gerontology exists to educate professional financial advisers on how to serve the planning needs of an "older" America. By "older" the institute doesn't mean old, any more than "gerontology" means the study of very old people. Gerontology, in case you passed on that elective in favor of rocks for jocks, deals with the process of aging and how we can improve the quality of later life.

The diminutive, bearded, and genial Cutler goes around introducing himself as a "sixty-year-old kid," a claim his youthful, impish vitality supports. His mother, who's in her nineties, lives in a nursing home not far from Cutler's suburban residence. Cutler uses the sixty-year-old kid quip to underscore an important point about baby boomers: they are, as we hear ad nauseam, the "sandwich generation," obliged to provide concurrent care to aging parents and their own kids. Research provides lots of sandwich meat. At the turn of the last century, only a tiny proportion of sixty-year-old men and women—7 percent, to be exact—had at least one living parent. In 1960, nearly one out of four did. By 2000, close to half of all Americans sixty and older had at least one living parent, a number that will increase further as the century wears on.

The sixty-year-old-kid phenomenon is—how could you not think?—a good thing. But lurking beneath it is an unsettling financial reality that most boomers failed to contemplate a decade ago, when they first glanced into what seemed like a secure, inheritance-juiced financial future. A lot of them quietly eyed their parents' nest eggs as college funds for their own kids. It was easy then to underestimate the degree to which those eggs would be scrambled by aging parents for their own needs. Just the other day, a sixty-something woman told me that her mother was paying $7,500 a month for a large apartment in a senior citizens home. The mother was as content as Gert Case to use up every last nickel of her net worth, as well she should. She assumed that at her current rate of spending, she and her money would expire at around the same time. Meanwhile the daughter, although not openly resentful, was reworking her own Number, aware that she was no longer sitting on an inheritable cushion.

Boomers who were looking forward to Number bailout in the form of an inheritance are now watching that inheritance pay for a parade of nursing aides. Having momentarily despaired, many are realizing there might be hope after all, defined in two words: *reverse mortgage*. This comes through loud and clear one weekend morning in Chicago, where Neal Cutler is the featured speaker at a trade association conference devoted to promoting reverse mortgages. After chatting with the sixty-year-old kid for a while, I decide to hang around for the program.

The reverse mortgage is an idea whose time has come. For some people, it's an appealing financial maneuver that allows seniors with lots of home equity to generate cash flow and still remain in their own comfortable surroundings. The reverse mortgage crowd calls this "aging in place." It's a straightforward idea: if a senior owns a home but needs income for anything from groceries to health-related expenses (prescription medicines, an elevator to the second floor, making a bathroom handicapped-accessible), a reverse mortgage will provide the cash. It amounts to a loan that's paid back when the late homeowner's estate is settled and the house is sold.

Although they're gaining in popularity, reverse mortgages aren't all that new. The first one was sold in 1961, when a banker at the Deering Savings and Loan in Portland, Maine, crafted one for the widow of his high school football coach. Now, with seniors living so long and boomer kids not eager to convert their media rooms into nursing quarters, RMs get a lot of press—which is why four hundred people who sell them have gathered in Chicago to buff up their marketing skills. One of the brokers, a spunky septuagenarian from California, points to the empty chair next to mine, shakes my hand, and asks, "Is this the old fart section?" The Old Fart proceeds to offer a short course on the reverse mortgage business, describing greenhorn salespeople vying to get into the action, slick biscuits who don't know how *forward* mortgages work, let alone those that move in reverse. Then, with curled lip, he derides the spend-thrift boomers who are colluding with those brokers to sell their parents on the wisdom of reverse mortgages. Reverse mortgages can be invalu-able, he says, but he's suspicious of the boomers' motives.

"They mostly want to keep Mom out of their house, all the while let-ting hers appreciate like gangbusters," the Old Fart tells me.

Because RMs are relatively new and a challenge to explain, and be-cause some middle-aged children are exploiting them as significant Number jumpers, the reverse mortgage industry is trying to live down some bad PR. Today's meeting is designed to lay some corrective groundwork, although it strikes me that there's still plenty of room for improvement. One slide in a presentation advises loan sellers to "play the emotional card," as in "Sally was able to move next to the sister she had not seen in forty years only because of a reverse mortgage." The presentation suggests that a successful seller would be wise to "dumb it down" because reporters are not trained in "geek speak." The presentation draws to a close with a welter of statistics that point to the boom years ahead: there are twenty-four million "pre boomers" born between 1936 and 1945, the first generation to be so uniformly raised in an "owned" home. There are thirty-eight million more "early boomers" who carry heavy home equity, also there for the plucking. These two age cohorts combined hold nearly two-thirds of their total household wealth in home equity—and a majority of these people report they will be unable to afford retirement. House rich. Cash poor. Getting older all the time. A marketing trifecta.

But my dyspeptic pal the Old Fart is alert to potential abuses. "If you lose people's trust," he says, "you lose everything. So remember," he admonishes, pointing a finger at me. "You better not fart with those old farts."

THE REST OF THE SANDWICH

On the other side of the generational hoagie, there's always the chance that Mr. and Mrs. Boomer's kids will move back into the old homestead, the so-called baby boomerang trend. This occurs when the job market goes dry or simply when Junior or Sissy Boomer can't decide what to be when (and if) they choose to exercise their option to grow up. This phenomenon, too, is lunch meat to a data-hungry financial gerontologist, but it's only a slice of what he thinks about in the course of a day. Three years ago Neal Cutler gathered up a sheaf of studies and wrote *Advising Mature Clients,* a handbook for financial planners, attorneys, accountants, CPAs, and insurance agents. A portion of the book revolved around a concept he adapted from work popularized by geriatrician John W. Rowe, former president of New York's Mount Sinai

Hospital, and Robert L. Kahn, a psychology professor at the University of Michigan. Rowe and Kahn were leaders of the team that produced a landmark MacArthur study on aging in the mid-1980s. Designed to find ways to improve the mental and physical abilities of seniors, it comprised dozens of studies on old age conducted by research heavyweights. Cutler saw at least two handy ideas in Rowe and Kahn's preternaturally optimistic white paper, titled *Successful Aging*. The first had to do with how Rowe and Kahn rejected common myths about getting old—as in "to be old is to be sick" or "the lights may be on, but the voltage is low." Instead, they advanced the view that we need to study what's *good* about getting old. Rowe and Kahn view aging as a series of stages that add up to a so-called health span. According to this model, if we make intelligent decisions about diet and exercise, and keep an upbeat disposition, we can forestall if not prevent many of the physical and mental afflictions we assumed are medically or even genetically inevitable. In his book, Cutler cites a survey by the National Council of Aging on how old we think "old" is these days. The survey found that old age is now widely defined more by vitality than chronology (thus lending authority to the immortal words of Sumner Redstone, the eighty-two-year-old CEO of Viacom: "Anyone who says age is chronological is an asshole"). Some 41 percent of the survey's respondents opined that old age kicks in when there's "a decline in physical ability"; a modest 14 percent felt it occurs when a person reaches a specific age, such as sixty-five or seventy.

The "sixty-year-old kid" saw an opening here, reasoning that just as we can view physical life as a health span, we can define our financial life as a wealth span, a series of stages of material accumulation followed, in later years, by a period of expenditure. If we make healthy financial choices in the earlier stages of life, we can forestall financial breakdowns later on.

Looking at his life in terms of a wealth span could clearly have benefited Tom Case Jr. Had he checked with the sixty-year-old-kid or any of Neal Cutler's disciples, Tom would have better understood how short a time he'd have to accumulate lifetime assets, and how long a time those assets would have to support him.

The wealth span has undergone a generational change. In Tom Sr.'s day, we entered the workplace younger than we do now and stayed there till we retired at age sixty-five. Soon after that we retired again, this time for eternity. Now we typically spend longer time in school, entering the workforce later. Even after we embark on a career, there are college loans to be paid off and other adult startup costs, which delay accumulation even further. We have the wealth span of Tom Jr.

Cutler asks budding financial gerontologists to picture a person's wealth span as a teeter-totter. The length of the teeter-totter board is life expectancy. In the table below, the boldface ages indicate your active accumulation years, the period in which you work like a dog and save as best you can toward your retirement. The italic years approximate your expenditure or distribution period, the time when you shift into retirement or quasi-retirement and begin to spend more than you're taking in (Tom Jr.'s move to the promised land of Arizona, for instance). What Neal Cutler and the financial gerontologists want you to understand is that you have fewer years to accumulate, more years to expend. Unless you have a good idea of how to get from one end of the teeter-totter to the other, you're tottering on the brink of a Number crash.

Tom Sr.'s Wealth Span

5	15	**25**	**35**	**45**	**55**	**65**	*70*	*75*	*85*		

Tom Jr.'s Wealth Span

5	15	25	**35**	**45**	**55**	**65**	*70*	*75*	*85*	*90*	*95*

Bold numbers = accumulation years
Italic numbers = distribution years

Adapted from Neal E. Cutler, Ph.D., *Advising Mature Clients: The New Science of Wealth Span Planning* (New York: John Wiley & Sons, 2002). Used with permission of John Wiley & Sons, Inc.

HOW TO SQUARE A CURVE

Don Haas is a diligent student of Cutler's theories, a true believer in financial gerontology and proud of the fact that he was the very first certified financial gerontologist in the state of Michigan. He is especially taken with a concept known as "squaring the curve," which he is forever explaining to clients. Squaring the curve is also not a new idea, just a slightly more felicitous term for what social scientists have long referred to as "rectangularizing the survival curve" and demographers call "the compression of morbidity." In plain English, squaring the curve refers to how we don't deteriorate and die the way we used to. In the old Rest of Your Life we deteriorated and died on a rather severe downward curve, ending with an abrupt demise often brought on by an infectious disease or God-knows-what for which there was no known cure. The old Rest of Your Life morbidity curve looked something like this:

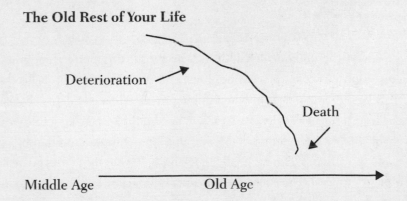

The Old Rest of Your Life

Deterioration

Death

Middle Age   Old Age

Adapted from Neal E. Cutler, Ph.D., *Advising Mature Clients: The New Science of Wealth Span Planning* (New York: John Wiley & Sons, 2002). Reprinted with permission of John Wiley & Sons, Inc.

Nowadays, as we turn into nonaging human lobsters, the morbidity curve is flattening out. Better diets, regular exercise, breakthrough medicines, diagnostic tests, and preventive procedures allow us to carry on. According to the authors of *Successful Aging,* ailments tend to be chronic but controllable: arthritis, hypertension, heart disease, and sensory impairments. We follow a morbidity curve that tracks something like this:

The New Rest of Your Life

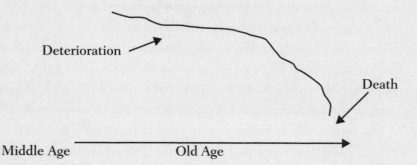

Adapted from Neal E. Cutler, Ph.D., *Advising Mature Clients: The New Science of Wealth Span Planning* (New York: John Wiley & Sons, 2002). Reprinted with permission of John Wiley & Sons, Inc.

Given the additional health care expense, this flatter morbidity curve is pricier than the old one. Financial planners like Don Haas do their best to factor that in when talking to ashen-faced clients. Every day brings further evidence as to why he should keep talking to them about this flattening curve. One morning I call him but am told he is out of the office. When we finally touch base, he tells me he has been at a client's funeral. The client died of cancer of the jaw, a cancer that took thirty years to kill him.

THE HIGH COST OF FEELING NOT SO HOT

Mercifully, Tom Sr. crashed in a flash and never suffered. Thus the Cases avoided the cost of a protracted illness, which is another good reason Gert's Number hangs tough. In the new Rest of Your Life you can never be too rich or too healthy. Everyone knows about the rocketing costs: health insurance premiums routinely increase four, five, seven times faster than the rate of inflation. Total U.S. health spending will double in the next decade, from $1.8 trillion to $3.6 trillion in 2014. These numbers are huge not only because people get sick, or because so many people are getting old, or even because big bad insurance and pharmaceutical companies are greedy, all of which are true enough. What pushes health care costs to the moon is spending on products and procedures that prevent or detect health problems. As journalist Gregg Easterbrook points out, we live in an age when "the notion of living with any treatable discomfort is unthinkable." He notes that billions are spent on, say, the implantation of artificial knees, which is just one of a gazillion surgical procedures unavailable a short while ago.

Ideally, a healthy person who leaves his or her job at fifty-five should have, according to financial services firms, around $200,000 set aside *just for health care expenses.* To amass this much, you need to invest (sensibly) $16,620 a year beginning at age forty-five; $5,260 a year if you possess the foresight, discipline, and the means at age thirty-five. That crushing figure does not include what you might also spend on cosmetic enhancements, which are not insurable and do not come cheap: Botox shot, $385; surgery to lift sagging eyelids, $2,600; routine chemical peel, $800. (Value to narcissistic boomer who refuses to go gently into wrinkled old age: priceless.)

RISK JOCKEY

Over forty million Americans lack health insurance. Too many people just can't afford it. Others can afford it, but lost it and can't get it back. And then there are the dummies who think they can sneak by without it. Tom Jr. is one such dummy.

Put yourself in his place. When you leave full-time employment to move to Arizona, you're sensible enough to extend your company health insurance coverage under the COBRA program. Although the premiums are steep, you keep your policy going the full eighteen months and tell yourself you'll cross the next coverage bridge when you come to it. Worst case, you figure, is that you'll have only a few years to go before Medicare kicks in.

That is nowhere near the worst case. The worst case occurs when you get nailed in the no-coverage gap. Finding interim coverage, whether through a personal policy or that rare part-time job that affords health insurance, is no slam dunk. Tom Jr. makes the fateful decision to try to make it across the gap butt-naked. Bam! He's diagnosed with a rare blood disorder. After a couple of years, he's forced to file for personal bankruptcy.

A recent study published in *Health Affairs,* an academic journal, analyzed the circumstances that bring people like Tom Jr. to their aching knees. The study, coauthored by professors at the Harvard Medical School and Harvard Law School, surveyed a sample of 1.5 million American families who filed for bankruptcy protection in 2001. The study found that around one of every two of these filings was precipitated by medical problems. "It doesn't take a medical catastrophe to create a financial catastrophe," noted one of the authors. Nearly a third of the filings represented people who were insured when their medical problems first surfaced.

Most medical-induced bankruptcies happen to families on the lower floors of the parking ramp, yet the study included ample evidence that middle-class households are by no means immune. Over half of those who filed these bankruptcies had at least some college education, and nearly 60 percent owned homes. They were a lot like you and me. The study showed that unpayable medical bills caused more personal bankruptcies than death of family members, alcohol and drug addiction, and gambling debts *combined.* It showed that while bankruptcy itself is no walk in the park, the path to it is particularly grim: 20-plus percent of those who filed for medical-related reasons had gone without decent food at some point; 60 percent had gone without needed medical or dental attention; nearly 50 percent couldn't fill their pre-scriptions. Medical bills hit with two barrels blazing: you're too poor to pay and too sick to work. The study cited the case of an insured em-ployee who was able to pay for hospital stays for lung surgery and a heart attack but could not return to his old job. When he eventually found a new position, preexisting conditions prevented him from ob-taining renewed coverage. His medical bills kept coming. So, eventu-ally, did a declaration of bankruptcy.

Perhaps Tom Jr. should have brought up his health insurance dilemma with a few of his prosperous golf buddies at his country club. They might have straightened out his priorities. The perils of high med-ical expenses are not lost on those who have enough money not to worry about them. A recent survey by Northern Trust asked people with at least a million dollars in investments which risks threatened their ability to enjoy retirement. Nine out of ten—people whose assets col-lectively amounted to $7 billion—said they were worried about devas-tation brought on by unforeseen and lingering medical problems.

It isn't uncommon to run into these worriers, men and women who stare glumly into what they regard as a Window of Potential Disaster. They're in their fifties or early sixties and either have the means to quit their careers or they've been laid off. When their eighteen months of COBRA coverage end, they face the daunting task of finding an insurer to take them on. Many are in pretty good health, but may have had at least one medical event dire enough to give pause to an underwriter. It could have been an angioplasty ten years ago or a cancerous basal cell long since removed. This is the age of zero tolerance.

Just as ominous is the situation that faces millions who once la-bored under the delusion that their company retirement plans would provide safe passage to the gates of Medicare. As a response to double-digit cost increases, the number of companies offering health plans to early retirees has dropped like a rock. Many companies are taking their existing retiree health-plan commitments to court in the hope of curtailing or, better still, vaporizing them. According to the *Wall Street Journal,* playing health insurance hardball is a "no lose" proposition for corporations. As pesky legal challenges grind their way through the courts, retired workers begin to lose hope, drop out, drop dead. In the meantime, these companies enjoy juiced-up earnings as they pare expense liabilities from their books. No wonder retirees feel queasy.

10

COVERING YOUR ASSETS

E ven a crash dummy has dreams. Dick Case, the middle child, had a disturbing one the other night. It happened hours after he and wife Jane met with an accountant to review their investment strategy and determine whether they were on the right track. Right track meetings invariably occur when people are about to go through some kind of life transition. In this instance, the Cases' daughter Caroline, the flutist, is about to depart for Stanford. With just a partial scholarship to offset the annual $40,000+ costs, Dick and Jane wanted to do a reality check on their Number, to get a firmer idea of what impact Caroline's years in Palo Alto will have on their retirement plans.

Money makes Dick one very nervous crash dummy. He has no instinct for personal finance, no stomach for it. He's always been extremely conservative with his investments, shunning the stock market in favor of supersafe government bonds despite Jane's carping about his portfolio being too flaccid to keep up with the cost of living. Meeting with the accountant, Dick found himself spiraling into confusion and anxiety as the conversation dragged on about tax-reduction feints and the best time to start receiving Social Security. How fortunate, he told himself, that Jane has a better grasp of this stuff. She was focused on everything the accountant was saying, writing key points in a little note-book.

In Dick's oddball dream he was dressed only in his crash dummy underwear. Stripped of his trademark blue oxford shirt and chinos, he stood alone on the playing field at Camp Randall Stadium, where the Badgers play their football games. Dick felt the eyes of eighty thousand people looking down, saw the throng passing cheese trays from row to row, the rabid fans screaming their lungs out in his direction. It was overwhelming. Through all his years as a faculty member, Dick had never attended a football game. He disliked football on two counts: he found it a brutish, violent sport, and he resented the way it hijacks the values and resources of higher education. But there he was in the dream, a child of the sixties, shivering and embarrassed in his skivvies, alone on a bleak, windswept fall afternoon. He looked around but saw no other teammates. Then, with alarm, he realized that the opposing team was about to kick off and that he was the only one on the field in a position to return it. He noticed for the first time that the players on the other team were neither crash dummies nor real people; they were ferocious-looking creatures, half animal, half men, ready to descend on him with violent fury. Curiously, they had dollar signs painted on the sides of their helmets. The kicker lofted the ball in Dick's direction. Terrified, he waited under it, palms to the sky. With the thunder of twenty-two hooves bearing down he knew it was only a matter of sec-onds before the wild-eyed special-team players smashed his scrawny crash-dummy body into matchsticks.

Just before contact, Dick awoke with a start. The next evening over paella and a pitcher of sangria, Dick tells Jane about the dream. She gets a big laugh out of it. "It's perfect! The dollar signs on their helmets! Don't you see?" she squeals.

Jane wasn't an honors English major for nothing. Her powers of in-terpretation are considerable. She proceeds to parse the dream, peeling back its layers as Dick listens sheepishly. The crowd represents a cacophonous, materialistic culture. (Now she's talking Dick's language.) It envelops you, she says. It exists to goad you, dare you to run as far as you can to achieve success. You have to run solo and into all kinds of dangerous resistance even though you have no confidence. Frightened, feeling totally lost, you've been thrown out there without preparation, like the classic dream in which you show up late for class, having forgotten about an exam. The players on the other team? The ones with the dollar signs on their helmets? They personify all the things that can bring you down, dash your hopes. The dream wasn't about you and football at all, Jane says. The field is your destiny. And the football you're supposed to catch and somehow carry down the field, however threatened and unprepared you are, that football represents money.

WARNING: DO NOT UNDERINFLATE

Dick wasn't sure that was the meaning of the dream at all. He actually thought that his dream, if anything, had to do with sexual potency. But Jane's interpretation rang true in one sense. For all his education, Dick never had a money coach, a financial Lombardi to teach him how to run to daylight.

Expert coaches like Don Haas or the Fidelity guys could make a player out of Dick Case. They would sit him down in front of a blackboard and with some quick X's and O's sketch out a game plan. Coach Haas, for instance, would take Dick to task for how timid he was with the eggs in his basket. Inflation will come along and smash them. Haas could show his novice how even a moderate rate of inflation sacks purchasing power. Too many people, Haas believes, underestimate inflation when they calculate how much they need to carry their lifestyle downfield. A 3 percent annual inflation rate over twenty-five years means you'll need twice as much buying power to live then as you do today. If you're forty years old, say, and it takes $200,000 a year to support your standard of living, it'll take $400,000 when you retire at sixty-five. If inflation runs at 5 percent, you'll need something approaching $600,000 to live comparably. Most people neglect this simple calculation when they noodle their Numbers during halftime breaks.

Financial advisers say that most of their clients have forgotten the hardships that result from rising prices and high interest rates. Boomers lived through, but didn't much learn from, the soaring inflation years of the 1970s, when prices rose, on average, 7.5 percent a year. Inflation doesn't much register when you're in your teens, twenties, maybe even thirties if you haven't yet started a family. But it's a killer when you're on a fixed income or trying to send your kids through college and you encounter sticker-shock prices on everything your family needs to survive. Two percent a year, as it's been running of late? Kid stuff. If the annual rate were to rise even to 3 or 4 percent, purchasing power would take a jolt. It would be enough to kick the legs out from under a fixed-income portfolio such as Dick's.

Inflation ranks as one of your Number's biggest dangers because it gets you coming and going: the value of your holdings diminishes while at the same time prices go up. Conservative investors like Dick will see their purchasing power eviscerated. A 4 percent annual inflation rate will reduce a million-dollar bank account to the equivalent of $675,000 in ten years; to $456,000 in twenty. A rise of only a point or two will be enough to put adjustable-rate mortgage payments out of reach for millions of homeowners. Millions of preretirees will be forced to delay or discard their career exit strategies; others will find themselves involuntarily retired.

Nobody knows how high inflation will soar through the boomers' retirement years, but the coaches will tell you it won't likely be as benign as what we're used to. When Don Haas runs numbers for clients, he assumes a future inflation rate of 3 percent over the next ten years, then raises it up to 3.5 after that, just to be on the safe side. And he tells them, as he'd tell Dick, that they're making a big mistake by playing defense, by being too cautious about how they invest.

Jane's been saying that to Dick for years now. At age forty-eight, she keeps 70 percent of her retirement funds in U.S. stocks, 15 percent in foreign stocks, the rest in bonds. Dick keeps his portfolio the other way round: 80 percent of his money is in bonds, the rest in a money market fund.

Compare Jane's approach to investing with Dick's (not that past performance is any indication of future results, etc.) and you see how asset allocation can pump a Number up or let its air out. Dick's portfolio allocation, computed over an eighty-year historical period, has yielded an average annual return of just over 5 percent. Deduct investment costs, figure in taxes owed on the gains, and his return is reduced to 2 to 3 percent, which is easily erased by even a moderate dose of inflation.

That's not a worst-case scenario. That's an average-case scenario.

Dick's best return over any thirty-year historical period was 8.2 percent. His worst was 2.4 percent. If he wasn't such a total financial crash dummy he'd realize that his portfolio, even in the best of times, carries little chance of keeping pace with the cost of living. Jane's long-term return, in contrast, is nearly twice Dick's, enough to keep her comfortably ahead of inflation and the tax man. Stocks, over time, yield higher returns than bonds. Jane's best thirty-year performance was 13.8 percent; her worst, 7.44 percent, five points better than Dick's. So while Dick presently sleeps like a crash dummy baby, his nights interrupted only occasionally by a corny dream about football, his bedtime hours will turn a lot more fitful when the crowd starts its Whip Inflation Now! chant.

THE TEN COMMANDMENTS

E. B. White, in *Charlotte's Web*: "There's no limit to how complicated things can get, on account of one thing always leading to another." White could have been thinking about his Number when he wrote those words. One risk leads to another. The Number is a delicate web of risks, some of which are within your control, some not, and some sort of are. The risks that are sort of within your control are how long you live and whether you live healthfully. You can floss twice a day. You can slather on the sunscreen. You can eat like a natural-born Mediterranean. What's not in your control is the genetic hand you are dealt, or a Ford Expedition driver talking into a cell phone while sipping a Red Bull while listening to Dave Matthews while you happen to be crossing the street with nothing but a sweet melody running through your mind.

The inflation rate is also not in your control.

What *is* in your control—it's a challenge, though—is how you can allocate your investments to help defend yourself against all the risks you can't control. Your spending is also in your control, barring extreme surprises. It's likewise in your control to hold to a reliable formula as to how much you can safely withdraw from your assets each year once you stop working.

With some additional help from the crash dummies, let's tackle the challenging part first. Dick and Jane's sample portfolios reveal what most people (like Jane) by now already know and what others (like Dick) are too squeamish to act on. Over time, stocks will return higher gains than bonds, bonds will return more than money funds, and money funds will return more than a mattress. In the interest of brevity, this discussion will refrain from evaluating passive or active real estate holdings, hedge funds, artwork good and bad, private equity, Hank Aaron–autographed baseballs, mint-condition copies of *Playboy,* collections of Pez dispensers, and all other investment vehicles that might be gathering interest or dust at the National Bank of eBay.

Despite their higher returns, stocks make many people nervous. There are a lot of Dicks in the world who are skittish about the stock market's volatility and whether they'll get back what they put in. Others know that the stock market is a sometime thing whose ups and downs are entirely oblivious to when they might need to sell something. As I write this in the early spring of 2005, I'm looking at a series of squiggles that show how the major stock market indices have performed since the bubble burst five years ago. Although the squiggles are trying gamely to make like the little engine that could, neither the Dow nor the S&P 500 has been able to haul its respective caboose over the hill it scaled in the final months of the Clinton administration. More sobering still is the squiggle that charts the performance of the tech-laden NAS-DAQ index. The little engine would if it could, but it just can't. It still gasps for fuel way down in the hollow there, some 60 percent lower than it was at its peak.

The financial press likes to talk about how more than half the households in America now own stocks, but there isn't much talk about whether those households understand what they're doing with those stocks and what role those stocks play in a household's nest of assets. If people are confused, it's not for lack of advice: there's no end to the conventional wisdom about portfolio management. Much of it, though, can be delivered in the form of ten modern commandments that should be etched onto an I-can't-believe-it's-not-stone Corian tablet:

- Thou shalt not put all thy eggs in one basket.
- Thou shalt have the patience of a nesting hen.
- Thou shalt know that past performance is no guarantee of future results, nor shalt thou become so exuberant so as to forget that eggs drop, cookies crumble, bubbles burst, and that which goes up will eventually come down.
- Thou shalt not invest in anything thou dost fail to understand.
- Thou shalt not question the divine power of compounding interest.
- Thou shalt not squander long-term returns by incurring frequent trading commissions or excessive management fees.
- Thou shalt honor thy company's retirement plan.
- In particular, thou shalt honor thy company's match—after all, it's free money.
- Thou shalt take on risk commensurate with thy ability to sleep well at night.

- Thou shalt honor thy age and timeline by properly apportioning thy ratio of stocks to bonds.

The reason these commandments exist, and the reason they remain eternally relevant, is because most people simply ignore them. Certain of the commandments have been echoing through the mass financial culture for several decades, having coalesced in the wake of Modern Portfolio Theory, conceived in 1950 by a University of Chicago graduate student named Harry Markowitz, who won the Nobel Prize for his work forty years later. To oversimplify, Markowitz used mathematical computation to show how the proper diversification of a portfolio could achieve acceptable returns with diminished volatility and risk. And, as a corollary, how the right basket of investments is less risky than any individual investment in the basket. In the years since Markowitz, highly diverse approaches to stock picking and portfolio building came into play. As recounted ably in Burton Malkiel's *A Random Walk Down Wall Street,* some of these ideas are wacky—as in predicting stock price based on sunspots and vibrations of the San Andreas Fault—while others depend on highly technical analysis and charting. Market momentum, persistence patterns, relative-strength theories, filter rules, they all have their proponents and they're all guaranteed to fail a great deal of the time.

The net result of all this gobbledygook is that it further mystifies certain gentle souls (like Dick) who should have part of their Number in the stock market but say they feel ill equipped or too dense to get all caught up in its technicalities.

There are at least three other common reasons that people ignore the commandments. The first, as noted, is that some people just can't tolerate having volatile investments in their portfolio. Risk aversion is an intractable emotional condition that frustrates financial planners as much as any other human foible. Don Haas is downright quixotic about trying to get clients over their risk aversion, insisting that financially timid people are made, not born, and that with patience, charm, empathy, and the power of a persuasive spreadsheet, a good adviser can get them to stiffen their spines. But estimating a person's risk tolerance, let alone adjusting it, is confounding. The inability to measure it, despite numerous studies and experiments, has been cited as the Achilles' heel of financial planning.

Haas and every other adviser I talk to seem to agree that risk aversion advances with age, and that the toughest nuts to crack are aging widows with more money than they could ever spend. Is there a neurological basis for our becoming more risk averse as we age? Van Harlow, a member of the Fidelity brain trust, tells me that earlier in his career he did some work with Vernon Smith, who would go on to win a Nobel in economics. Smith and Harlow ran big-time risk takers—skydivers, mountain climbers, other thrill seekers—through a series of tests and discovered they carried low levels of a specific enzyme that is generously present in highly risk averse older people. Others question a biological connection. Michael Roszkowski, director of institutional research at LaSalle University, debunks any correlation between physical and financial risk taking: "It's not improbable," he observes, "to find a bungee jumper who's conservative in his investments, and someone who's aggressive in his investments but would never bungee jump." Still, there may come a day when the cause of Dick Case's portfolio deficiencies might be clinically measured along with his annual lipids count.

The second reason people say they don't honor the ten commandments is because as investors they're just plain overloaded with choices. One out of every two American households now owns mutual funds; over 260 million separate shareholder accounts hold assets in excess of $7 trillion. For better or worse, they've got a lot to choose from. Today there are over 8,000 mutual funds, nearly three times as many as there were in 1990. Almost 90 percent of company 401(k) plans offer ten or more funds from which workers are asked to allocate their retirement portfolios. The average number was sixteen.

Choice is good, to a point. But when people have too many mutual funds to choose from, they find they can't make a confident decision, so the result is sometimes no choice at all or a really bad choice. If you find yourself in a bookstore overwhelmed by how many titles there are to choose from, you might want to try *The Paradox of Choice* by Barry Schwartz, who teaches at Swarthmore College. Schwartz explains how too much choice can demotivate, even tyrannize us, citing a study in which workers are presented with too many mutual fund choices in a 401(k) plan. Many simply opt for a default strategy: they punt by allocating funds equally across the options they are given. This may seem like diversification, but depending on which funds are on the menu, it could result in a portfolio that's way too conservative or wildly aggressive. Another thing that choice-addled workers do is pick just one fund and put everything they have into that. It could be a slow-growing fixed-income fund or a jackrabbit high-growth fund that takes years to squiggle its way out of a nasty bear market.

The third reason people ignore the ten commandments is because some of them are just too full of themselves. While overheated day traders and self-proclaimed market timers are convenient stereotypes, the world is full of normal people who labor under the delusion that they can outsmart the market and get to a handsome Number without the tedium of putting together a well-balanced portfolio. Warren Buffett has said that it isn't stupidity that screws up investors, "it's not having the temperament to control the urges that get other people in trouble."

Princeton psychologist Daniel Kahneman (who as it happens shared the 2002 Nobel with Vernon Smith) suggests that it's hubris as much as risk aversion that gets people into trouble. Kahneman sees many investors plagued by bouts of "delusional optimism." During a recent presentation to financial planners, he told of numerous studies that show how we commonly tend to overestimate our abilities across a range of activities. When it comes to driving a car, over 85 percent of those asked say they are above the median skill level, and over 50 percent regard themselves as better than average investors. According to a PaineWebber survey conducted before the market tanked, inexperienced investors were shown to be particularly overoptimistic and superconfident about their ability to achieve outsized returns. Other studies reveal that garden-variety stock pickers are quick to take credit for their successes and just as quick to palm off responsibility for losses on things they say are beyond their control: the system's rigged, or the deck's stacked against the little guy—not that there isn't some truth to both.

Risk aversion. Overload. Hubris. That these qualities get in so many people's way, that they louse up investment returns, that they screw up the Number, is deeply regrettable, if only because they can be tempered by a trio of reliable, if boring, traits of character: moderation, balance, common sense.

The wisdom of keeping an investment strategy simple is documented thoroughly in Burton Malkiel's *A Random Walk Down Wall Street*. After a lengthy stroll through the thicket of asset pricing theories, beta as a measurement of risk, chartist modeling, demand-pull inflation, covered calls, inverse floaters, first movers, price-to-book value ratios, wash sales, and naked puts, Malkiel leads the ordinary investor to a clearing: *successful investing doesn't have to be all that complicated.* Here come those pies again. Malkiel likes the idea of a Number pie with just four slices: stocks, bonds, cash, and real estate. The stock and bond slices can consist of low-expense mutual funds, preferably index funds because they're cheap and usually perform as well as or better than costly ones managed by erratically performing experts. The relative size of the slices is determined by how near or far your investment horizon looms and is gently tweaked by how brave you are and certainly by whatever special circumstances you need to take into account— dependents, or the current state of your health, for instance.

THE COUNTS OF MONTE CARLO

A good litmus test for determining those obsessing over their Number these days, and those avoiding it, is to ask them to say the first thing that pops into their mind when they hear the term "Monte Carlo." The answers "hotel in Vegas," "zippy Chevy coupe," or "jewel-box principality perched atop quiet waters of the Mediterranean favored by tax cheats in exile" suggest that the Number is not keeping a respondent awake at night. If the answer is something on the order of "a kind of simulation that employs random numbers and probability statistics to produce a reliable snapshot of how likely this, that, or any number of outcomes is likely to occur based on inputted variables," then you know you've got a real live Number freak on your hands.

In financial planning circles, Monte Carlo simulation is much the rage. Every self-respecting financial adviser now routinely uses it to show clients whether the rest of their lives will likely be festooned with peacocks or feather dusters. As a forecasting tool, Monte Carlo analysis is old hat, having been used for years in economics, chemistry, nuclear physics, radiation therapy, city planning, military war gaming, and the programming of slot machines. But it's especially handy in Number planning. Here's an example of why, courtesy of the Fidelity team:

Say you're a sixty-five-year-old crash dummy with $500,000 invested in a portfolio that consists of 50 percent stocks, 40 percent bonds, and 10 percent short-term investments. Based on seventy-five years of historical data, this particular allocation of assets has resulted in an average annual rate of return of 8.9 percent. Assuming an annual inflation rate of 3 percent a year, and assuming you withdrew 6.8 percent of your assets each year as living expenses (which is too high, as we'll see, but okay for this example), that hypothetical return of 8.9 percent would be sufficient to carry you to beyond age ninety-nine before you would run out of principal.

However, markets don't operate according to linear projections. Markets have this thing about going up for a while, then down for a while, then sideways, with occasional interruptions for a heart-pounding upsurge or a sick-making downdraft. If, say, in the years immediately following your long-awaited retirement, the markets return less, perhaps much less, than 8.9 percent, there's little chance your $500,000 nest egg will carry you to age ninety-nine. Indeed, when you overlay real market conditions onto the example, the portfolio described above has only a 57 percent chance of providing you with requisite income to age ninety and a 46 percent chance of getting you to ninety-five. Eventually, of course, the nest egg will revert to its mean. The trouble is, it could happen long, long after you've died unhappy and broke.

WITHDRAWAL SYMPTOMS

When Tom Jr. stayed up nights back in Chicago, running and rerunning assumptions on whether he could move to the desert, he wasn't just burning the midnight oil, he was burning his candle at both ends. He was counting on too much income from investments and part-time work and not being strict enough on the expense side. Avoiding the first set of delusions would seem straightforward enough: use assumptions about market returns and outside income that are conservative, at least well tempered. But how do you know what you might reasonably spend based on those sensible income projections?

Your retirement picture so far: You're going to live to whatever age you're going to live to. Your asset allocation is properly diversified, and your expectation of what those holdings will return is reasonable, even a bit cautious. Your health care costs are contained. Inflation, even though you had nothing to do with it one way or the other, is in check.

The only puzzle piece remaining is how much you think you can draw down from your assets to pay for things you deem to be necessary or, just to live a little, nice: help your grandson through college, cruise the Greek islands, customize a golf cart, dinner and a movie every Saturday night. If you draw down your Number too much, too soon, you're in trouble. If you draw it down too little, too late, you're not in trouble but you'll miss out on life's dwindling opportunities to squeeze out some fun and satisfaction. So how do you know how much drawdown is too much, how little is too little?

These questions are nowhere near as fiendishly complicated as they sound. In fact, drawdown is one topic about which there is little disagreement, at least for those with okay assets on account. Assuming that these assets are more or less rationally allocated, which is to say you've got anywhere from half to three-quarters of your money in stocks, the rest in bonds, then the magic-number withdrawal rate is 4 percent of the value of your assets per year.

Four percent. That's what it says in a guide to lifetime income planning published by a big financial services firm.

Four percent. That's what I hear from a money manager with clients whose invested assets start at $20 million and go as high as Pluto.

Four percent. That's what they say time and again at a four-day conference hosted by the leading association of independent financial planners.

Four percent. Four percent is the reliable drawdown number if you want your assets to wind up somewhere north of zero when Final Accounting time rolls around.

But it wasn't always 4 percent. It used to be higher. Through the 1980s and '90s, financial advisers and money magazines touted generous withdrawal numbers of 7 percent, 8 percent, 9 percent, 10 percent. Many retirees withdrew and spent accordingly. But—oops!—the financial advisers and magazines had overlooked the you-would-think-it-was-obvious fact that stock market returns through that era were unusually robust. What almost everybody assumed was that those heady returns would refill people's retirement buckets sufficiently to allow them to withdraw 6 percent, 7 percent, 8 percent, and more over the long term. In the 1980s, for example, respected money magazines told their readers they should set a spending target of 5.9 percent in their first year of retirement, then adjust that figure annually, up or down, for inflation. The formula, according to financial planners who look back on it now, seemed perfectly rational, even restrained at the time. Then, in 1994, long before the stock market boom had reached its crescendo, a man named Bill Bengen came along and announced that the universally accepted drawdown number should be, give or take a basis point, 4 percent.

MR. FOUR PERCENT

Bill Bengen didn't become a financial planner until he was forty. He was trained as an aerospace engineer, then spent a number of years managing the finances of his family's soft-drink business in New York. Eventually, when the business was sold, the Bengen household picked up and moved to a peaceful town outside San Diego, where the climate was perfect and Bill got to play a lot of tennis. In time he started looking around for a new career and became intrigued with financial planning. A year after he gained certification, he found himself wondering whether he was giving clients the right answer when they asked how much money they could safely spend in retirement.

The question prompted Bengen to fire up his Lotus software and wade through seven decades of investment returns analyzing a hypothetical portfolio of 60 percent stocks and 40 percent bonds. He devoted—he's ready with the answer the second I ask, he's that kind of guy—four hundred hours to figuring out the sample portfolio's real return based on historical performance. Rather than look at a straight-line average of those returns over seventy years, though, Bengen took snapshots of what the portfolio would look like during shorter increments of time. He asked what would have happened to clients had they retired in the wake of three significant stock market declines: the "Little Dipper" (1929–1931); the "Big Dipper" (1937–1941); and the "Big Bang" (1973–1974). (If he had done this more recently he could have used the "Eclipse of the Boom" [2002–2004].) What Bengen found was that you can be very unlucky if you happen to pick the wrong thirty-year period in which to retire. You can also get lucky if you pick the right one. To be safe through *all* of them, Bengen concluded, a person would have to adhere to an annual drawdown of—you guessed it—4 percent. (As a curious footnote, Bengen says, it wouldn't have mattered if your portfolio contained 50 percent stocks or 75 percent stocks, the drawdown number would still work out to 4 percent.)

Although Bengen isn't surprised that everyone I talk to now advises their clients to stick to 4 percent, he actually thinks this is erring on the safe side. He says that if you, or your adviser, manage your portfolio with reasonable finesse, you'll almost certainly be okay with a drawdown rate of 4.5 percent, even 5 percent. And you could continuously fine-tune beyond that, based on inflation trends, and so on. While not for everyone, obsessing over your drawdown number could make for an offbeat and productive hobby. But if, over the last decades of your life, you'd prefer to read, swim, golf, play bocce, or cook Italian in what hard-won leisure time remains and not worry about running out of money, Bengen says stick with 4 percent. Q.E.D.

CRASHLESS

If a person is lucky and smart, the new Rest of Your Life doesn't have to be just one damn crash after another. Harriet, Tom and Gert's perfect daughter and youngest child, is living proof, as it were.

She and Ozzie are in their early forties. Their combined annual income (100 percent hers, 0 percent his) is around $250,000. They have two kids, who still have a way to go before college. By age sixty-two, Harriet says, she wants to leave her lucrative private practice and devote her considerable medical skills to ailing kids in the Third World. Ozzie wants to discover his inner Julian Schnabel. Today, thanks to their ability to save and keep a lid on their spending, they have $655,000 in assets salted away (not counting home equity), 77 percent of which is invested in low-cost, indexed equity funds. Keep in mind that good things happen to those who save and remain Debt Warp–free, so that by the time Harriet reaches her altruistic target date everything should be in place for her to join Doctors Without Borders and for Ozzie to buy himself a fine set of nickel-plated, brass-ferruled Italian hardwood brushes in the hope that inspiration suddenly strikes.

Harriet and Ozzie serve as excellent role models. Follow their example and the chances are solid that the Number god will smile kindly on thee and thine. Consider the following *ifs* and *thens*:

If, once retired, Harriet and Ozzie can keep their monthly expenses to $9,000 (in today's dollars), which they easily can . . .

If they begin drawing their combined monthly pension and Social Security benefits ($7,700) in their midsixties, which they certainly will . . .

If they assume that inflation over the long term will come in at historical levels, which is a reasonable guess . . .

And *if* they live into their nineties—which could be high or low, who knows? . . .

Then the word from Monte Carlo is that Harriet and Ozzie can have a confidence level of 90 percent that their money will last into their nineties, even if the markets perform somewhat worse than their historical average.

If the markets perform *significantly* worse than their historical average, Harriet and Ozzie would still have a high confidence level (about 75 percent) that they could leave a couple million dollars or more to their kids, or to Doctors Without Borders. Yes, inflation will bring that down to a million or so in future dollars, but that's still fine for everybody involved.

It's all very complex, predicated as it is on cold historical data microprocessed by slivers of silicon. But for Harriet and Ozzie, there's peace of mind in Monte Carlo.

11

ADVICE SQUAD CONFIDENTIAL

Peace of mind is not that easy to come by. Harriet and Ozzie may have it, but most others don't. It doesn't matter whether you're rich, somewhat rich, or not rich at all: the Number game is complicated, the choices are overwhelming, and it is stressful for nearly everyone. You may be good with figures and recognize a standard deviation when you see one, or you may be unschooled, unconfident, and unprepared regarding anything affixed to a dollar sign. Either way, it's hard to imagine anybody who doesn't need at least a receptive ear, a shoulder to cry on, or just a tough-love smack upside the head.

There's a giant and unruly industry out there ready to provide you with support and counsel. While this country may have a shortage of nurses, special ed teachers, and tool and die makers, it certainly does not lack for asset managers, financial advisers, accountants, insurance agents, securities brokers, bankers, and trust officers, all eager to make your acquaintance, impress you with their wisdom, and grab their share of the market. Most advisers present themselves honestly and forthrightly; some are a little funky and strange.

Today the financial services business finds itself swimming in an alphabet soup consisting of dozens of designations that seem to promise ethical service, candor, trust, rigorous training, competence, experience, and peace of mind. Here are but a few of the titles—some American, some Canadian, some both—that might turn up on the business card of somebody pitching for your business:

AAMS = Accredited Asset Management Specialist
CA = Chartered Accountant
CFA = Chartered Financial Analyst
CFP = Certified Financial Planner
CFS = Certified Financial Specialist
CFTA = Certified Financial and Trust Adviser
CGA = Certified General Accountant
ChFC = Chartered Financial Consultant
CMFC = Certified Mutual Fund Counselor
CPA = Certified Public Accountant
CRC = Certified Retirement Counselor
CRPC = Chartered Retirement Planning Counselor
FC = Financial Consultant
IA = Investment Advisor
IC = Investment Counselor
Pl. Fin. = Planificateur financier (pour les Québecois)
RFC = Registered Financial Consultant
RFP = Registered Financial Planner
RIA = Registered Investment Advisor

What does each of them do? It depends. How extensive is their training? It varies. Can you trust what they tell you to do? If you're lucky.

Advisers will place one or more of these designations after their names for the same reason a doctor covers his walls with framed diplomas and association memberships. However, the designations may or may not mean much or offer you recourse if you get rotten advice. The SEC is presently up to its EBs (eyeballs) trying to sort out a squabble between the Financial Planning Association and the big brokerages. The planners' trade association has charged that it's wrong for someone who's just a salesperson, a broker, to masquerade as a qualified financial adviser. Few brokers have been so "certified" or appropriately educated, the planning industry argues, and many possess no more meaningful professional qualification than bright smiles and glossy shoeshines. These charges are also leveled in "Secrets of the Wirehouse."

It's a matter of opinion as to whether this confusion is the result of a conspiracy of sorts: Wall Street maintaining a hammerlock on elected officials and regulators who might otherwise take sensible steps to clear things up. Why should a bank, for example, assume fiduciary responsibility when you hand over your nest egg to one of its trust officers, but have no such obligation when you walk across the floor and shake hands with someone in its brokerage department? And even if an adviser *is* "certified" by a professional board, well, so what? The board in question almost never actively polices its members and will decertify a guilty miscreant only after a citizen's arrest or a fellow professional cries foul. Why isn't anybody protecting us? The most charitable thing one can say is that financial planning is still in its infancy, and regulation hasn't yet caught up with it—that is, if you consider a big, strapping thirty-year-old still an innocent, babbling baby.

It's a mess, okay? Which is why almost nobody chooses a financial adviser on the basis of the initials next to his or her name. So if an ambiguous credential isn't what sells you on an adviser, what does?

Generally, financial helpers who troll for your account bait their hooks with the three T's: trust, temperament, and touch. The air is thick with the three T's when I arrive at the annual conference of the Financial Planning Association in Denver. The FPA is a trade group whose membership includes accountants, attorneys, bankers, charitable-giving specialists, insurance agents, stockbrokers, money managers, investment consultants, broker-dealer and corporate executives, anyone with an avowed interest in "professionalizing" the planning process or at least having marketing proximity to those who do. The organization runs a certification program that confers CFP status on those who pass a comprehensive planning exam, serve several years in practice, abide by the organization's ethics code, and commit to approved continuing education programs.

From presentations and conversations at this year's conference, a visitor forms the impression that conscientious people in the Number game are dealing from more or less the same deck of ideas: the need to finance longer lives, the value of Monte Carlo simulations for this or that, the 4 percent drawdown principle. It's all pretty much commoditized. Beyond these basics, however, the planning community gives a lot of thought to how products and services can be distinctively packaged so that a planner or firm can separate itself from the rest of its kind. Or, in the words of Gypsy Rose Lee, who knew something about maximizing assets, "You gotta have a gimmick."

A so-called Super Session at the conference features a presentation by a financial adviser from Quincy, Massachusetts, named Scott Fithian, who's an intelligent, articulate guy apparently respected by his peers. Fithian gives a forty-five-minute dog-and-pony show entitled "The Battle for Brain Share" that outlines the concepts underpinning his own planning practice and rings many of the bells that are now chiming clamorously in Numberland. Fithian's bio doesn't actually refer to him as a planner; he dubs himself a "Wealth Coach" and notes that he is the founder of the Legacy Wealth Coach Network, which exists—deep breath here—"to provide leadership for the transformation of the financial services industry from a singular focus on financial capital, to a holistic focus that incorporates human, intellectual, spiritual and experiential capital as well." Grandiose, yes, but it captures a slew of themes much in vogue throughout the planning universe:

Wealth is where the action is. There are reasons why intelligent people are confused. People need help integrating their affairs—certainly their financial affairs—but also in tying those financial affairs to personal hopes, dreams, and principles held dear.

T1: TRUST

Fithian dedicates his planning practice to the proposition that a high-wealth client requires and deserves a "most trusted adviser." "Trusted adviser" is a catchphrase much in favor within financial planning circles. A few years ago a book was written by three management consultants who'd clearly caught wind of an emerging opportunity. The opportunity rested on the insight that you and I have a soft spot for trustworthiness. Silly, but true. If an adviser can gain your trust, the authors contend, good things will happen to him and his professional practice. You'll see him more frequently. You'll recommend him to others. You might buy additional products and services from him. You'll be less fixated on what he charges. And you'll be apt to "play more fairly" with him, meaning you won't broom him on a whim.

To Fithian, a most trusted adviser stands shoulder to shoulder with you—assuming, of course, that you're sufficiently financially endowed. The two of you occupy space at the center of a hub-and-spoke system. In the hub there's him and you (and your spouse, as in that commercial about the dream house by the lake). The hub's spokes lead out to other advice-giving specialists: lawyer, tax adviser, banker, broker, insurance agent, philanthropic counselor, even family members with whom you might be encountering financial conflict. Your most trusted adviser is thus optimally located to serve variously as your gatekeeper, sounding board, devil's advocate, mediator, discreet and intimate friend, copilot, navigator, demystifier, strategic planner. You're the Cisco Kid and he's Pancho, a financial compadre who is versatile, reliable, and so honest you could shoot dice with him on the telephone, as Dan Rather would say. Wouldn't it be terrific to have that? Well, all it takes is money, as my grandfather would say.

But whether you're rich enough to have your own most trusted adviser or you're just looking for an honest broker, how can you know someone is knowledgeable, ethical, up to the task? Ordinary people say they haven't a clue. Many seem to evaluate a financial rep the way my mother assesses a doctor: Is he nice? Does he take sufficient time and interest?

A big concern people have is whether an adviser puts his financial well-being ahead of theirs. The truth is, it's sometimes hard to be sure. Financial planning for the masses is still trying to get its act together. Performance standards can be highly subjective, given our widely varying goals and risk tolerances. Are the investment returns your adviser generates for you good, fair, or unforgivable? And compared to what? Are they worth the fees or commissions you pay? Some people couldn't care less. They're fine with "good enough" as an acceptable measure of performance. Barry Schwartz, author of *The Paradox of Choice,* calls people like this "satisficers" (as in "I'm satisfied"), a term wanting in elegance but it gets the job done. In contrast, there are people who never like where they're seated in a restaurant or send back a bottle of wine if it's two degrees centigrade off perfect chill. Schwartz calls these people "maximizers," people for whom no piece of advice is likely to be good enough. Both my own impressions and Schwartz's more disciplined research indicate that satisficers tend to be happier and better adjusted than maximizers. But I wouldn't be surprised if maximizers tend to wind up with bigger houses, bigger boats, and bigger Numbers.

Whether you're easy or hard to please, you shouldn't pay more than you have to. There are three fundamental ways you can pay a professional to manage your Number, and the question of trust levitates over all of them. The first one makes an adviser, at least on the surface, more trustworthy than the others: this is when you pay someone an hourly fee or a retainer. Advisers who work this way are "fee-only" or "asset-based" planners. This is when you pay someone an hourly fee or a retainer, and/or a percentage (usually .5–1.5%) of your invested assets if the planner actively manages your money. They offer assurance that your Number won't be whacked by conflicts of interest. (This does not mean that your fee-only planner's hopelessly incompetent advice won't whack it—that's always a risk.) Based on counsel from your fee-only adviser, you yourself go out and buy your stocks, bonds, annuities, and insurance policies directly from reputable sources such as Vanguard, Fidelity, TIAA-CREF, among many others.

Compensation option number two is to use an adviser who charges hourly fees but also brokers mutual funds, bonds, annuities, and so forth. These people are "fee-*based*" advisers. There's nothing necessarily wrong with this option if you understand what the deal is and do enough homework to know you're not overpaying for products you can buy directly.

Finally there are individuals and institutions—like the wirehouses— who make their money by selling you stuff. Commission-based advisers can sell you good stuff, not so good stuff, and occasionally stuff you simply don't need. Commissions on these range from fair to steep and from transparent to opaque to completely concealed.

T2: TEMPERAMENT

Independent financial planners, who work on a fee-only or fee-based arrangement, are an interesting lot. I find most of them intelligent, decent, and genuinely concerned about their clients' well-being. They're also keen observers of how we fumble with the mechanics and emotions of Number management. Relative to their risk-averse, nervous-Nellie clients, these planners are slightly more adventurous with their own money. Few fret over the possibility of a cataclysmic market collapse. They tend to be sourpusses on bonds, wary of meager real returns. Persistent advocates of the Long-Term View, they don't sweat the market's twitches the way the rest of us do.

Their personalities, however, vary widely. There are broad differences in deskside manner. Some advisers are blunt enough to render a client speechless. In the summer of 2004, one Number chaser, totally

unnerved by what he perceived to be the Bush administration's foreign
and fiscal policies, woke up at an ungodly hour and, on the verge of
panic, e-mailed his money manager. Should he bail out of the market altogether? Hang tough? Move to Saskatoon? Perhaps all he needed was
a soothing voice to talk him down off the ledge. The e-mail reply from
his adviser, however, had all the serenity of haiku composed by Bruce
Lee:

> Here it is straight.
> You are uncomfortable.
> Sell everything. Then you will be
> comfortable. Comfort is an important part of the client
> relationship. This is meant from the heart.
> To date I think we have achieved what you expected.
> So maybe we just cash in.
> You have heard from this camp.

The client wasn't prepared for such a karate chop. Too startled to do
anything else, he kept his financial plan intact. He now tells himself
that even if the world goes to hell, at least he has avoided paying unnec-
essary capital gains.

If having a martial artist for a financial planner strikes you as too
harsh, then maybe you should keep things simple and folksy. There are
a lot of planners who find inspiration in time-honored precepts: The
Hare and the Tortoise. Chicken Little. The Little Red Hen. You can get
a good idea of a planner's values by the tattered book he goes by. For
Don Haas and others of his generation, the admired book is *The Richest
Man in Babylon* by George S. Clason, a slender collection of parables
published in 1926. The book reinforces Haas' conviction that it is impossible for anyone *not* to wind up wealthy if he or she consistently
saves 10 percent of every dollar that comes in. This principle is one of
seven Babylonian money lessons in *The Richest Man,* the idea that you
should "pay yourself first." That is, before you pay Miuccia Prada for a

calfskin shopping tote or John Deere for a shiny new lawn tractor, pay yourself a fee of ten cents out of every dollar you take in. Pay yourself first long enough and soon you'll be the richest man or woman, give or take, in Babylon, Hempstead, Garden City, or whichever font of civilization you happen to call home.

T3: TOUCH

How your financial advice gets delivered is largely dependent on how big your Number is. Many advisers will tell you their practice embraces people at all levels of the parking ramp and that in many cases they'll waive or reduce their fees for those who are strapped. These advisers are mostly telling the truth. In general, though, Scott Fithian has it right in his Denver presentation: there's a service model designed to fit the size of your Number. If you've got a million or two, Fithian says, expect to be engulfed by the old-fashioned "sales model." Banks, insurance companies, and brokerages are always knocking on your door with prepackaged products and services. Nobody will make enough money off you to devote long hours working up a highly complex custom plan.

As your Number climbs to between, say, $5 million and $10 million, you start hankering for the "advice model," Fithian notes. It is at this level that a lot of trusted (but not *most* trusted) advisers request the honor of your business: trust companies and private banks are the prospective helpers who discreetly inquire after the availability of your assets. Your holdings can throw off enough fees to make it worth their while to personalize your tax, investment, and estate planning strategies.

If your Number sits on the $10 million ramp or above, you graduate to the "discernment model." Here is where Fithian and his associates extend their *most* trusted adviser's pledge to provide the highest levels of "trust, clarity, competence, management, and confidence." It's here that you and your most trusted adviser stand cheek by jowl in that hub, that network of professionals orbiting around you, their trajectories coolly coordinated by your most trusted copilot.

Fithian doesn't say, but I'm confident he wouldn't disagree, that within each of these three models a client can underpay or overpay, and can get really good or really awful, financial advice.

THE SHAPE OF THINGS TO COME

The next ten years will bring a sea change in how people think about and manage the Number. Are you ready for Wealth Care Reform? As the age of self-determination matures and we settle into it, financial jargon will sound less and less like Greek; we'll speak personal finance as easily as we have come to master the languages of wine and gourmet cuisine—just look at the Food Network. A visit to a financial adviser or even a life coach will be about as momentous as visiting a dentist.

Exactly how the advice game will change is open to debate, but nearly everyone believes the board it's played on will be quite different from the one we know today. At least two scenarios for change currently exist: one takes a top-down view of the future, the other sees it from the bottom up. They are not mutually exclusive.

The top-down view belongs to Mark Hurley, CEO of a Dallas advisory firm called Undiscovered Managers. Several years ago Hurley published a research report on the future of the advisory business that set the industry's hair on fire. It said the present model for providing advice to millions of semi-affluent investors was doomed to imminent extinction because clients are becoming more financially literate and demanding higher-quality advice. He opined that technology was making a commodity out of the planning process. Most important, he said, too many financial services and planning firms were entering the market, dazzled by the billions at stake in fees. Darwinian competition would squeeze profits and force consolidation, and thus individual planners and small firms would have a hard time competing. The result, Hurley predicted, will be something like what has happened in the institutional money management business: several dozen large firms will survive, each with revenues of $10 billion or more. They will aggressively compete for tens of millions of customers. He compared today's planning business to the health care field before managed care came along. Just as individual doctors lost their one-on-one relationships with patients, most independent financial advisers will lose personal relationships with clients as they wind up in large, efficient, impersonal firms that offer commoditized financial advice to the mass affluent.

Hurley said something else that really got the industry's goat. He called the advice game "fundamentally a marketing business. The issue isn't whether you have the best service or not. It's your ability to market the service." He conceded that this sounded cynical, but he was unwavering about it. The financial services business vehemently disputes this.

A bottom-up view of the future belongs to Sheryl Garrett, a tireless entrepreneurial planner who really does believe that going to your friendly neighborhood financial adviser will be like popping in to have your teeth cleaned. Now forty-two, Garrett grew up middle class in Emporia, Kansas. "Even as a bitty kid," she tells me, "the thing I liked best was starting little businesses." When she was eight, Garrett sold grasshoppers for a dime a dozen. The business flopped. Undaunted, she opened her own bike repair shop. She delivered newspapers on horseback. She polished her parents' shoes, a nickel a pair. Several years after college, Garrett met a woman at a cocktail party who worked for what was then IDS American Express. Garrett was impressed by her knowledge, poise, and the ease with which she could talk investing strategy with total strangers. It was enough to encourage Garrett to take a job at Amex, where she began to pick up the rudiments of personal finance, which in turn led to her certification as a planner.

Sheryl Garrett's dream is to do for financial planning what H&R Block did for the tax return, what Jiffy Lube did for the oil change, and what Cost Cutters did for the haircut—take it to the people. She founded the Garrett Planning Network, which is a nationwide federation of independent planners, each with professional certification. The network supplies the business model, some training, and the promotional energy of an effervescent, talk-show-savvy, trade-show-loving apostle who spreads the word. Affiliated planners work on a fee-only basis. If you need a portfolio checkup or a retirement cash flow plan, you pay anywhere from $120 to $300 per hour to have it done. If you need an annual physical done on your Number, you can do that, too. Garrett says that 98 percent of her clients have had no prior experience whatsoever with planning, but that the new Rest of Your Life has become too complicated not to have some help now and then.

Official Garrett agitprop characterizes its broad target market as "hardworking, everyday people who play by the rules and who need folks they can trust." Garrett refers to her customers as "normal people" who make, on average, $75,000 a year, which may be considered "middle market" but hardly "middle income," as we saw back on the parking ramps. This segment represents a huge untapped opportunity for the advice squad. "Thirteen percent of Americans are living in poverty," Garrett says. "And about 3 percent of Americans are on the upper end of the scale, with invested assets of $500,000 or more. That leaves 84 percent of Americans who need, and can afford, occasional hourly consultations"—and for whom, she says, "one-size-fits-all" planning advice from the likes of David Bach is frequently too boilerplate. She recalls a recent conference she attended, at which Bach told a jammed meeting room that anyone who doesn't own a home is a loony bird. Afterward, says Garrett, an elderly woman—a renter, not a homeowner—came over to say that she felt like a fool. But after listening to the details of the woman's life, Garrett concluded that the woman was doing exactly the right thing by not tying up her assets in a house.

Predictably, the press pins the McPlanning label on Garrett's vision of the future. While she's not especially offended by it, she quarrels with its lack of nuance: "What I'm doing is less like McDonald's and more like Applebee's. Not real cheap, but not real expensive, either. And where what you get is good, satisfying, middle-of-the-road, consistent."

It's possible that Scott Fithian, Mark Hurley, and Sheryl Garrett all have it right. In Hurley's vision, financial advice will be dispensed by the equivalent of huge managed care companies. In Garrett's view, it will come from an urgent care clinic just down the block. In Fithian's, a lucky few will have 24/7 access to their own Number docs, who are eager to make house calls. So get ready for it: radical wealth care reform is coming on fast.

12

NIGHT SWEATS

I t's ten P.M. Do you know what your Number is?

The Number keeps many people awake nights, with only the tree frogs to provide solace, yet most of them refuse to seek professional help. They think they can work it out themselves. Bounding out of bed, they log onto the site of whichever financial services firm handles their company's retirement plan. The Internet can be a refuge, a place to collect thoughts and gather advice. For these people, online Number check-in is now part of everyday life—except their destiny hangs in the account balance. Once logged on, people must choose from among mutual funds whose exact purpose in a portfolio they may not understand. Do-it-yourselfers stay online for a second or linger for an hour; they leave but they'll be back sometime soon. The Web site where they keep their Number is sticky.

The people on the other side of the firewall, the financial services industry, have a great deal riding on what customers do once they get to a site. They want customers to feel comfortable, informed, and secure whenever they log on; they also want them to log on often, to check out new features and tools. What keeps *them* up at night is the fear that customers might leave them for other bookmarks, go elsewhere to manage their Numbers, which can easily happen when people change jobs or retire. Family pictures and rubber plants aren't the only things carried out to the car. When the Number moves to a new site, it leaves no forwarding address.

People manage their Numbers at Vanguard, Merrill Lynch, American Express, T. Rowe Price, Salomon Smith Barney—the list goes on forever. The big player in the field is Fidelity Investments. Fidelity has over nine million "retail accounts"—accounts not affiliated with workplace plans or other such—and over nineteen million institutional accounts, 401(k) or other retirement plans offered at the office. Every day, a million customers log onto Fidelity.com to do some piece of business.

At Fidelity, as at all financial services companies, they don't think of the Number as a metaphor, illusion, existential premise, pipe dream, recurring nightmare, anxiety pang, or anything remotely like a last taboo. They regard your Number much as Home Depot regards your house. They offer an array of tools, a large inventory of products, and enough know-how to give you some assurance that you can take up the project on your own, even if you're a hopeless klutz of an investor.

HOUSE OF NUMBERS

On what is surely the hottest, sweatiest day of the summer, I find myself on the doorstep at 82 Devonshire Street, in the heart of Boston's financial district. Despite how insufferable it is outside, I detect a bracing nip once I step inside Fidelity headquarters. What better time to be in the Number business? Tens of millions of people are approaching age fifty with considerable assets to be managed. If they're the kind who won't seek professional help, they face a new and complicated life stage, one that demands financial socket wrenches and nail drivers. They need step-by-step instructions. Never before have so many people realized the immediate need to take on a financial improvement project.

The main reason I've come to Fidelity is to get a sense of how a big Number company thinks about those who are wrestling solo with the Number. Fidelity's do-it-yourselfers live in the sweet spot of mass affluence. Most have enough money that they have to manage their Numbers, but not so much that they need, seek, or feel like paying by the hour for financial counseling. By and large, these are people with anywhere between a few hundred thousand to a couple of million dollars on account. Fidelity assumes that when you get much higher than that, a Number of $4 million, say, you tend to bring in a by-the-hour professional to do the job.

Fidelity generally deals directly with its customers, and like all seasoned retailers, the merchants at 82 Devonshire are tuned to the moment. A great deal of money is about to roll around. Millions of preretirees will have to make choices about what to do with their 401(k)s. Clients have already shifted $200 billion out of company retirement plans into individual accounts. Over the next few years, as more and more people retire, another $600 billion will be in play. With so much at stake, Fidelity is intent on figuring out how it might make a complex financial project like retirement as doable as possible. How can it make a handyman out of a klutz? How can it teach him to spackle and solder and rewire his Number without making one gigantic and irreversible mess? How can it help him sleep better at night?

More than most firms, Fidelity believes in the efficacy of self-help, a business model that succeeds or fails depending on how well it delivers the tools and the step-by-step directions. For better or worse, it helped create the new world of financial self-reliance. The company started just after World War II as a reasonably conventional mutual funds operation, when mutual funds were still but a stubby tail on the dog of the equities market. When mutual funds took off, so did Fidelity. From the 1940s to the 1970s its managed assets zoomed from $13 million to $3.5 billion, and its growth spurt was yet to come. Fidelity's heir and current

CEO, Edward C. "Ned" Johnson III, somehow figured out that the coming decades would produce millions of people who would be obliged to develop do-it-yourself skills. Accordingly, he directed the company to invest heavily in technology and customer service, knowing that any successful big-box financial retailer would have to stay open twenty-four hours a day, Christmas, Kwanzaa, Yom Kippur included. Johnson further decided that Fidelity would extend its reach beyond the usual tradesmen, the network of commission-based brokers and sales reps, and deal personally with its customers, which is primarily how it does business now. Technology was the key. Today, 20 percent of the workforce at Fidelity is technology related—not surprising given that over 90 percent of Fidelity transactions take place online, much of it by do-it-yourselfers.

GROWTH SPURT

Fidelity, while it made a lot of timely moves, also had gusty economic and demographic breezes at its back. Its growth coincided with the baby boom's big earnings years and long-running bull markets. Then, not incidentally, came the advent of private retirement plans—IRAs and 401(k)s—which hit the market in the 1970s and '80s, an opportunity Fidelity was notably quick to seize. Bob Reynolds, now chief operating officer at Fidelity, enjoys remembering those years. Over coffee in a small conference room at 82 Devonshire, Reynolds observes that self-determination has defined the larger culture for the past couple of decades. "It is simply everywhere in our lives now," he says, "this need to take control of our own health care, our kids' education, certainly our financial well-being."

A hearty guy, ruddy-faced and with a linebacker's build, Reynolds is oblivious to the temperature outside, decked out in a bright pin-striped shirt and perfectly coordinated pink tie. Twenty years ago Ned Johnson called Reynolds into his office. At the time Reynolds was a rising star at 82 Devonshire, a young man overseeing a $12 billion division. More or less on a hunch, he says, Johnson asked him to run with something. Congress had recently enacted the legislation authorizing 401(k) plans. Although the idea hadn't gotten that much attention in the press, Johnson sensed that this new workplace plan would change how people saved for retirement. "I have a feeling this is going to be very big," Johnson told him. Reynolds was assigned to put together a team to address the 401(k) opportunity. "I'm not sure the industry really understood what was happening," he says. "These first 401(k) plans were, if you can believe, actually called Salary Reduction Plans. Not especially appealing, was it?"

Getting someone to give up take-home pay was one thing; getting that someone to do the right thing with the holdback was job two. Most people, financially untutored and risk averse, opted for "gicks," guaranteed investment contracts, fixed-income products that wilted in the face of inflation. Reynolds says Fidelity had to teach the wary and the innocent to strive for higher rates of return if they wanted their Numbers to outpace the cost of living. Over the ensuing decades Fidelity became a huge player in the management of corporate retirement plans, but even this growth is a mere prelude to the opportunity that lies immediately ahead. Retirement, Reynolds says, is "the biggest do-it-yourself project ever." He believes that most people don't really think about how to finance the rest of their lives until they approach, then exceed, age fifty.

Thirteen million people turned fifty in the late 1990s. Nineteen million more turned fifty over the past few years. Twenty-one million more will turn fifty in the next few years. And twenty-three million more will turn fifty soon after that, with the last boomer hitting fifty in 2014. They'll all need more than a little baling wire and nails and tape measures and duct tape. The financial services industry wishes happy birthday, and long life, to every one.

LUNCH PLANS

The initial adventures with IRAs and 401(k)s are ancient history at 82 Devonshire. The modern DIY era began on the afternoon of Wednesday, May 29, 2002. The occasion was an executive luncheon at 27 State Street, a Fidelity office building just around the corner from 82 Devonshire. Fifteen people were seated around a large rectangular table, open in the middle. They were all top Fidelity executives, including Bob Reynolds and Abby Johnson, Ned's daughter, recently turned forty. Lunch was a three-course meal prepared by a company chef and served in a private room with teak trim and antique floral prints on the pale blue walls.

Prominent on the agenda was a presentation by Roger Servison, head of strategic initiatives and a top Fidelity hand for nearly thirty years. On this day in 2002, Servison's thoughts were turning not to strategies past but to the decade ahead. He considered his presentation a blueprint for the future, although he didn't hype it with a kicky headline or dazzling graphics. Titled "Income Planning and Distribution," Servison's fourteen PowerPoint slides sketched out his vision of the mass affluent do-it-yourselfers' most vexing conundrum over the next thirty years: how do you keep a portion of your assets growing while at the same time drawing down funds to live on? The opening section of his four-part presentation dealt with demographics and market opportunities. Then he got to the nub.

He said that you, me, the crash dummies, *everybody* would be wise to cultivate "a new mindset," a more holistic view of our lifetime income similar to what Neal Cutler and the financial gerontologists talk about: that a well-planned lifetime consists of an accumulation phase, during which you work and save for the future, and then a distribution phase, in which these assets are drawn down in an appropriate way, with taxes and other considerations taken into account. In the accumulation phase, he said, time is your buddy—if you start young and keep your financial house in order, you'll probably do fine, according to the Monte

Carlo bookmakers. In the distribution phase, however, time is not a friend. Not only is it too late to accumulate all that much, what you have accumulated is subject to all those risks our crash dummies faced: longevity, health care costs, misallocated investments, excessive spending, inflation.

Servison didn't come right out and say what would have been obvious to the people in the room, that arranging assets in the right proportion and at the right time while withdrawing other assets for maximum tax efficiency and minimum investment risk, isn't something most investor-tinkerers should try at home. That is, not without the right toolbox and someone standing over their shoulder or, at the very least, no more than a log-on away. He told the group that sound financial strategies could be welded to both the accumulation and distribution phases. To cover essential retirement expenses such as food, shelter, and health care, a person should earmark his or her Social Security, pension, and fixed-income investments. For more discretionary spending such as travel, hobbies, facelifts, people could take a chance on the market. Should these investments run into stormy weather, discretionary spending could be scaled back without jeopardizing the income stream that keeps food on the table, a roof overhead, and your blood pressure in check.

A new mindset and new tools could come together in a new strategic initiative, Servison suggested. The initiative would leverage technology to give DIY investors a convenient way to do a bunch of things: monitor how their portfolios are performing, keep tabs on their budget, and keep them apprised of what inflation and health care costs are doing to their best-laid blueprints. Thumbs up all around the table. No one suggested that outside consultants scrub the concept, nobody asked for a feasibility study. They knew it wouldn't be long before Vanguard, Merrill, T. Rowe Price, Amex, and all their other competitors were forging their own retirement-based financial tools. Everyone would be elbowing to get into this space. This is where the future was; this was where the money was. And so Fidelity placed a bucket of resources—technologists, financial planners, marketers, customer reps—at the service of what would come to be called the Retirement Income Advantage program. It named a top exec, Cynthia Egan, to oversee its launch as soon as the right toolbox had been built, refined, and tested. A white paper distributed throughout the organization described the change in thinking that must occur if the massive baby boom generation was to face down the perils of retirement. It also offered a mea culpa: "the financial services industry has not done a very good job in preparing its customers for [the] distribution phase of their financial lives. . . ." Only one in five people, it noted, had anything resembling a plan for managing income, assets, and expenses during retirement. Most retirees simply "play it by ear."

The white paper fired a warning shot over the head of every one of you procrastinators: develop a realistic lifetime income plan—*now*. Cushion your investment portfolio against unforeseen financial shocks. Update your plan regularly as circumstances change, or live with the consequences.

At an employee meeting that year, Chairman Ned Johnson issued an edict that the Retirement Income initiative was to be regarded as one of the company's top priorities. What eventually rolled off the assembly line was a Web-based tool that had at its core an overall financial plan for the do-it-yourselfer, one that stipulated targets for income, investments, and spending. This was the part of the program that customers would need some guidance with, so they'd consult a Fidelity rep on the phone or in one of the firm's walk-in centers around the country. Connected to this plan was an Income Management Account, which offered an on-screen overview of a customer's finances, whether all of her assets were kept at Fidelity or not. The system could alert her to when taxes were due and when spending went off the rails. It could also function as a paymaster. Say you're retired. There's something like a green funnel into which goes deposits from all of your income sources, including Social Security, pension checks, interest from CDs, investment dividends, annuity payments. Out of the bottom of that funnel drops a monthly check in whatever amount your plan calls for. Any remainder gets automatically invested. This would cut down the hassle that confounds many retirees, not just wealthy ones, who have to keep track of four, six, nine small checks a month.

Fidelity capped its launch with a television and print ad campaign featuring a series of couples and showing how their lives had evolved from childhood through the counterculture, through career stages, and ultimately to the brink of retirement. The spots have been running for a month when I meet Cynthia Egan for breakfast at 82 Devonshire. Egan, who made sure the campaign chugged along in the right way and on schedule, stresses what should be obvious to do-it-yourselfers but isn't to most: you've got to have a plan—if not from Fidelity, then from somebody else. And not just a-lot-of-numbers-on-a-page plan, but a plan that continuously updates itself according to investment performance, spending, cost-of-living changes. "The old days are gone," she says, between bites of an omelet. "It used to be that even if you had a plan, it was some leatherette-bound report someone gave you, which you soon after put behind the piano and never looked at again. Gone, too, are the days when it was usually enough to take your 401(k) and roll it over into CDs that your neighborhood bank was happy to sell you. Or build a bond ladder. Or buy an annuity. While this kind of planning can sometimes work out fine," she notes, "longer lives and health care costs require something more dynamic."

Whenever she sits in on planning seminars with investors, Egan sees evidence of rampant unpreparedness. She says that when attendees are asked for a show of hands—Who has a will? Who has a retirement plan?—a large majority say they have a will but only a smattering say they have a financial plan. This boggles her mind. "Think about it," she says. "A retirement plan exists to allow an orderly distribution of assets while you're alive. A will exists to allow an orderly distribution of assets when you're dead. It amazes me that people are comfortable doing one but not the other." She assumes that many people would rather not know how dicey their future is. When this denial is overcome, however, and people do finally get a plan together, they go through what sound like Elisabeth Kübler-Ross' stages of grief:

First, as they take in reality, there's *disappointment*. Prospects are bleak. This is depressing. I'm screwed.

Then there's *anger*. They get angry with themselves (or, too often, with a spouse) for getting into this mess in the first place.

After that—sometimes—comes a dose of *relief*. At least they know where they stand.

Finally, if they're lucky, *liberation*. With delusions and denial stripped away, they might get a sense of what has to happen next. It is at this point, Egan says, that people can make some headway. Gross indulgences and excessive spending may finally be curtailed.

It's now midnight. Do *you* have a plan? Do you know what your Number is now?

SOUL OF A NEW TOOL

Fidelity's retirement income tool doesn't run on smoke and mirrors. A vast boiler room of data and algorithms lies beneath its surface. The do-it-yourselfer doesn't need to know how it works, just that it does work, and that the tools are built on solid assumptions and data. This job falls to Van Harlow, a soft-spoken Ph.D. from Texas. Harlow doesn't try to win debating points with fanciful theories about why people do or don't get their planning acts together, he just wants the numbers in the plan to be right. Getting the data right is a challenge, or has been till now, Harlow says. Setting an accurate Number is complex, given all the risks and variables of the new Rest of Your Life. It takes more than a little computing power to shmoosh all of them together and project out investment returns, life expectancy, inflation trends, health care costs. Technology finally exists to collect and sift all these data, he points out, and gives the do-it-yourselfer some simple-to-use controls with which to hammer away.

Fidelity reports that it's working. More people, the company says, even some younger ones—"young" as in forty—are beginning to roll up their sleeves. They're not clearing off the kitchen table to take a meeting with their accountant Bernie, they're logging on while sipping their morning coffee, throughout the day at work, after a movie, late into the night. Sometimes they log on just to check the market, sometimes to play with the controls Harlow and his people have provided. In the first seven months following the launch, some 600,000 people are logging on to engage in—love the phrase—"planning interactions," pounding on Van Harlow's algorithms to see where they stand at any given moment.

Keep in mind that these 600,000 are self-selected. They are obviously comfortable with technology and have gone to the trouble of working out their financial plans, then sitting down at the controls. Although not representative of everyone out there, they could represent many millions. Here's what the toolbox is telling them:

About one out of four of them seems to be in OK shape. They are, presumably, old enough, frugal enough, and healthy enough to be able to live off their investments and other income. Another one in four, though, is in hot water. They can click their mice all they want, but the toolbox is telling them they're a long way from realizing their dreams, let alone surviving if they lose their jobs or get sick.

For the rest, about half the people sitting at the controls, a warning light is flashing, telling them maybe, maybe not. Here come those ifs again. If they save more, spend less, take their withdrawals out with an eye on tax implications; if their insurance premiums and the inflation rate stay under control; if the markets do what they're supposed to; and if they make it a habit to log on and not hide the computer printout behind the piano, then everything might work out fine.

HIDDEN COMPLEXITIES

A final stop before hitting the steamy bricks. Tucked away in a small corner office in another of Fidelity's downtown buildings sits a boyish fifty-eight-year-old man named Charlie Brenner. He's a product of the Bronx, a graduate of Hunter College who got turned on to computer science while in the military. Brenner runs a division, the Center for Applied Technology, whose primary function, he says, is "to hide complexity." His job is to make sure that a do-it-yourselfer can actually work the controls and not screw things up because he or she is too old or nervous to use the Internet. Brenner questions the conventional wisdom that baby boomers are generally computer- and Internet-savvy enough to manipulate Fidelity's tools as adroitly as Fidelity would like them to. "An awful lot of them are still technophobes," he allows. This is why it's important to design Web pages that are equally well conceived for a wide spectrum of investors, whether financial hobbyists who like to delve into the nits and gnats of their portfolios or mere novices. Brenner says plenty of highly affluent, successful professionals have barely touched a keyboard in their forty-year careers and are still extremely uncomfortable with computers. And there are still dinosaurs—male and female both—who have "gals" in the office to do it for them.

Even if a do-it-yourselfer is tech savvy, Brenner points out, things change over time. You begin to experience, well, teensy-weensy slipups. Hand-eye coordination begins to go. Your eyeballs, your brain aren't quite as reliable when asked to follow multiple paths of logic on a Web site. Your mouse takes on a mind of its own, clicks when you don't want it to. Years from now, right? Unfortunately not. "These things occur well before people get to be seventy or eighty," says Brenner. "From the testing we've done, we know that many skills begin to decline in one's fifties, when we start to experience a drop-off in short-term memory. You know how you begin to race to dial the phone before you forget a phone number?" I nod, perhaps too vigorously. "Well, to remember seven digits is not very difficult when you're twenty-five, but it gets harder and harder when you're middle-aged."

According to sources cited by marketer David Wolfe, there's evidence that our eyes begin to lose acuity after the age of eight, let alone what happens at fifty. Visual memory starts to decline in middle age, eroding sharply at around seventy. Performance on logic tests likewise declines around that age. By the time you reach your forties, not only do you need cheaters to read, you lose some ability to distinguish between gradations of color. Depth perception grows less acute. Add in attention-span deficits and short-term memory lapses and you can appreciate why Brenner is spending so much time on the design of Web sites that will be easy and friendly when preretirees and older customers come logging on.

A comfortable online experience is half of what Brenner worries about day to day. His other mandate is security. He frets over how spam, viruses, identity theft, and security alerts might cause people to lose confidence in the whole idea of do-it-yourself online Number management. "My concern," he explains, "is that people will be scared to touch the computer, and frankly, the technology industry has not been good at providing reassurance. Telling everyday people 'to check your Windows updates' and 'keep your virus protection updated' is not going to cut it. It's like car maintenance: the manual tells you to check your tire pressure once a week, walk around your vehicle and look for fluid drips— but nobody in the world does that. And we know we can get away without being so diligent because cars generally work pretty well. But computers aren't there yet. What the tech world says is that if you want security, you're going to have to trade off convenience. You're going to have to remember fourteen-digit passwords that you'll have to change every six days. Well, that's just not going to work."

I ask Brenner where all his work is taking us, whether the Holy Grail is one single, powerful online tool that keeps track of virtually every number in your life. The ultimate financial Veg-o-Matic:

It doles out retirement checks.

It badgers you to pay your bills.

It then pays them with a single click (assuming you're still sure-handed enough to effect a crisp, single click).

It monitors mortgage rates and tells you when to refinance.

It automatically rebalances your portfolio.

It audits investments for tax efficiency.

"I'd call that an achievable if utopian goal," Brenner replies. "Achievable because the technology is certainly there to do it. Utopian because it would be a challenge to carry it to its full potential. Think about what else it might do," he goes on. "Let's say I have a 1994 Volvo station wagon in the garage. Should I sell it? Should I trade it in? Should I buy or lease a new car? What if this tool could gather new car prices but also understand your lifestyle and taste? Bernie your accountant might tell you to buy a hybrid-powered car to save on fuel costs, but the tool, who knows you better than Bernie does, says Hey, forget gas mileage, you're a sports car kind of guy. You won't be happy with a hybrid, you need something sexier, which is probably more expensive, which means you're going to have to cut down your spending somewhere else. So I've prepared a few suggestions." A machine shrewder than even Bernie the accountant? The mind reels.

A last question for Brenner. I ask him how he thinks things are going in the new Rest of Your Life. After all, he's on the front lines. He pauses for a moment.

"While self-management has given people enormous power over their own lives," he says, "I'm not sure it was entirely a kind thing to do to them. With old-fashioned, defined benefit plans all you needed to worry about were two numbers. If I retire at such-and-such age, this is how much money I will get. Then society took that away and gave people this gift of self-management. It's as if your doctor suddenly said, 'You're a bright guy. Here are your blood test results, and here's a copy of the *Physicians' Desk Reference*. It has a lot of stuff about medications in it, so you now have the tools you need to manage your hypertension and your diabetes and here's my Web address if you have any questions.'

"The doctor needs to do better than that," Brenner concludes. "And so do we."

PART THREE

FINDING IT

13

DOWNSHIFTING WITH JUNG

Is the Number about money, or is the Number about meaning, fulfillment, and life's true calling? When you wrestle with Uncertainty Principle 6—what is the Number good for, anyway?—the questions can get big and hairy. Seven decades ago, Carl Jung, psychoanalyst laureate of the money-and-meaning movement, offered his interpretation of the stages of life. The second half of life is a time to reflect, he said. Midlife is the time to let go of an overdominant ego and to contemplate the deeper significance of human existence.

One day I'm chatting with David Wolfe, whose book *Ageless Marketing* offers an interesting account of the life, times, and values of the over-forty consumer market. Wolfe puts a Jungian spin on what midlifers are all about and contends that the media and marketing people just don't have a clue. He's confounded by how Madison Avenue wastes money sucking up to demographic targets that are younger, smaller, and decidedly less affluent than midlifers. Referring to the midlife market as "the New Customer Majority," he notes that consumers forty-five and older will spend a trillion dollars more than the eighteen-to-thirty-nine-year-old cohort. Why don't marketers get this? Because they don't read Jung? To sell financial products, health care, retirement homes, in-

surance, even walking shoes, it helps to know what makes a midlife person tick. Instead of chasing the hip, David Wolfe would advise marketers to get cozy with a copy of *The Portable Jung*.

For years Wolfe has been trying to convince clients that there's a
"New Senior" out there, a person who cares as much about "life satisfaction"—glancing nod toward Jung—as about boating and golf. He has
said New Seniors turn four faces to the world:

- They are creatively and intellectually involved. They read newspapers, take adult education courses, travel to enlightening
  places, or would if they could afford to.

- They have a strong desire to share their experiences with others,
  to mentor, teach, tell stories.

- They are generally far more vital and productive into their eighties and nineties than Old Seniors.

- And they are compassionate about others and concerned about
  the well-being of the world around them, not just out for themselves.

While Wolfe doesn't dispute that per capita spending tops out when
people reach age fifty, he reminds us that New Seniors certainly continue to buy things, not only things to maintain the lifestyle they're accustomed to, but things that provide meaning and value to others, such
as tuition for grandkids.

Wolfe, who's in his early seventies, is an impassioned champion of
what Jung and Erik Erikson and Abraham Maslow tell us about how
values evolve in the later stages of life. Each man in his own way posits
that we become less materialistic and more introspective as we age.
This is why, Wolfe says, older people are frequently misrepresented and
misinterpreted by political polls, marketing surveys, and research studies, which typically call for a yes, no, or no opinion answer. Seniors'
views are more nuanced, Wolfe tells me, and with nuance comes the

urge to answer: it depends. This explains in part why clients frequently come to him asking why a product launch failed or why older consumers act in ways counter to what surveys predict.

Wolfe then explains his theory of "the psychological center of gravity," which posits that if businesses want to understand how New Seniors influence the larger culture, they can't just look at the dead center of a population segment, they need to look at the values of those who fall to one side or the other of the median age. He points out that the makers of the counterculture were, for the most part, not boomers (who usually get the credit for it) but people like Jerry Rubin, Martin Luther King, Jr., Ralph Nader, Timothy Leary, Gloria Steinem, Bob Dylan, the former Hanoi Jane, all of whom were older than the boomer cohort.

This observation holds promise. I make a note to try to find some people who might exemplify the Number life of tomorrow—call it the Number Center of Gravity. So before we end our conversation, I ask Wolfe if he knows someone he considers emblematic of the values we take on in midlife and beyond, when the meaning side of the Number comes into play. He mentions a friend of his who, he says, has "learned how to mind his passion," a man who once thought a lot about the money part of the Number, "then came to build a different structure around who he wants to be."

RE-NUMBERED

It's a stroke of luck that I manage to catch James Weil just before he flies off for India. He's heading there to take a series of classes in religion, then move on to Bhutan, where he plans to bike-trek the eastern Himalayas. Bhutan is the land of mask dances and prayer flags planted on the mountaintops, blue sheep, golden langurs, and snow leopards. If in midlife it's good to stop and smell the rhododendrons, there's no better spot than Bhutan, where there are fifty distinct varieties.

Seven years ago Weil's life wasn't so piquant. He was an out-of-shape senior executive sweating over whether he'd made his Number. He spent the big chunk of his career in the—heart, be still—insurance industry, working in marketing and sales at MetLife, running accounts in the company's group insurance and pensions department. Beginning in the early 1980s and for twelve years thereafter, he helped MetLife enter the long-term-care business. He then started a division dedicated to getting MetLife policies into the hands of customers fifty and older. Along the way he served on the boards of nonprofits devoted to support services for the elderly.

When he retired at fifty-five, Weil believed he had things pretty well thought through, at least financially. Within five years, however, he realized he had been barking up the wrong rhododendron. "I'm in a totally different place," he says to me. "I'd spent hours and hours working on my Number, looking at cash flow, projecting out to age ninety. I felt I was finally there, even though one's never sure. You can figure you need $5 million, but then you immediately think $6 million would provide a margin of comfort, $7 million would be better still. Today, I don't think it's about the money at all. Not that you shouldn't try to make sure you have your Number—I always tried to save between 15 and 20 percent of my income. It's about what you then go on to do with your life."

No matter that Weil spent an entire career in the belly of a business that brought him into routine contact with the aged, the costs of aging, and with what people can do to protect themselves from the financial ravages of age. He says he truly didn't understand what later life was about, or could be about, until he started traveling with people who were ten, twenty, or more years his senior. He took a few Elderhostel trips. He biked from his home in Connecticut to Boston, an outing put together online by a retiree. He hiked Kilimanjaro with two others, a woman in her sixties, a man in his seventies, following which he joined up with his wife and daughters and went on safari. Weil says nearly all of his journeys are with people he has never before met, people who are "phenomenally vital and who have never once complained about their arthritis." He says that when he started he was in terrible physical condition, but he isn't now. The people he travels with have disabused him of the notion that life is about the Number. Very few of them, he says, can be considered wealthy. He says that if they can't afford a sailing trip, they volunteer to crew. If they can't afford a ski trip, they work at a lodge.

Weil's travels with elderly strangers take him away from home a couple of months a year. When he's not on the road, he puts in sixty hours a week at a consulting firm near his home that advises private companies and government agencies on benefits management. Weil mentors his colleagues on marketing and aging issues. He's twice as old as most of the other people he works with, but he finds it stimulating to be around them.

One other piece of the puzzle has fallen into place, and that's his marriage. Weil tells me that he and his wife of thirty-four years have figured out how to engage in "parallel play for grownups." When he arrives in Bhutan, she'll be landing in Paris. He says it wasn't always like this. His wife enjoys garden tours—he doesn't. (He says going on a garden tour is like a prison sentence.) He enjoys riding a bike through the countryside—she doesn't. So she does her thing, he does his.

Traveling with old-timers, working with relative babies, parallel play with your own wife. None of these was in the plan when Weil worked out his Number, yet they turned out to be his most valuable assets.

TAKING THE CURVE

The old Rest of Your Life came equipped with an automatic transmission. Your trusty compound planetary gear set moved you along steadily without a lot of bumps or jerks. You glided through school, then with easy acceleration through a job or two, then eased off when you reached retirement. The new Rest of Your Life, on the other hand, comes with a stick shift. You use it to whip on past a dead-end job, switching career lanes like some kind of Jeff Gordon.

You need to downshift. Downshifting is the life passage du jour, what you need to know how to do when you enter the curve between the time you leave your career and the time you decide, or the time that time decides, to switch off the engine.

That everyone is talking about downshifting is entirely understandable. People nowadays are so fit and alert they keep rolling on long past their first retirement, albeit at gradually reduced speeds. A huge majority of boomers say they intend to work well into the indefinite future. And, appropriately, there are now an endless variety of flexible models in the workplace to allow them to do just that. Many companies have instituted phased retirement programs that offer part-time hours with or without ancillary benefits. Others have launched job sharing schemes and lifelong learning classes to give older workers a broader set of skills. Every industry understands that there is a serious labor shortage just around the corner. Be on the lookout for greater numbers of senior burger-flippers, baristas, and hospital aides. For some, like James Weil, downshifting the postcareer curve will turn out to be a blast: adventure travel, a tailor-made part-time job, a compatible spouse. For others, downshifting will mean scrounging for money *and* meaning.

The challenges of downshifting have been under discussion for quite a while now. Back in 2000 *Fortune* published an article under the memorable title "Candy Striper, My Ass!" It told true tales of high-powered retired executives, sufficiently Numbered, who went looking for meaning in the nonprofit sector only to find that their inquiries went unanswered or they were offered part-time positions that didn't exactly amount to lateral career moves.

The former president of one of Kodak's international divisions, who had visions of joining the board of a local charity, contributing strategy and vision to its efforts, was told that he could go out and raise funds if he wanted to. "I was pissed off," he says. A group president of a Fortune 500 consumer-goods company, willing to work for nothing, went 0 for 10 in his search. The final indignity came when one position he was interested in, and for which he expected no compensation, was filled with a paid staffer.

The moral of these stories is not that the world slams the door on those who seek to downshift, it's that adjustments need to be made, expectations lowered, grandiosity brought to heel. Yet a lot of people in their forties and fifties, even though they say they want to keep on working, are fuzzy about where, when, and how. Their sense of the future is, to be generous, a loose sketch:

"Work defines my life more than anything else. I don't have hobbies. But I'm going to wind down at fifty-five."

"We would love to move back to a two-bedroom apartment on Riverside Drive, where we would be close to cultural activities. We will both work in some capacity, but we don't know what."

"My husband might be a business consultant. He could make at least half of what he brings in now. Maybe."

"We'd like to move to the Carolinas and buy a year-round house near the water. I want to stop at fifty-five and not work again. He would try to work half-time."

A few others supply specifics. They see the dots and a way to connect them:

"I'm very good at reducing expenses. I'll work at lower rates. I've already rented out an extra room in my apartment. It got me through a rough spot. I'm very resourceful."

"My husband will stop working in five years. He already has a side job that he will continue in retirement. Or he might open an automotive shop with his brother."

Tradeoffs and sacrifices are all part of the curve. Handling the curve calls for dexterity. It helps to know how to drive a stick shift.

DOWNSHIFTING AND THE JOY OF MOTORCYCLES

Downshifting doesn't have to be all compromise and no play. Consider Ron Cavill, who's a piece of part-time work if there ever was one. Cavill's a financial planner, divorced, sixty years old. He's a big bear of a guy who is today dressed in a white shirt with a Colorado Rockies logo on it; also khakis and boat shoes without socks. He pulls up to my Denver hotel wearing aviator shades and a wide grin. Cavill is a gregarious downshifter who spends a lot of time on the road. He's behind the wheel of a yellow four-year-old Sebring JXi convertible, top down, vanity plates reading CAVILL. He says that he remembers the exact sound of the engine in the old Sunbeam Alpine he drove when he first visited Colorado years ago. Cavill likes to drive almost everywhere he goes. Planes are too cramped for his bulky frame and creaky knees—they're cattle cars. Besides, there's another vehicle in his life, a Kawasaki Vulcan Nomad V Twin Cruiser. The bike figures prominently in Cavill's notion that downshifting makes life worth living.

Cavill moved to the Denver area from Washington, D.C., in 1995, after his divorce. He'd built a successful planning practice in Washington, raising a family there. Even though he knew he might go broke in Denver, at least he'd be broke in Colorado. "It's so beautiful out here," he says. "The climate is great, the people are terrific, or at least they were till all the Californians moved in." Beating up on people from L.A. is major-league sport among Coloradoans, native and relative newcomers both. Californians are too flashy, they say. Cavill likes people who are real, not showy. "On the East Coast," Cavill says, "it was very hard if you didn't have money. You were surrounded by it. I used to marvel at how many cars on the Beltway had university stickers on their rear windshields. Princeton. Dartmouth. Georgetown. Constant reminders of wealth and privilege. You don't much see things like that in Denver. It's easier to kick back here. I go to work in shorts and TopSiders and nobody thinks a thing about it. Back in Washington, if I stopped at my office after being on my boat, people on the elevator would back away from me like I was some kind of bum."

Prior to my meeting up with Cavill, I'd been corresponding with him about downshifting. He'd forwarded a batch of the newsletters he sends occasionally to clients. "Cavill's Comments" comes prepunched for a three-ring binder and is more or less equally devoted to Cavill's life and times as a downshifting middle-ager, interrupted by thoughts on which way he expects the market to move and other pieces of practical financial advice.

Back in 2000 Cavill suffered a bout with angina that was duly chronicled in "Cavill's Comments": "I am happy to report that I have been taking my own advice and since November 4, when I had my attack, I have had a marvelous turnabout in my own physical health. I have lost 40 pounds . . . my cholesterol has dropped to 129, my blood pressure is down to 120/80 and my resting pulse rate is 20 beats better than before." In the same issue of the newsletter Cavill addressed what he called basic steps in good financial planning. These include keeping enough cash on hand for emergencies and building reserves for college educations and estate planning purposes. Then he asked, "But what about the 'worth living fund'? Do you have one of those? Do you consciously set aside a sum of money to engage in some sort of frivolity?"

RULES OF THE ROAD

The gospel according to Cavill posits three requisites for successful downshifting. Ideally these components are interwoven on a daily basis. None require much of a Number. The first is that an accomplished downshifter must appreciate the importance of fun, joie de vivre, kicking back, laughter. The second is that a good downshifter should know the value of friendship, camaraderie, and support, and hang with those who share his interests—in Cavill's case, interests that include getting on a motorcycle, sleeping in crummy motels, riding sometimes all the way to Alaska. The third is that a proficient downshifter should know how to give something back to others: kindness, a helping hand.

Per my request, Cavill has arranged our day to give me an inside look at each of these components. He wheels the Sebring into the parking lot at Denver's Ronald McDonald House, for which he raises a fair amount of money. Some would-be downshifters don't like raising money for others—as in the retired exec who resented the fact that a charity had only one use for him. There are many reasons guys like that get ticked off. Some just hate to be turned down; some fancy themselves above it all. Cavill, though, loves asking for money because it gives him an excuse to get out and talk to people, which he does exuberantly. He also likes to raise money because it involves organizing motorcycle rides on behalf of the cause, which means he gets to ride his bike and do good at the same time.

Cavill has been active in Ronald McDonald activities since his days back in Washington, where he sat on the board and hobnobbed with Barbara Bush, also a supporter. His involvement stemmed from contact with children who needed a great deal of help. One of his sons was born with Down syndrome. A client's kid had leukemia. When he visited that child he saw kids who were just out of chemo or awaiting delicate heart surgery and thought, "Whoa, I gotta do something here." Cavill wants the world to understand that downshifting isn't just a fancy excuse to goof off. "It isn't just riding your motorcycle, or whatever else pops into your head," he explains. "A good downshifter devotes his time efficiently to things that bring pleasure but also have meaning." The M-word again.

Cavill and I spend some pleasant time with Pam Whitaker, who has been running the Ronald McDonald House here for the past ten years. A sixth-generation Denver native a few years younger than Cavill, Whitaker spends every day of her workweek around ill children, some of whom are certain to die within days. It wouldn't be surprising if she thought about downshifting from time to time, yet "No, I never do," she says. "I couldn't have a better job. Not once have I gotten up in the morning and said 'I don't want to go to work today.' "

Mutual admirers, Cavill and Whitaker chat amiably about the city's ups and downs over the past two decades. One gets the impression it's particularly hard to work out the Number in a place like Denver. How do you do a financial plan when you're on an economic yo-yo? The energy business goes boom, the energy business goes bust. Telecom booms, telecom busts. Because the economy, the job market, and real estate prices are all especially volatile out here, downshifters need to be resourceful. At the moment, Cavill says, he's house-sitting a beautiful place in the hills with a well-stocked bar and every imaginable luxury.

I ask Whitaker whether she thinks her lifelong Colorado friends are Number-ready. "I'd say they're split," she replies. "I have good friends who think about their finances a lot and have made plans for their future. But there are others who are dreading it. These are people with enormous credit card debt, who have mortgaged and remortgaged their homes over and over. I mean, really, these are people in their *fifties* whose mortgages run out to twenty-five years or more."

I decide to leave it at that. In a Ronald McDonald House, these questions don't matter.

THE GANG

Cavill and I climb into the Sebring and head for lunch. He's made a fine choice: the dining room at the Brown Palace (known locally as the Brown), Denver's antique jewel box of a hotel. Teddy Roosevelt stayed at the Brown when he ventured west to hunt bear. It was at the Brown where he once addressed a throng of business leaders who smoked a reported fifteen hundred cigars. In the fifties, Eisenhower used the Brown as his base camp for golf and fishing outings. Lore has it that the president dented a fireplace mantel while practicing his swing in an upstairs suite. (Even in office, Eisenhower displayed many earmarks of a committed downshifter.) Ike liked the Brown, and the Brown liked Ike. Its head chef once created a special dish for him, Tenderloin a la Presidente, which Eisenhower so enjoyed he ordered it three nights in a row. It may also be worth noting that Ike suffered a heart attack in his second term.

Cavill has taken me to the Brown so we can gab with the gang of gray-haired bikers who comprise the second element in his weltanschauung of downshifting: the need for good buddies. His gang is linked in curious ways. For one thing, they refer to each other by *noms de bike*. Cavill is Slinger, so called because his illegally parked bike was once picked up by a mechanical sling and towed off while he was having a drink at the Broken Spoke Saloon in Sturgis, South Dakota, home to the notorious late-summer Motorcycle Rally, which brings 600,000 fanatic bikeheads to the town's dusty little streets. Spoleto it's not.

Then there's Bruiser, real name Brad Pelsue, who owns a company that sells all the things workers need to toil in and around manholes, from safety lights to the yellow tents you see when the local utility digs up the street. Bruiser got his name after he fractured his leg on a bike ride with the boys. As they drove him to the hospital in somebody's Caddy, they rested his cracked leg on the console between the front seats. Pelsue's toes, Cavill says, were pointing "180 degrees away from where they usually do." Pelsue kept insisting, all the way to the emergency room, that the fracture was only a bruise. And he's been Bruiser ever since.

I also meet Ray Bob, aka Ray Pope, who until last year was a hard-charging senior executive at a giant paper and packaging company. A couple of others I don't get to meet today. One is Road Snake, who had to cancel because he's on jury duty. Otherwise known as Steve Peterson, Road Snake got his name after his bike went into a wild skid when it hit a tar snake during a hitherto uneventful trip. Also missing is Mongo, who's unavailable because he and Mrs. Mongo have just departed for Romania, where they plan to spend two years helping out in an orphan relief program.

In addition to their macho handles, Slinger, Bruiser, and Ray Bob have something else in common: each has a junkyard of sheet metal in his body, as Cavill explains once drinks arrive. Cavill's corpus is home to an arterial stent and a chrome knee. Bruiser has sixty-seven screws in that fractured leg. Ray Bob has a piece of metal in his throat that runs down his windpipe, the result of an old football injury. And they also have gray beards in common. Slinger's is, you might say, free-spirited; Bruiser's is low on his jaw and impeccably trimmed; Ray Bob has a close-cropped goatee. Each in his way keeps busy doing nice. Bruiser is active at his church and in the community. Ray Bob is an attentive god-father to the children of a friend who recently passed away, and just about every day, he says, he visits a couple of elderly women in a senior-care home, taking them supplies, reading to them, or just talking.

The guys don't get all earnest or self-congratulatory when they describe how they give back to others. Often it's a chance to party. Cavill tells how eight years ago he and Bruiser were up in the mountains riding their bikes. They rolled into the pretty little town of Frisco—actually, their noses led them to the pretty little town of Frisco. There was a big Rotary Club barbecue challenge in town that day, where cooks compete and visitors exchange dollars for Buck-a-Bones, which they then use to pay for as much BBQ as they can stuff into their bellies and still haul themselves out of town. The food was pretty good, Cavill recalls, but he looked over at Bruiser and said, "Hell, we can win this thing." So in the years thereafter they and other biker buddies cooked up their secret recipe, "working our asses off," he says, raising money and copping a few awards, which made the giving that much tastier. "It drew us all together in a real way," Bruiser tells me.

There are also differences among the Cavill downshift gang. If the guys' hair is an indication, downshifters can form tight friendships while letting a hundred follicles bloom. Slinger's grows kind of shaggy. Bruiser's is full and luxuriantly silver, by far the most elegantly styled. Ray Bob's head is completely shaved, buffed and brown as an acorn.

A more significant difference is how each is coming to terms, or not coming to terms, with his life as a downshifter. Cavill is a full-blown addict. He proselytizes, builds his calendar around it. Bruiser is a recovered downshifter. At fifty-nine, he says he is currently "unretired." He's a good example of what can happen when you plan the Number in an up-and-down economy like Denver's. When the telecom business was booming and companies were laying thousands of miles of fiber optic around the country, Bruiser's company grew like crazy, doubling its sales year over year. He felt he could safely turn the reins over to others, follow Cavill's lead, and do the old downshift for the rest of his life. A few years ago he thought he had it all set up that way: from time to time, as chairman of the company, he'd pop into a trade show, take a big client to dinner, but otherwise leave himself free to take two- or three-week bike trips out west with the boys. Then the telecoms went south and sales plummeted 50 percent one year, another 50 the next. "Now, *there's* a pucker factor," Bruiser says. For two years he went back to work full-bore, without a paycheck, telling employees they needed to reinvent their business model. With Cavill's help he rejigged his portfolio so it could throw off minimal living expenses, while holding on to the savings he and his wife would eventually need for their retirement. And that's where things stand now, even as business gets better. Bruiser is a once and future downshifter.

Ray Bob, however, is still trying to get the hang of things. Not long ago he was *told* to downshift, in no uncertain terms. He was suffering from a variety of health problems including bipolar disorder. Still, Ray Bob was able to function effectively, or so he thought. A respected, productive, and tirelessly driven executive, he was always on a company plane headed for paper plants all over the world. Then one day about a year before this lunch at the Brown, he left his doctor's office feeling, he says, like he'd been whacked by a two-by-four. The doctor told him that he either had to decompress or he'd be pulp in no time. Her message was unequivocal: "You're done." So Ray Bob worked out an amicable split with the company and found himself, by fiat, not choice, a full-time downshifter.

The first few months, he recalls, were a nightmare. He watched daytime TV and slouched listlessly around the house. Then, with a little help—he points to Slinger and Bruiser—he changed direction. "These guys helped me focus on building one-on-one relationships with people. That's when I started spending time with an eighty-six-year-old aunt and some ladies who live in the same home. Now we're good friends. I do what I can to help emotionally, sometimes financially. Lately I've started to paint. And of course I ride my bike as often as I can." Ray Bob says his life is richer now. He recently wrote a letter to the doctor who'd grounded him, telling her that "if you hadn't taken me by the ears and head-butted me, I'd be gone now." Downshifting— friends, fun, and giving something back—had saved Ray Bob's life.

SURPRISE ENDING

After lunch, Cavill suggests we have a single malt across the hall in the Churchill Bar. The bartender there knows Cavill (everyone in Denver seems to know Cavill) and waves at him when he walks in. The waiter brings over the wooden cigar box Cavill keeps in the humidor beside the bar. For the next couple of hours we chat about this and that, me-andering on about the search for meaning, the state of financial planning, the downshift imperative. Then Cavill out of the blue mentions that ambition still flares up from time to time. He thinks about writing a book about how to downshift or maybe building some kind of franchise, the Downshift Institute or some such, which would teach the fine points of downshifting to high-net-worth individuals. He's run some numbers and thinks he might be able to get well-heeled middle-aged couples to spend $10,000 for a five-day retreat at an appropriately plush Colorado resort, where they'd explore the emotional and logistical aspects of downshifting the upcoming curve.

"Do you really want to do this? Upshift and all that?" I ask him.

"Yeah," he says. "Sometimes I think about getting in the game again."

I take this to mean that a road sometimes turns back on itself. Or, now that Cavill has downshifted partway down the long curve, he believes he might be a different driver, older but wiser, better able to take life's straightaways.

14

SUN SPOTS

Remember when Small was Beautiful? Thanks to all the down-shifters out there, it's back. The realization hits one afternoon as I'm lunching with a New York media executive, a man who wears his high-net-worth stripes comfortably and has never lost his salt-of-the-earth values. I've just released him from his Number interrogation ("To tell the truth, I've never done a financial plan; maybe I should") when he thinks of a story he wants to share. It's about his uncle, a blue-collar Joe from Ohio who diligently raised eight children on modest wages. He decided to retire not to a sunless apartment across town or to a patch of hardscrabble in Florida. Instead, he bought a snug one-room schoolhouse on the coast of Ireland. He figured out that contentment could be drawn down from a salty breeze and a glorious setting. His little stone schoolhouse provided joy and romance.

The simple life represents an honorable way out for boomers, who have always had a knack for rationalization. If expectations outstretch your Number, then change your stated values, rewrite the rules. Put simple pleasures first, money second. This way nobody will think you failed. In the words of that noted financial gerontologist Sheryl Crow: "It's not having what you want. It's wanting what you've got."

A couple of years ago Abigail Trafford, a columnist for the *Washington Post*, believed she was onto something and wrote a book called *My Time*. Unlike "downshifting," the term has a touch of verve. It says this is all about *you*, meaning *me*, of course. Reassuringly self-centered, it evokes the boomer's journey. The Me Generation, remember? Me. Now we're talking. Me. Me. Me. After all, isn't *me* what the Number is for?

Trafford's book announced that "something huge is happening," not to be confused with what 007 might whisper as he slips off Pussy Galore's skirt. Trafford believes that millions of people now "have an aura about them" that proclaims: *"I'm free. I've paid my dues. Now it's time for me to be who I am, do what I really want to do."* "My Time," Trafford wrote, is "a complicated process of regenerating yourself and your life to take advantage of [your] extra innings."

Trafford quoted a noted Harvard epidemiologist, Lisa Berkman, who was also looking for an appropriate term. "We need a name that denotes the dynamics of adolescence for fifty- to seventy-five-year-olds," Berkman said. Trafford nominated the obvious: "Second Adolescence." Like the first adolescence, the second is a time to break away, but not from childhood, from middle adulthood. Either way it's a time of mood swings and changing relationships, a time when the body goes through major changes—not puberty this time around, but menopause for her, andropause for him. My Time's a dynamic time, an overwhelming time, a time to figure things out.

Is *this* what the Number is for? To acquire enough money to subsidize a second adolescence, only in Round Two your face is covered with liver spots, not zits? Or, as in the case of George Burns, liver spots *and* zits? Burns, who lived to be one hundred, went around saying that he had pimples till age sixty-five.

David Wolfe noted that the sixties' cultural center of gravity lay not within the boomers but in those a half generation ahead. Forebears from the Silent Generation were the true trailblazers; the unwashed hordes just fell in behind. By the same logic, the Number's center of gravity, where second adolescence is in full flower, may lie in the desert Southwest or along the Florida coastline.

People with big, really big, Numbers downshift in places such as Palm Beach. I spend a day in late autumn house shopping in Palm Beach, just to acquire a sense of how dear a PB downshift might be. Knowing my limits, I pretend I'm a rich but not superrich downshifter and ask a broker to show me some places at the low end of the market. A low-end house in Palm Beach—a standard-issue sixties ranch, pretty creepy, nowhere near the beach—costs $2 million and up. I do a little arithmetic to determine what kind of Number you'd need to swing it. Since property taxes in Palm Beach are based on sales price, not assessed value, that unprepossessing ranch carries an annual tax bill of $40,000. (Taxes on a smallish condo run around $30,000.) Figuring conservatively, that's $800,000 in Number right there. Add in routine landscaping on this modest property ($500 a month), a pool man ($150 a month), a just-once-a-week cleaning person ($20 an hour), and a "house manager" who'll stop in twice a week ($350 a month) when you're back up north, and you've added another $20,000 a year to the annual expense column, or an additional $400,000 of investable Number. So before you've even gotten to big-ticket items such as health care, repairs, utilities, food, entertainment, insurance, clothes, golf, personal training, travel, let alone the cost of a summertime place to live, you're already at a Number in excess of a million dollars. Figure you better have twenty to downshift shabbily in Palm Beach.

So forget Palm Beach. That's not where mainstream Americans dream about downshifting anyway, not by a long shot. What they dream about is Del Webb's Sun City.

Del Webb was to the American way of retirement what Ray Kroc was to the hamburger patty. He was the one who, for better or worse, hammered together a new American Dream designed expressly, as it turned out, for midlife downshifters. In the late 1950s, Webb saw that the times were changing as profoundly for middle-class retirees as they were for kids who were trading in acoustic guitars for lacquered Strats. He didn't know from any second adolescence but he did know there were millions of postwar, reasonably affluent fifty-and-overs with Numbers big enough to own their own small plots of retirement heaven. They had just enough Number to buy their way out of decaying cities in the United States of Stressful: crime, dirt, and noise—and crazy teenagers who blasted music on their transistors and drove around the once quiet neighborhood in Bonnevilles, Impalas, and Fairlanes, none of which had mufflers.

Just over sixty at the time, Webb had already made his Number, a vast one, in commercial construction, concentrating on the Sunbelt. His headquarters were in Phoenix, where he settled after moving from California in 1927. To that point he'd been a hard-drinking (twenty bourbons a day) semipro baseball player who had come down with a near-fatal case of typhoid fever. Seeking recovery, he dragged his six-foot-four-inch body to Arizona, where the arid climate worked magic on his health and eventually dried him out as well. He stopped drinking entirely, became a no-smoking zealot, an all-around control freak. According to a 1962 *Time* cover profile, he insisted that all Webb company cars be painted black; that every office worldwide use the same desk calendar; and that every company door, no matter where, be lettered in precisely the same typeface.

By the thirties and through the decades that followed, the Del E. Webb Company was awash in contracts for huge construction jobs. Webb built bases for the military, Minuteman missile silos, post offices and government buildings such as the Arizona State Capitol. He built airports and giant factories, including aviation plants for his good pal Howard Hughes. He built the Las Vegas Strip—the Sahara, the Mint, the Thunderbird, the Flamingo (which was owned in part by Bugsy Siegel, whose name, Webb would later claim, never rang a bell when they worked out the deal).

Webb also built one of the greatest dynasties in sports history, the New York Yankees. In 1945, with Dan Topping and Larry MacPhail, he bought the club, its farm system, and stadiums in New York, Newark, and Kansas City, for all of $2.8 million—not a bad deal, a mere tenth of what A-Rod earns in a single season. Webb's Yankees were the Yanks of Stengel, DiMaggio, Mantle, Rizzuto, Ford, Berra, Larsen, Maris. He owned the club for nineteen years, through which time the Yankees, incredibly, won fifteen pennants and ten World Series.

This was one gigantic American life. Between the time Del Webb opened his first little Phoenix construction office until his death in 1974, he could pick up the phone and get through to just about anybody: FDR, Goldwater, the shah of Iran, Richard Nixon, LBJ, right down through Bing Crosby, Gene Autry, George Gobel, Earl Torgeson. The man had range, yes. But in the end, what was his true legacy? By the time the hotels and factories and missile silos have turned to dust and half the names in Webb's Rolodex have long been forgotten, history will show that Del Webb did much more than pour massive amounts of concrete wherever he went. He changed the way a couple of American generations thought about what the Number was good for. He changed the Dream.

PARADISE FOUND

In 1960, the Del Webb Company was still erecting the big stuff—hospitals (now in places with names like Maricopa and Loma Linda), stadiums (Madison Square Garden), cultural centers (the Art Museum in Pasadena), and bridges, resorts, office complexes, and urban plazas from San Salvador to Taipei. That year it also decided to become the leading developer of homes for Americans entering the postcareer curve (or second adolescence or downshift years, whatever term you prefer). From his office in the heart of the Sunbelt, Webb had no trouble foreseeing the invasion of U-Hauls, gray heads at the wheel laughing and singing as they drove in from every direction.

Nineteen sixty was the year America came face-to-face with the fact that it wasn't getting any younger. It was the year stories began to appear saying that old age was an emotional and financial condition to be reckoned with in the coming decades. These articles were much like the ones we read now, compare-and-contrast stories full of foreboding. In 1900, 600 out of every 1,000 Americans lived on family farms, with Granny and Gramps camped out in their attics. In 1960, only 87 out of every 1,000 Americans lived on farms. The rest had moved to apartments and houses in the city that were too small or too distant to serve as retirement quarters for the old folks. First a trickle, then a torrent of stories appeared about how creaky Americans would be in the next century—meaning now.

Del Webb read the numbers on the Number clock as well as anyone. He gave a thumbs-up to associates who'd been urging him to think housing, not just hospitals and hotels. Webb began to buy up tens of thousands of acres in the desert northwest of Phoenix, barren ranch lands and old towns lying wilted and affordable in the sun. His blueprint wasn't for houses and carports to shelter the giant wave of families with young children—June and Ward Cleaver and the boys. That's what every other builder was doing. The Webb Company turned its back on 80 percent of the housing market, "a big gamble," as one of its executives said in an understatement as dry as the desert itself. Instead, Webb built a town called Sun City, a place where retirees could swim, golf, play bridge, and shuffleboard all day every day, for as long as their hearts could pump the requisite life force.

Sun City's houses were made of concrete blocks gussied up in yellow, pink, and light blue paint. Averaging around 1,200 square feet, not much bigger than the steam shower in a modern master bath, they cost between $8,700 and $11,600, a bit more if they overlooked the golf course. According to Time, monthly mortgage payments ranged from $73 to $114, with more than half the buyers—people who had struggled to raise families through the Depression—paying cash. Sun City homebuyers were, according to Time, "men of solid substance—former engineers, successful salesmen, foremen, dentists, small businessmen, schoolteachers." The middle class had seen what the good life could look like in its sunset years, and it liked what it saw in Sun City, so much, in fact, that nearly three hundred of the little pastel houses were sold the first weekend.

Those houses, the community center, the golf course, all of it, *that* was what the Number was for. But there were rules to follow if you wanted to kick back in Sun City, quite a few rules. They were an integral part of the Dream, and they were nonnegotiable. You had to be at least fifty years old to be a full-time resident. In other words, you had to be going through what we would later come to call a second adolescence. And then there was the No Kids Allowed rule. School-age children could visit but they couldn't stay, a shocking prohibition in a land where family values were paramount.

As a business decision, the banning of kids was on its face incredibly bold. In 1960, 36 percent of the American population was under the age of eighteen, the historical high-water mark. Baby boom kids were everywhere, under the covers, under their desks during air raid drills, underfoot. The Webb Company, though, had done its homework. It had talked to seniors all over the country and had concluded that older people had changed. Retirees were neither docile nor selfless; they were bored, restless, not ready for prime-time pasture. Having raised their own kids, the people who came to Sun City said they had no desire to be around other people's and they said so without shame or apology. "We love children," a woman told *Time*. "But as you get older, [the fact] that you can have your own yard and flowers without having children traipsing through is appealing."

When it was entirely built out, the original Sun City consisted of 27,000 little concrete-block houses and was a runaway success, so much so that Webb began to put Sun Cities all over the map, or at least on the warm parts of it. Within a couple of years there were two new Sun Cities in California, another in Florida, and more communities rotating in the cement mixer.

Tsk-tsking over the kids issue continued. Some condemned Sun City as a ghetto for the old. Maggie Kuhn, who founded the Gray Panthers in the early seventies, was aghast. Her followers were to ageism what the women's movement was to sexism, seeking to free seniors from social stigma, cultural stereotyping, and segregated housing. Kuhn famously called the new retirement communities, with their clubhouses and quilting rooms and dance floors and putting greens and tennis courts, and especially their no kids allowed policies, "playpens for wrinkled babies." In the heat of the moment, Kuhn may have missed the point. Today, those who lobby for improving the lot of seniors practically deify Del Webb. For downshifters, Sun City isn't segregation, it's liberation. As Marc Freedman writes in *Prime Time,* an admirable book about "how baby boomers will revolutionize retirement and transform America," Del Webb took hammer and nails to death's anteroom and put on a huge addition. Del Webb had given us, after all, what we came to know as the Golden Years.

SAME, ONLY DIFFERENT

The Del Webb Company is today a profitable division of a larger home-building corporation. It doesn't do retirement communities anymore, it does "active adult communities." Like AARP, the Del Webb folks don't much like the R-word. They say people aren't into retirement these days, they're into *activity.* They run, they jump, they do the backstroke. They volunteer, they work. They check their Numbers online. They keep themselves busy from morning to night. Coming soon: Ritalin Silver.

Is this "active adult" message just marketing claptrap, or has some thing fundamentally changed since the little cement-block houses went up in the desert? One day I put in a call to Dave Schreiner for a center-of-gravity, second adolescence, New Rest of Your Life, midcourse reality check. Schreiner works in new business development at Del Webb, wrestling daily with what Alan Greenspan has called, as only he can so solemnly intone, "the need to look at the aging of our population as a permanent condition." It's Schreiner's job to monitor that condition, to keep a finger on the senior pulse—yes, it's still there—and to stay tuned to the evolving American Dream. In short, it's Schreiner's job to know what people think their Numbers are for. If the company's motto is any indication, the Number is what gives middle-aged people a ticket to "Explore the Possibilities." It's a message the company lives by. It's exploring (bulldozing is more like it) possibilities by the thousands of acres, planning active adult communities in what's left of the once empty desert in Arizona, California, and Nevada. Also in Colorado, Pennsylvania, Virginia, Massachusetts, New Jersey, Illinois, and no doubt other places to be announced.

It isn't long into the conversation before Schreiner, who's sharp and direct, is giving me a hard time over the notion that a baby boomer's second adolescence is altogether different from the prior generation's. I've floated the notion that boomers are generally allergic to regimentation and restricted covenants, and won't live on streets where your graybeard pals can't glide around the neighborhood astride their motorcycles. Schreiner doesn't entirely agree. He says that midlife boomers are different in some ways, but many resemble those who first beat a path to his company's desert door. Retirees who came out to Sun City in 1960 had dedicated their lives to others: to their kids, to their country during successive wars, likely as not to a single employer. They were frugal, patriotic, community-minded, he says, and when they retired, with a pension and the proceeds from selling their former homes in the city, they realized it was time to do something for themselves—fish, golf, quilt, bake in the sun. This was what the Number was for.

Schreiner observes that sixty-year-olds today are less dedicated to serving others. Having plowed through multiple marriages and serial employers, they're more self-involved and self-indulgent. But he insists these differences don't amount to a paradigm shift, that they're evolutionary, not revolutionary. He suggests that the Webb Company has had to tweak the Dream of forty years ago but not redream it. In the newer Sun Cities, he says, a lot of little stuff has changed, but not the fundamentals.

Because baby boomers have flealike attention spans, Webb now plans some of its physical spaces differently. Specialized interests— sewing, knitting, bridge—were once accommodated by dedicated rooms near the clubhouse. Today, physical space needs to be more versatile, designed to go with the flow of trend-right crafts and sports. Yesterday everybody was into tennis, today they're into pickle ball, which means Webb designs tennis courts to be used either way. He says that there are now "nine million different varieties of needle arts," which can't all be served by a room built for rows of sewing machines. In addition, Schreiner says, every house must now have a home office, and each is wired for cable and high-speed Internet. And not just to keep tabs on the Number; a lot of Sun City downshifters work from home. Webb thus needs to arrange "lifestyle programming" 24/7, so that different work schedules can be accommodated. And, he says, the company now thinks about siting communities not only where it's warm, but within striking distance of employment opportunities—for example, the fairly new Webb community outside Chicago.

The huge new fitness centers, the Pilates rooms, the spas, these have come about since the original Sun City. But overall, Schreiner says, the activities and facilities aren't all that different. "What about shuffleboard?" I ask. "Do you still put in shuffleboard courts?"

Schreiner has a prickly, droll side, and seems exasperated by this question. "We don't build many shuffleboard courts anymore," he says. "Haven't for a while. But do you know what we put in instead?"

Not a clue.

"Bocce courts. And do you know what bocce ball is? It's a slow, low-stress, highly social game."

A long beat here.

"In other words, it's shuffleboard."

I throw Maggie Kuhn back at him. What about the rules, the regulations, the restrictive covenants? Can't imagine baby boomers going for all that. Schreiner makes no bones about the fact that there are people who not only like regimentation, they crave it—e.g., his father, who worked for three decades at one of the Big Three automakers and is big on order, everything in its place. And there are those who hate all the uptight regulation—e.g., his father-in-law, a small business owner. He says people who downshift in Sun City are obviously the former, people who typically spent careers in a bureaucracy, whether a large corporation, the military, the post office, a big university. They want to use their Numbers to buy neat and clean. Hunter Thompson, Allen Ginsberg, Baba Ram Dass, Eldridge Cleaver, William Sloane Coffin, I venture they would not be good candidates for a Sun City, but I did know an awful lot of people in college who may well have gotten into its brand of adult swim by now.

Before signing off, Schreiner offers an insight into why some people want to use their Numbers to resettle in the new editions of Sun City. There's a "push-pull dynamic" at work. They're *pushed* to Sun City by a growing concern about congestion, environmental quality, and safety in the places they're coming from. A dark suburban parking lot makes them nervous. And they're *pulled* to Sun City by the prospect of new friends, lots to do, little maintenance, a life of neat and clean.

So which is it? Do we chase the Number because it enables us to push back on yesterday, or do we chase it because it pulls us to a different tomorrow? I'm off to Sun City to find out. Those who know about my imminent trip react in different ways. Some friends have a good laugh—they'd never in a million years dream of using their Numbers to buy a faux casita in a giant planned community where the songs they used to smoke dope to in the sixties now whisper through the restrooms at the community pod. Others are sincerely curious to know what life there is like.

My destination is Sun City Grand, the newest and, yes, the grandest Sun City in the chain of three that presses yet farther west out of Phoenix. If you chose to make a documentary about the evolution of the late-twentieth-century retirement lifestyle, this string of Sun Cities would be a terrific location. Title it *Amenitize Me!* The three communities meld into one another the way the passage of time and changing styles do. With each new installment the houses grow bigger, the amenities posher and more varied. The smallest house in the new community is about the size of the largest in the previous one. These Sun Cities are a living museum: you start with an authentic display of the Depression Generation's take on the Good Life, move on to the Postwar affluence collection, and finish by admiring the countertops and pocket doors in the Aging Yuppie wing.

I tell myself that my trip to Sun City is a game of pretend, a foretaste of what's to come, at least for some people. If relocation to a spanking-new, high-quality active adult community is what the Number is for, then this is how it might feel to you when you actually do it. Imagine yourself a young and active sixty-two. You're coming out here from Cleveland, with a good career behind you. You've made your Number— let's say you have $3 million socked away, including the proceeds from your former home, plus Social Security and a small pension. You're moving to Sun City Grand because of that push-pull dynamic. Cold, old Cleveland is pushing; golf, bridge, and volunteering are pulling. You fly in on a night when there's no moon over the desert, then set out along ramshackle Route 60 toward the towns of Peoria, Youngtown, and Surprise. You drive in total silence past mile after mile of dance joints and nudie bars, Taco Bells and KFCs, auto body and paint shops, used car lots, late-night bodegas locked down behind iron window grates, tattered strip malls, abandoned except for a fluorescent-lighted nail salon or barbershop, all closed for the night. So far nothing is neat and clean, happy and new. The outskirts of Phoenix have nothing over the sadder parts of Cleveland. So far this is indisputably *not* what the Number is for.

After twenty miles of wondering why the hell you did this, you come to a train of slatted livestock cars sitting gray and ghostly on a siding. In the dim light you can make out that these ancient cars are remnants of the old Santa Fe and Union Pacific lines. By now you're totally freaked out, an adolescent again feeling at once like a lost, frightened kid and an impatient grown-up, longing to get settled for the night with a good stiff Black Russian. You still see no stars in the sky, no people on the streets, only an occasional pickup that passes with a low growl, its driver a silhouette behind the steering wheel, faintly glowing cigarette in hand.

After what seems an eternity, sparkles of life appear way far out in the desert but getting closer, an oasis in the middle of nowhere bathed in pure white light. In minutes, you've driven right into this blaze of illumination. It's as if someone has thrown a giant electrical switch. There are lights everywhere, bursts of colored signs. There's a gargantuan Lowe's, glowing blue and white, and just down the road its equally immense orange-clad archrival, Home Depot. Then there's an Applebee's, a Bed Bath and Beyond, the Chicago Title Company, a three-story U-Haul facility with rows of self-storage lockers and a fleet of rental trucks outside. Opposite is a Starbucks, the first you've seen, so this must be a dream—it's either the American Dream you're looking for or you've made a wrong turn and driven smack into death's anteroom. But it's too late to go back. You turn off the highway into the silent, entirely deserted streets of Sun City Grand and search for your casita, which in this part of the development looks like every other. Finally you spot the right one and enter. Four things catch your attention right away, each of which partly explains why you decided on this version of the Dream according to Del Webb:

1. *Fun.* Management has been thoughtful enough to provide a little green E-Z-Go golf cart, which sits there in the otherwise completely empty garage, looking even lonelier than you.

2. *Security.* When you go to turn on the light you notice a panic button on the wall. In the event of an emergency, you flip the switch and you'll automatically signal your location to the Sun City security patrol.

3. *Orderliness.* There's a copy of the Sun City Grand magazine on the breakfast counter. You open it to a feature devoted to reminding residents, gently, of the rules. This issue covers the keep-your-garage-door-closed-at-all-times rule. An open garage door, the article warns, is an

invitation to troublemakers and, no less important, unsightly in the extreme.

4. *Neatness and cleanliness.* The spotless refrigerator is empty, aside from a small box of Arm & Hammer Baking Soda left thoughtfully in the door to guard against any intrusive odor.

These are what the Number is for, right?

In the morning, the anxiety of the drive has vanished. Let the good times, *your* time, roll. You take a walk. The air is warm. It's only 7:15, but the adult community is not only active, it's practically frenetic. The card and billiard rooms are jumping. You stop in at the posh sales center, where, in big black numerals not unlike the sort that show gas prices at filling stations, you see that there are only 349 home sites left to be sold. (When the last few houses are finished, Del Webb will turn over management of the community to its residents and move on to sandier pastures—in this case yet another community west of Sun City Grand, this one called Sun City Festival.) A giant banner proclaiming "Best Selling Active Adult Community in Arizona!" is draped across the front door of this Taj-ish sales center. The doormat reads "Live On." Inside are photos of available home styles, and it's just a short walk to a block of actual-size models that will one day be lived in. Unlike the first Sun City and to a lesser degree Sun City West, the 9,000 housing units here run the gamut: big ones, little ones, with every kind of finish inside. Dentil moldings, wainscoting, decorative columns, aren't these what the Number is for? In the sales center music plays through the speakers in the ceiling. Jim Morrison singing "Hello, I Love You." You wonder what year you're living in and how old you are.

You stop for a cup of coffee at Joe Zuni's, a Starbucks knockoff located in the center of the community's activity pod. A cup of coffee and a scone costs $4.98. Two blond-streaked women are whispering confidences at a corner table. One wears a peasant blouse and high-heeled sandals, the other warmup pants and an Athletica workout shirt. Although you do run into a few Gabor sister wannabes here, with cosmetics-counter grooming and lots of face work, most of Sun City

Grand's women are wholesome and tidy rather than glam. On the other side of the café one man is explaining to another (both wearing khaki Bermudas) the fine points of tricks, trump suits, and redoubling a bid. A resident walks by, belly stretching his Del Webb Softball League T-shirt. Friendship, isn't that what the Number is for?

Wandering down the hall, you check out the course offerings at the tiny office of Arizona State University's Lifelong Learning Center. Here you discover that over three hundred residents out of the fifteen thousand at Sun City Grand have enrolled in courses, many of them conducted by residents who were teachers in their former lives. The nice woman behind the desk is quick to tell you how inexpensive and interesting the courses are. And the best part, she says brightly, is "there's no homework or tests!" Enlightenment, isn't that what the Number is for?

You wander into the immense fitness center, which is packed with midlifers on treadmills, StairMasters, stationary bikes, elliptical trainers, weight machines, working out by themselves or huddled around personal trainers. Healthy living, isn't that what the Number is for?

You stop and watch some bocce matches. A gaggle of men and women slowly roll colored balls across an artificial surface not much longer than a shuffleboard court. Nearby, in the immense swimming pool, a raucous volleyball game is in progress. Throaty hoots and hollers accompany every winning point. On the PA the Beatles sing "Love Me Do." You try to get a closer look but an elderly woman behind the desk says you need a temporary pass. There was supposed to be one in your guest packet. She commiserates, "Well, shame on them if they forgot to include it." Empathy. Courtesy. Decency. Isn't that what the Number is for?

Later on, you hop into your E-Z-Go and explore the farther reaches of Sun City Grand. Aside from the occasional Cadillac or Chrysler cruising back from the supermarket or a morning's volunteer shift over at the Del E. Webb Memorial Hospital, the streets are deserted at high noon. Most of the curtains and blinds are drawn on the windows of the houses and—maybe you're getting paranoid in your old age—you have

the weird feeling people might be staring out at you from behind them.
It's Singapore meets the Southwest, not so much as a chewing gum
wrapper or cigarette butt on the street. Or maybe it's what nuclear winter might feel like if a nuclear winter was warm and dry and you could
wear shorts to it. Out of nowhere, another golf cart glides by, a resident
with his visiting four-year-old granddaughter riding shotgun. It's easy to
forget that humans this tiny still exist. Then they're gone. You look up
and down the empty block. Even though Election Day is right around
the corner, you see but a single political sign—for Kerry/Edwards, surprisingly—its presence doubtless a violation of a rule. Otherwise,
there's not a hint of individuality in the neighborhood, unless you count
the cool customized golf carts parked here and there, with fancy print
upholstery and burled-wood dashboards.

On the ride back to the casita, you find yourself thinking that neat
and clean is nice, especially at your age, but you find yourself making a
mental list of things you might miss now that you've decided to downshift to a place such as this:

The changing seasons. Walking down the street, reading stuff on
walls and in windows. Good live music. Ethnic humor. Ethnic anything, for that matter. Sitting at a funky bar, watching people smoke.
Getting real garden dirt on your hands. The ocean. Studying humanity
in all its diversity on a city bus.

Stop bitching, you tell yourself. What if Maggie Kuhn saw you like
this? Nobody likes a complainer, especially an old one. Besides, you
can't have everything. Who says the Number entitles you to *everything*?
Your casita in Sun City Grand certainly beats an apartment in Cleve
land, where the faucet drips and the old woman down the hall fell and
broke her hip and wasn't discovered for a day and a half. And it beats
being dependent on your kids, living in one of their spare rooms with
hockey skates in your closet, knowing that your presence is only grudg-
ingly tolerated by your self-centered son-in-law. You're safe here.
There's fun here. It's clean here. You're among solid people, many of
whom devote countless hours reading to Latino kids in the county

schools, people who pick you up in a golf cart from a distant corner of the hospital parking lot, urging you to get in because it's a long walk and it's a scorcher, and so you agree rather than hurt their feelings.

Okay? Maybe this *is* what the Number is for.

There's a curious postscript to all this. It raises the question of whose dream was it, anyway, these retirement communities for adults only, this idea of the golden years, the longing for a perfect place in the sun? The original Sun City, it turns out, grew up around, then entirely engulfed, a retirement community down the road called Youngtown. Youngtown, in fact, was the first place restricted to seniors and, fittingly, hosted the very first chapter of AARP. Compared to Sun City, Youngtown was a speck, just a scattering of little houses and a general store, some recreational facilities that are still in use but that are to the activity pods at Sun City Grand what I am to Lance Armstrong. Modest in scale and with but a trace of Del Webb's capital and marketing power, Youngtown never had a chance to be Sun City. Perhaps the person who put it there just didn't understand the territory as well as Webb did. Youngtown, you see, wasn't an idea that sprouted in the Sunbelt. It wasn't a vision the New America foisted on the old. The idea for Youngtown belonged to Ben Schleifer, Russian-born by way of Brooklyn, who bought 320 acres of ranch land in 1954. Schleifer's concept was a daring stab in the desert dark, so startling that Alistair Cooke featured Youngtown on one of his *Omnibus* programs, and there was a segment about it on *Today* with Dave Garroway. Indeed, the Webb people say that it was all this media attention that alerted them to the full potential of a Sun City in the first place. Compared to Del Webb, Ben Schleifer is a forgotten man. Hours of phoning around yield scant insight into exactly what on earth he was thinking when he conceived Youngtown. Even libraries and associations devoted to Arizona's Jewish heritage— which isn't, let's face it, all that deep—know virtually nothing about Ben Schleifer; some have never heard of him. The best I can do is track down a man who says he once went over to Schleifer's place to fix the

TV. This was years after Sun City was built. By then Schleifer had lost all connection to Youngtown. Divorced and living in an apartment above a garage, he was complaining about "shysters in Mesa" who ripped him off in some deal or other and, for all we know, robbed him of Youngtown, fame, fortune, and credit for the lasting dream about what the Number is really for.

15

A NEEDLEMAN IN THE HAYSTACK

Is the Number about downshifting, or is the Number about something more profound? Are places like Sun City the true destination or just a step in the right direction? Is the Number about *where* we want to be, or *who* we want to be?

Today the financial planning community is wrestling hard with whether it should stick to what it knows how to do—manage money and tax strategy—or whether it should, *must*, poke and prod our psyches to help us figure out the answer to that last question. Financial planners are not trained to do this kind of poking and prodding. They're numbers people, not therapists, who keep ticklers to remind themselves to change the batteries in their smoke alarms, even before the first chirp. They generally go by the book; there are no intuition keys on their calculators. They're comfortable around spreadsheets, longevity projections, and pie charts. They know how to talk us down from a mountain of debt and guide us through the narrow straits of reverse mortgages and independent annuities. But what if all that financial blather amounts to a row of beans? If life is about the human spirit, and money just plays a part, what do they know about that?

"Money isn't everything," we tell ourselves. Some people roll their eyes when they say it; others say the words as if they just thought of them. What if the life we want, really want, requires less, not more, money? Ever think of that? Why not, then, figure out what we want, what's truly meaningful to us, and *then* do a financial plan to light the way? Trouble is, traditional financial planners don't ask about the spirit. A client's quest for self-knowledge is beyond their scope. But a growing cadre within the planning profession is not at all reticent about asking questions about the soul. These people call themselves Life Planners. That I came to know about them, even expose my own psyche to their prodding, testifies to the fact that sometimes life plans you, and not the other way around. Here's how it happened:

A few months after I started research on this book, I wrote an article about the Number for a national business magazine. The article generated a batch of letters and e-mails. One was a handwritten note from a man named John Nelson who, it turns out, lives in a little Wisconsin town just a cow-chip toss from my house on the prairie. After commenting kindly on the article, Nelson mentioned that he, too, was working on a book, not exactly like *The Number* but along a parallel track. Would I care to get together for a cup of coffee?

We meet at a nearby Mexican restaurant. Nelson turns out to be bearded, smart, a genuinely nice guy in his early forties. The book he's working on, he says, was inspired by Richard Bolles' *What Color Is Your Parachute?*—which everybody but me has read—the perpetually best-selling guide to how to look for the right job and fix a dead-end career. Nelson's book, which he has discussed with Bolles, will do for retirement planning what *Parachute* did for career planning. This project strikes me as solid, a potential blockbuster. And Nelson is well prepared for the task. After earning his MBA, he spent years as a consultant, advising companies and their employees on matters relating to pension planning. He kept running into two problems, he says, over which he had little control. Most people who came to his planning sessions were not saving enough for retirement. He advised them to try to save more, but few listened. Worse, those who did save usually made less than astute investment choices—the old story. For years, Nelson pushed that rock uphill, getting nowhere fast. Realizing that the usual bromides— save, don't spend—didn't work, he came up with an intriguing new color for his own parachute. He decided to go back to school and pursue a Ph.D. in a field that doesn't yet exist: Retirement Education. Cherry-picking the fields of psychology, sociology, career development, business, and education, he eventually crafted a concept he calls Integrative Retirement. What he means, I gather, is that broad areas of overlapping academic research can be drawn together to create a coherent approach to studying why some people are satisfied in retirement while others aren't. If we understood why that was, we could teach others how to think more successfully about planning their later years.

Nelson draws three overlapping circles on a yellow legal pad. The first circle he labels Money. "In the past we've mostly focused on helping people save enough money to retire, and that's closely related to where they want to live. So I call this phase of retirement Geo-Financial," he says, adding that this and the other circles have a wealth of research embedded in them.

In the second circle he writes the word Health. "People are obviously concerned with healthy aging," he explains, "and with access to medical care. These concerns are addressed by studies that fall into the Bio-Medical category."

He labels the third circle Happiness. "If you think you don't have enough money or health you'll probably have a hard time being happy," he says. Money itself isn't enough to make you happy. So what is? This question falls into what Nelson sees as the Psycho-Social area of current academic research. It's this circle that seems to have the firmest grip on Nelson's attention right now. Two or three decades of low-impact R&R—golf, bridge, bus trips to Branson, Missouri—aren't the answer. People are better off, much happier, when they're intellectually, spiritually, and emotionally engaged. Engagement. Now there's a good use for the Number. Engagement promises nourishment for the soul. It's also affordable. Engagement doesn't require a credit card; no need to pay someone to scrape barnacles off an expensive boat every spring. Money. Health. Happiness. Stitch them together, according to Nelson, and you've arrived at what the Number is for.

Nelson then mentions a life-planning workshop he attended a year or two before that had a profound impact on how he thought about his new career. At one point in the workshop, Nelson explains, the session's leader asked participants to think about an early memory having to do with money, one they considered to have had a meaningful impact on them. Nelson says that the question caused him to remember an incident he'd completely forgotten about. The incident occurred when he was around five. One day he and his mother were in his parents' bedroom. She was doing chores, he was doing what kids do: rooting around in his dad's dresser drawer, playing with spare change, old watches, and assorted curios. He picked up two items that caught his attention. One was a small glass jar filled with liquid and some sort of little gooey thing, the other was a small book filled with numbers. Although Nelson was barely able to read at the time, he recognized his name on the front of the book, and he noticed that the numbers got bigger and bigger, then smaller and smaller again.

Asking his mother to explain what the two items were, he held up the glass jar. The little floating thing, she told him, was his father's gall-bladder. She explained what a gallbladder was, and that it had recently been removed by a doctor. The surgery was just one of the many health issues his father had had around that time, Nelson says. He was barely aware of what these problems were and certainly didn't understand their seriousness.

The little book, she continued, was called a bankbook. Just after he was born, she and his dad had opened a savings account in his name. From time to time they'd put money into it to pay for important things he would someday need, such as going to college. But when his dad got sick they had to close the account and use the money to pay medical bills.

John Nelson says that when all this came racing back to him in the life-planning workshop he was struck by its connection to how he came to think about money when he grew up. He says he remembers feeling very proud and happy that day in the bedroom—his little bankbook helped make his father better. Years later, Nelson says, when consulting with people on their pension plans, he felt especially satisfied whenever he reduced or erased the fees of clients who'd fallen on hard times. He believes there's a definite connection back to the gallbladder and the passbook.

If I really want to understand what good life planning is about, Nelson suggests, I ought to pick up a copy of a book called *Money and the Meaning of Life*. It was the intellectual spark that indirectly led him to find a glob of truth floating in the glass jar.

THE NEW TESTAMENT

The man who wrote *Money and the Meaning of Life*, Jacob Needleman, teaches philosophy at San Francisco University. Published in 1991, the work is a circuitous journey through the lessons of King Solomon, the moral and economic teachings of the early Christian church, Protestantism and the rise of capitalism, peppered with references to Dante, Gurdjieff, John Kenneth Galbraith, and even Donald Trump, who makes a cameo appearance. Needleman plows through all of this to illustrate what lies beneath our love/hate relationship with money and our relentless, myopic quest to make and spend as much of it as we can, heedless of its deeper meaning.

Needleman also seems to have written *Money and the Meaning of Life* as a way to disentangle some money issues of his own. As he writes at the beginning of the book:

In the household where I grew up, the most intense and violent emotions centered around money—the lack of it, the need for it, the desperate difficulty of having enough of it, and the fear of what would become of us without it. Money was power, reality, happiness. Money was a reality stronger than anything else, and the gods of money had no compassion; they were hard, unyielding, hostile. They broke my father's spirit again and again and, through his violent despair and anxiety, they continuously broke my own spirit.

Just before that passage, Needleman confesses to an incident that occurred when he was around eight. It goes like this: he's visiting a rich boy in the neighborhood, a kid whose playroom is filled with shelves of neatly arranged, shiny new toys. Among them is a model train set worthy of F.A.O. Schwarz—silver tracks, all kinds of switching and loading stations, bridges, tunnels, quaint houses, a locomotive pulling a long line of gleaming cars. Young Jacob is beside himself with excitement, but when he looks over at the rich boy, he notices that the kid appears to be sad and disengaged. When he returns home, Needleman remembers, he gets out his own train set and realizes it's cheap, rusty, and busted. At this moment two opposing thoughts collide. One is how much he envies that kid down the block; the other is how empty they both feel. One kid had nailed his toy Number. Needleman hadn't. Neither was a happy camper.

THE NUMBER'S NEW AGE

Needleman's book was an inspiration to a small group of financial planners who regarded money as a more powerful force in people's lives than their traditional colleagues could imagine. Money, they believed, operates both above and below the surface of our existence. Above the surface it's green stuff we exchange for every imaginable thing. It's just a tool, albeit the most versatile tool mankind has ever known. But money also works below the surface, which is why these life planners believe it's important to probe deep down to help people answer some difficult questions:

Why does money make us knotty?

Why do we impart evil to it?

Why do we invest it with magical feel-good properties?

Why do we run from it?

Why do we lose love and friendships over it?

Why do we work so hard to get it?

Why do we waste it once we do get it?

Why don't we spend more of it on things that matter?

Oh, and by the way, *what does matter?*

Needleman cogitates on all of these. We need to take a more qualitative view of money, he and like-minded life planners say. Money and
the spirit are connected. Money and meaning must be brought into
alignment. Or, as one life planner puts it—not surprisingly, she lives in
Santa Fe—"to be a useful life planner you need the heart of a social
worker and the head of a capitalist."

The acknowledgments page in Needleman's book says pretty much
the same thing. Thank-yous are offered to a number of prominent New
Age writers and thinkers from the Bay Area, people who speak fervently
about the value of spirituality over materialism and how society's priorities are out of whack. And yet the very first thank-you goes to Laurance
Rockefeller, capitalist extraordinaire, whose philanthropy granted
Needleman time and money to write *Money and the Meaning of Life.*
Another gracious nod goes to Charles Schwab, who, although a citizen
of the Bay Area, was never the kind of guy you would have run into hot-
tubbing at Esalen.

One day I have a pleasant conversation with Needleman, who's at
home in San Francisco. His voice is deep and rich, his manner courteous and direct. He is a man who can be forceful, ironic, reflective, and
sharp-tongued all in the same spoken paragraph. We should all have
such teachers in college. When I tell him that many people clam up
when I ask them how much money they need, he promptly suggests
that I'm probably asking the wrong question. When I ask him how
much money he thinks *he* needs, he tells me without a second's hesita-
tion it's none of my damn business.

In interviews given in the years following the publication of his
book, Needleman offered observations that all Number-anxious baby

boomers would be advised to download onto their PDAs and consult from time to time. He says, "Money has the power of giving people the idea that they are powerful, happy and important. That's where the danger lies, because it is a false sense of comfort. If you worry about little things when you are poor, you will continue worrying about bigger things when you are rich." We're now living in an age—we're growing old in an age—in which "everything is monetized." He recalls a time "when issues involving personal relationships, doctors and medicine, academic relationships, artistic life were considered out of the realm of monetary measures. An artist could be appreciated for who he was without being financially successful. A doctor was willing to perform a medical treatment without necessarily being paid right away or even at all if the patient could not afford to pay. Now, however, if people talk about disease often the health-care cost is an important part of the . . . discussion. [That everything is] priced . . . has to do with the breakdown of values in our culture."

When I tell Needleman how much I think he has influenced a new movement in financial planning, one that could be hugely influential to baby boomers, he modestly deflects the credit. That was never his intention, but it's exactly what happened.

THE DISCIPLES

Money and the Meaning of Life helped the early life planners bond with one another and it eventually inspired a handful of them to establish a free-form think tank they called the Nazrudin Project. Nazrudin was a Sufi holy trickster who, in the words of the movement's leading disciple, "upended people's blinkered, conventional ways of thinking and forced them to look at themselves anew." The "people" in the foregoing sentence, well, that would be you and me, blinkered by Debt Warp, dead-end jobs, Lifestyle Relapse, illness and bankruptcy, the Eisenberg Uncertainty Principles.

The Nazrudin Project, the snowball that grew into the life-planning movement, began in 1993 as little more than weekend bull sessions in pastoral settings in New Hampshire or Colorado. Just thirty or so life planners showed up in those early years; today, maybe a hundred get together on a regular basis. There's no formal membership process, so people come and go. With no established agenda, they canvass one another about what's on their minds, then go at it for a couple of days. These are lively and garrulous people. Nazrudin remains a movable colloquy on the relationship of money to the heart and soul. Now well known throughout the independent planning world, the group has also influenced large chunks of the mainstream financial industry. Those brokerage ads with soft-focused images of family life and sappy music that may as well be selling Xanax as financial products? They're all part of a cultural shift in no small part due to ideas batted about the Nazrudin campfires.

Life planning. It's a tricky and, to some, regrettable term. For the Nazrudins, life planning is a disciplined attempt to get people to wrestle with hidden demons. To others, life planning is hokum, practiced by yentas in Great Neck who hang out Life Coach shingles and proclaim themselves ready to straighten us out.

The disciple who gave Nazrudin its name and mission, George Kinder (rhymes with "tinder"), is a somewhat gaunt, bookish fellow with wispy hair and wire-rimmed glasses. Well read and well educated, he doesn't toss around folksy platitudes the way life coaches in Great Neck do. Kinder is a financial planner beyond category. He's built a theory of how you and I can gain "money maturity" based on the philosophy and literature he studied as a student at Harvard. Much as Needleman did in his book, Kinder shuffles the principles of Eastern religion and Western mythology, topped off by what ancient Hawaiians referred to as "the passing of a blessing." We'll get to all this. At first it may sound flaky. By the end it may also sound flaky. For the time being, keep an open mind.

Now in his late fifties, Kinder grew up in St. Clairsville, a small Ohio town near the West Virginia border. He says that his family was neither poor nor especially rich, but better off than most in a rural area that felt more like a southern town than a midwestern one. His father was a lawyer, his mother a housewife, although she eventually became president of the Ohio Historical Society after Kinder and his two brothers had gone off to find deeper meaning in the world.

Kinder ardently believes that our attitudes and hang-ups about money are established early in life. His own upbringing was Puritan ethic, dawn to dusk. Hard work and self-reliance conquered all, his parents preached. Frivolity, self-indulgence, and mindless amusement were verboten. George wasn't allowed to listen to rock and roll, read comic books, waste his dimes on soda pop. In 1966, Kinder went off to Cambridge, where he initially majored in economics but quickly felt more kinship with Blake and Shakespeare than with Keynes and Max Weber. So he turned his back on the dismal science and eventually enrolled in a doctoral program in English. But he soon chucked that, too, and moved to a Massachusetts farmhouse "to live a life of spiritual practice and writing." This life plan struck his parents as an enlightened pathway to material nowhere. When his mother suggested that he try accounting, which would at least provide him with some income, Kinder assented. He passed the CPA exam and for the next thirteen years made a living as a tax accountant, building a broad base of clients, some of whom he attracted with flyers that he attached to windshield wipers on frosty mornings. Now and then he found himself counseling a client on an emotional issue. Around town, people began to refer to him as "the tax therapist."

Kinder's ultimate calling took shape in the early 1980s, when he says he began to lose patience with the "bonehead advice" given to many of his tax clients by their financial advisers. He remembers the case of one young, hapless fellow who was making $50,000 a year and should have been socking his money away in long-term growth stocks. Instead, the man's adviser had sold him a tax shelter—which he needed like a hole in the head—with up-front fees of 30 percent. Out of righteous indignation (and no doubt a dash of enlightened self-interest),

Kinder began to broaden his own services to include conscientious investment counseling, retirement and estate planning, insurance, the whole enchilada of a traditional planning practice. He offered these services on a strict fee-only basis. No longer would he paper windshields. He decided to go narrower and deeper, limiting his client base to fewer than a hundred individuals and families with a combined net worth of $100 million.

By now Kinder had caught a glimmer that his destiny lay in something more than helping people avoid the alternative minimum tax. He was by nature intellectually curious. He was something else, too—a dynamic, captivating presenter of ideas. George Kinder knows how to work a meeting room. He has the invaluable and enviable knack of making everyone around him feel intelligent and capable. He doesn't field a question without complimenting the intelligence of the person asking it.

Kinder put these qualities to good use back in Cambridge, where his knowledge of planning, his literary and philosophical allusions, all played well in that cloistered community. He started giving seminars that interwove the financial side of life with the spiritual side, first to groups in Boston, then around the country. He began to spend more time in Hawaii, where he now owns a home and lives half the year. It was on one such sojourn in 1993, he tells me, that life handed him the plan. He was on Maui, living in a modest beach cottage. One day his girlfriend at the time reached down and picked something out of a wastebasket, a brochure promoting the upcoming Personal Economic Summit in Washington, D.C. Bob Dole was going to be there, along with a number of congressional heavyweights and leading national economists.

"You should be speaking at this," his girlfriend told him.

"Who am I, compared to those guys?" Kinder answered.

"Well, if you don't try to get a spot on one of the panels, I'll do it for you."

So Kinder talked himself onto a panel discussion. He delivered a presentation on savings and the value of compounding interest laced with Kinderian insights drawn from literature and philosophy. The reaction to it, he says, was electrifying. The organizer of the event came over and raved that his presentation was great, "out of the box." Kinder remembers the event with relish. The comment made his day, his year, and ultimately his career.

Fate was doubly generous to Kinder on that occasion. The meeting's sponsor was an organization then known as the Institute for Certified Financial Planners. Its president, Dick Wagner, was a financial planner from Denver who was a mover and shaker in this evolving field. He believed that planning could be more than just a "tax-shelter delivery system," as it was, deservedly, called at the time. Wagner believed planners had to develop a professional code, act with integrity, and impart technically astute counsel, not just push products on people. To Wagner, the Personal Economic Summit was an important milestone for the planning profession that brought to the national stage the idea that a person's lack of financial literacy can be a source of anxiety and fear, and demonstrated how planners might align themselves more closely with their clients' needs, financial *and* emotional.

Kinder says he had to screw up his courage to walk over to introduce himself to Wagner. He asked Wagner if he was familiar with Jacob Needleman's book. Half joking, Wagner put his finger to his lips and leaned in close to Kinder's face. "Shhh, not here," he whispered. The two of them retreated to a quiet corner and had a good long yak about it. Out of this exchange eventually came the Nazrudin Project and the branch of financial planning that finds clues to happiness not just in our wallets but more fundamentally in our brains and gallbladders.

MANO A MANO

The term "life planning" can be off-putting even to some who fervently believe in its tenets. Dick Wagner thinks "life planning" is an unfortunate term, open to distortion and exploitation. George Kinder is an un-

abashed, unapologetic champion of both the term and the practice. He
believes life planning will one day *be* financial planning. Both men
know how to dazzle a crowd when they get together to debate life planning's use and abuse. A favorite Wagner shtick is to open a talk by rip-
ping a twenty-dollar bill in half, letting the pieces flutter to the floor.
This usually brings a gasp from the audience. His point is that money is
only a piece of paper. Why then is it so shocking to see a twenty treated
with no more respect than a grocery list? More comfortable asking big
questions than providing glib answers, Wagner is careful with his
choice of words, mindful of how any important idea in our society runs
the risk of being marketed or otherwise exploited into total uselessness.
He's a builder, an organizer, an integrator, and it was these qualities,
back when he presided over the Financial Planning Association, that
enabled him to persuade his industry that it needed to develop a meaningful professional code. Today he's still in full, holistic build mode,
even though he takes time off to meditate and walk in the woods, practices he says he owes to Kinder and his workshops.

Kinder is a builder, too, but of a different kind. He builds ideas and
brands them. His principal brand is now the Kinder Institute, which
grew out of Nazrudin and through which Kinder believes the life-
planning movement will come to flower.

When Kinder and Wagner face off in public, as they did in 2004 at
a financial planning conference, they're like two guys enclosed in a
handball court, players who have been competing for years, admiringly
for the most part, and who know each other's moves all too well. They
are obviously fond of each other, but competitive, too, with completely
different playing styles. Kinder moves with finesse; Wagner is more
stolid. If Kinder tries to get away with an idea Wagner deems too subtle
or cute, Wagner is apt to hammer it hard.

Kinder asserts that a traditional financial plan is fundamentally hollow if it's not wrapped around a life plan. He believes that life planning
is the industry standard waiting to happen. Give it ten years, no more.
Wagner doesn't buy the easy rhetoric. He parries by noting that the fi-

nancial planning business models are still in flux and, while the idea behind life planning is sound, "we're still at a baby stage." He says that to
encourage a relatively untrained financial planner to move on to emotional turf could be granting "a license to kill." He stresses how vulnerable people are. "Where's the accountability?" he asks. Kinder doesn't
disagree with any of this but believes that empathy, compassion, and
emotional support are teachable and nonthreatening.

At the core of the debate lies the question of whether Kinder and
others are attempting to play in the sandbox where psychotherapists
keep their pails and shovels. Kinder hears this all the time and is un-
fazed. "Therapy," he says, "involves going back, looking at childhood,
and trying to resolve inner issues. Life planning is about the most efficient way to deliver a financial plan. We require some of the same skills,
notably the ability to listen. It's our job to help a person find out whether
he wants to play the guitar like Eric Clapton or write the great American
novel while living in Belize. Then it's up to us to try and develop a financial plan to make it happen."

Wagner demurs. Life planning is to therapy as snorkeling is to scuba
diving, he says. "In scuba diving you have to go deep. You need training
in how to work the equipment. You need to know what's difficult and
dangerous about it. When you snorkel, you still get wet, you still get to
see fish, but generally speaking you're within a safety zone. Like
snorkelers, life planners must know when they're venturing out of the
safety zone into depths they're just not ready for."

STAGING GROUNDS

Eight years after Needleman's book came out, George Kinder published his own, *The Seven Stages of Money Maturity*. Like its inspiration,
Kinder's draws on the history of religion, philosophy, and literature in an
effort to give money its due as one of life's profound forces. It's full of
case studies based on his years as a planner in Cambridge.

For example: A female M.D. comes to see Kinder and tells him straightaway, "I want a million dollars. That's what I'm after." (This was a few years ago—her Number might be higher now.) Prodding, Kinder learns that even though the woman says she is intently focused on making that much money, her career choices belie the goal. She hasn't set herself up in a lucrative private practice; instead, she works for far less at an inner-city health clinic. Why is that? Kinder asks. She tells him it is because she didn't put up with the rigors of medical school just to cure rich people's acne. Like our principled crash dummy Harriet Case, this woman wants to use medicine to make a difference. After another round of prodding, Kinder learns that she recently ended a relationship with a wealthy man who lived in a grand house and who had convinced her that it took a million bucks to raise a child. Kinder probes some more. The woman eventually admits that she desperately wants a child, which is the sole reason she wants the million dollars so much. Even though her relationship is in the past, it's clear to Kinder, and eventually to her, that it left her with financial values that are now calling her career choice into question. After they talk things over, she comes to see that her ex-lover was wrong: you really don't need a million dollars to raise a child lovingly or well. In fact, she comes to see that there's even a way to continue her work at the clinic *and* seek the right relationship *and* plan to have a child—all for a whole lot less money than she thought she needed.

A conventional financial planner might have simply told her, Yeah, kids are damned expensive, and it's always one thing or another, yada yada. Or he might have encouraged her to take unreasonable investment risks as she reaches for that million-dollar goal. Kinder's life planning is about the opposite: stay true to your values and figure out a way to make what matters happen. That's money maturity, or in simplest terms, "gaining ease with dollars and cents."

Sounds simple, but it isn't. Money—the Number—messes with your head and heart. Money—the Number—makes you stay in a job, live in a place you really don't like. Money—the Number—makes trouble between you and your spouse. Doors slam. The silent treatment.

Money—the Number—makes you shortchange how you'd really like to spend your time. You want to listen to Bach or Bob Marley, you want to write or paint, you want to play catch with your kids, you want to devote more time to a school or a church. Instead, you're a hamster and life's a cheap tin treadmill. Money—the Number—makes you feel stupid. Where should I put it? When should I buy? When should I sell? Money—the Number—makes you feel empty. You're rich, the Number's secure. You live, travel, eat, and tee off at the best. You'd think all this would make you happy, but it doesn't. Maybe the reason is hidden away in a squishy organ somewhere in your body. Maybe the organ could use a bit of probing, a surgical skill taught in that Kinder workshop where John Nelson found his answer in a little glass jar.

Enough said. I'm on my way, determined to make a connection with my inner billfold.

16

DEEP BREATHING

Entering the Denver hotel where Kinder's workshop is scheduled to take place, I spot a red, white, and blue banner above the lobby bar that reads "Welcome Hump Pilots." My psyche hasn't been poked yet and already I'm confused. Then I realize that hump pilots are not financial planners trained to get us over life's money-related emotional humps. Back in the early 1940s hump pilots were flyboys who undertook critical supply missions across the treacherous Himalayan "hump" between India and China. In their lumbering C-47 transports, hump pilots were sitting-duck targets for Japanese gunners. Their planes were famously unarmed and ill equipped, lacking even basic radio gear. The hump pilots' derring-do was the stuff of legend in what aviation buffs say was the world's first major airlift.

Standing in the lobby for a moment, I'm pleased to see that a good number of the old humpers are still among us, scuttling stiffly across the lobby toward the continental breakfast table. Tom Brokaw material, they are frail yet spirited men in their eighties and nineties, shining examples of the Greatest Generation the world has known. For the last few decades they've been dependent on pensions, Medicare, and Social Security to meet their retirement needs. Talk about a hump. Getting by on government benefits, and maybe a pension that hasn't kept pace with the cost of living, is a hump of a challenge.

In a windowless room in the subbasement of the hotel, ninety or so financial planners are milling about. Looking young enough to be the children and grandchildren of the hump pilots, these baby boomers are members of the Greatest *Spending* Generation the world has known. Men outnumber women in the room by ten to one, most of them dressed in polo shirts and khakis, standard-issue business casual for guys prepared to hunker down and devote long hours to a tight agenda. Unlike the wartime hump pilots, these financial planners are well fortified for the mission at hand, with bottled water, hard candy, pens, notebooks, and a prodigious supply of business cards. Hundreds of these cards will be exchanged amid much friendly chatter during the workshop's coffee and potty breaks.

Within moments of entering the windowless room I meet Steven S. Shagrin, or Shags, as he likes to be called. (Hump pilots? Shags? Who's next? Dr. Evil?) Shags is an especially friendly planner who's been on the lookout for me thanks to an e-mail from John Nelson, whose father's extracted organ got me into this in the first place. Shags' planning practice is in Youngstown, Ohio, not exactly a top-tier market. But Shags plugs away there, he says, forging a new personal path. As is true of many planners in the room, he's retooling his career. Even though he has a law degree, he spent over twenty years pushing investments at a couple of the big wirehouses. Like Scott Dauenhauer, who blew the whistle on the wirehouses, he grew uncomfortable in a world of panting commission lust, and like Dauenhauer he gave up career security in the hope he could make a positive difference in clients' lives. Dauenhauer became an independent planner of the old school, not a poker and prober. A veteran of a Nazrudin conclave or two, Shags gravitated toward the newer life-planning branch of the business.

Shags is short and balding, and so eerily resembles Jason Alexander you would swear that it was George Costanza who was working up your life plan. Perhaps because he is trying to gain traction in this new career phase, or just because he genuinely likes people, Shags savors the non-stop schmoozing that happens at workshops and professional conferences. He's aware that I'm writing a book, and I get the distinct impression he wouldn't mind a supporting role. Shags knows it's good to keep your name in circulation. He promptly hands me a business card, which, though a standard 3½ inches wide by 2 inches deep, is without question the most credential-intensive business card I have ever laid eyes on:

PLANNING FOR LIFE
Steven S. Shagrin, J.D., CFP®, CRPC®, CRC®, CELP
CERTIFIED FINANCIAL PLANNER™ Practitioner
Chartered Retirement Planning Counselor
Certified Enhanced Lifestyle Planner
Specializing in Life & Retirement Planning Concerns
Steven S. Shagrin Company, Inc.

With the intensity of a machine gunner at the Battle of the Hump, Shags rattles off his life-planning philosophy. The fusillade comes so fast I have trouble keeping up, but just as I'm getting my bearings he changes the subject and confides details about personal issues he and his family are battling. If Shags is any indication, a life planner's existence, compared to that of a traditional financial planner, is transparent. Shags says that things at home are improving, which I'm pleased to hear. Shags is a likeable guy, but as for inviting him to probe the inner folds of my psyche, that's another story.

Shags reaches into his bulging briefcase and pulls out a shrink-wrapped deck of what look like playing cards. In his rat-a-tat style, he says he uses them with many of his clients back in Ohio. Called Money Habitudes, the cards were created, Shags says, by a life planner named Syble Solomon to help people figure out how they relate temperamentally to various money matters: why they mainline debt, why they shop till they drop, why they fret about their financial wells running dry even though their holdings may be wide and deep. The Habitudes deck is designed to unmask just about every common financial affliction found in this cold, cruel, Number-ridden world. The premise is that money per se is not the issue. What plagues you are your so-called Habitudes about money (habits + attitudes = Habitudes, ya?). Habitudes are buried in your psyche and need to be dragged into the glare of understanding.

A Habitudes deck, Shags explains, is divided into six sections to help us focus on why we do what we shouldn't (or don't do what we should) when it comes to saving, spending, earning, giving, and investing. Each of the fifty-four cards carries a statement (sometimes a rather tortured one) that defines a given Habitude we may have sequestered deep within our spongy gray matter. The Status section of the deck contains the Habitude "I love getting a great reaction when I give an expensive gift more than I enjoy the actual shopping experience." Or, from the Spontaneous section, "I have money secrets that I keep from even the people closest to me because I am so unhappy about the way I spend money or the amount of debt I have."

Shags may sense that these cards are making me cranky. He doubtless thinks I'm a welter of Habitude hang-ups, and maybe he's right. He keeps trying different approaches, hoping to persuade me of the deck's power. One of the ways a person can gain financial self-knowledge, Shags tells me, is to play Habitudes solitaire. You pull a card from the deck and place it on one of three piles—a *"That's me!"* pile; a *"That's sometimes me!"* pile; and a *"That's not me!"* pile. You then count up the cards in each pile and, faster than you can say prestotude! you get an instant read on whether your money Habitudes gravitate toward the Selfless, the Free-Spirited, or whatever.

The game strikes me as ridiculous. I am under no illusion that I will one night mix myself a martini, put on some Thelonious Monk, and settle in for an intense evening of Habitudes solitaire. I should come right out and tell Shags what I really think: "Shags, this particular pathway to financial enlightenment is, well, it's *just not me.*"

• • •

The Habitudes cards safely nestled back in his briefcase, Shags and I sit side by side at one end of a horseshoe composed of ninety-odd financial planners. It is a couple of hours into the session and I've more than once gotten the impression that some of the planners are wondering what on earth they're doing in this Kinder workshop and whether this unusual experience was worth the price of a ticket. Other planners, though, are clearly getting into it. They're here because something told them there had to be a better way to practice their craft, that they were playing at financial planning with just half a deck. Maybe that's why so many of their clients don't save, don't stop spending, never take their advice: they're not getting through to them for some reason. The planners sense that the life-planning express has pulled into the station and they'd better get on it before it leaves without them. Still other planners grow restive because they want to know how to use life planning to double their billable hours. They want to get straight to alchemy: how do you turn people's fears and dreams into a thriving practice?

Kinder, the man in the middle of the horseshoe, gently waves away their impatience. What's happening here may not be clear yet, but it will be, he says. He asks everyone in the room to find a comfortable body position in which to remain motionless for several minutes. Obligingly, the planners settle into their chairs and the room falls silent. No clacking of keys on calculators, no shuffling of hard-copy presentations. Even the peripatetic Shags has managed to immobilize himself. Eyes gently closed, lips slightly parted, the planners sit ramrod straight in their seats. No one so much as crosses a leg; every last foot in the room rests flat on the hotel carpet.

The financial planners are learning how to breathe. It's an exercise right out of Meditation 101, although it isn't used here as any kind of prelude to mudra or mantra—not explicitly, anyway. In a slow, calming cadence Kinder tells the planners, "Relax your feet . . . now your legs . . . feel how your body touches the chair . . . feel your chest open wide . . . now relax your shoulders, that's where we hold so much of our tension." He says softly, "You want to let your thoughts go, and let your feelings be."

Let your thoughts go, your feelings be.

Kinder says it over and over again. I confess, I'm cheating. Yes, I'm sitting ramrod straight, feet resting flat on the carpet, but my eyes are not entirely gently closed. I'm squinting around the room, sneaky as hell. What I spy is very odd: normal-looking financial planners, not exactly pocket-protector types but close, from Kansas, Utah, Missouri, Ohio, and all points heartland, sitting straight in their folding metal chairs, learning how to breathe. Their clients never see them like this, ever. Their clients see them as certified number geeks who spend days, nights, weekends poring over the fine print of defined-contribution retirement programs and 529 college-savings plans. They see them as people for whom "sunset" invokes not peace or tranquility but a provision relating to the expiration of the federal estate tax law. Market goes up, they see them as heroes; market drops, they see them as dolts. I begin to understand how stressful the life of a financial planner must be. Their counsel can make or break a Number. Their clients are pursued by everybody and his sister: Charles Schwab, Raymond James, A. G. Edwards, and Muriel Siebert. So maybe it's good they're finally getting the chance to relax. Maybe it's good they're learning how to breathe.

According to Kinder, the breathing exercise has one important payoff: it teaches the planners how to listen better. To listen better to you, the client. To listen better so they can really hear your hangups about money, about what lies smoldering under your concerns about the Number. But breathing, listening, these are difficult skills to master, says Kinder. You have to practice deep breathing every day, for at least a few minutes. Better still, a half hour. Best of all, ninety minutes, as he himself does. But be warned, he notes: a conscious thought will always try to barge in when you're sitting with a client, even if your breathing skills get pretty good. Also, you'll be tempted to do all the talking. You'll be too quick to decide what someone needs. You'll be tempted to sell them something. When these kinds of thoughts muscle their way in,

Kinder tells the now rapturous planners, it's critical that you learn to swat them gently away so that you can better hear what the client really truly wants.

Kinder believes that a good financial planner should be a torch-bearer. Sounds pretentious, but he sincerely believes that a good financial planner needs to know how to light a client's way through career ennui, marital static, health scares, and the assorted other blahs that visit a life. The life planner's job, he maintains, is to help his or her client make it through the seven stages that end in gaining the assets you need—the Number—to achieve the life you really want. Some of these stages are emotionally difficult to work through. Kinder calls them Innocence, Pain, Knowledge, Understanding, Vigor, Vision, and Aloha.

FROM OZ TO OAHU

The seven stages are not strictly sequential; you don't necessarily graduate from one stage to the next. You don't feel money pain until one day you get money knowledge, and then the pain goes away. Kinder's stages leading up to full money maturity are additive. They mix and mingle. There's an analogy to *The Wizard of Oz,* says Kinder. The Tin Woodman needs a heart (Understanding); the Scarecrow needs a brain (Knowledge); the Cowardly Lion needs courage (Vigor). So they all fall in together and join Dorothy and Toto on the road to Oz—or, in this case, Vision and Aloha. This all sounds more confusing than it is. Shags and I and the others move through the stages without a hitch.

Stage one: Innocence. Stop for a moment and think about your earliest money memories. Which platitudes got passed around at the dinner table? What was said about the importance of work? About how it was just as easy to marry a rich guy/girl as it was a poor one? About all the children who were starving in China? In the innocence stage, Kinder says, values about money attach themselves to our psyches like ticks to a hound and influence how we relate to money later on. To drive home the point, he asks the planners to volunteer some early memories. The group responds with a few predictable ones: Waste not, want not. Better to spend your money on the cheapest thing in a good store than the best thing in a cheap store (which I suspect doesn't hold anymore because now you can get some really cool things at Target—but that's another story). The innocence stage, Kinder says, is when we develop a belief system about money, albeit an incomplete and shallow one. It is certain to run into obstacles, contradictions, frustrations, and disappointments. Life happens. Shit happens. This brings on Pain, stage two on your way to money maturity.

Kinder asks the planners to return to their childhoods. What are some of the painful memories you have about money, Kinder asks, even ones that seem pathetic or funny to you now? What sort of response did they set off?

Here's how I answered that one, and it's about as pathetic as a painful memory can be. When I was seven or eight, I nicked a Tootsie Roll from the little grocery store around the corner—a five-finger discount as we called it in the neighborhood. It wasn't even one of those big Tootsie Rolls, the kind that sold for a nickel and were lightly scored so that you could break them into five equal-size chunks and share them with others (not that you ever wanted to). Nor was it one of those tiny, bite-size Tootsie Rolls people keep in a bowl and grab by the handful. The Tootsie Roll I stole was the middle-size one, about three and a half inches long, that cost a penny. My mother, preoccupied at the cash register, never saw me tuck it in my jeans. Back home, I was caught the second I pulled the prize out of my pocket. The pain came five minutes later, when my mother marched me back to the store and I handed the Tootsie Roll back over to the crotchety old grocer, who gave me a terrifying stern look. Not only did I lose the Tootsie Roll, I felt deeply ashamed and scared. I never lifted anything again. There, I've gotten it off my chest.

In the workshop, the planners offer up a litany of money-pain stories having to do with bailing out spendthrift relatives and personal bankruptcies that followed what were once promising professional dreams and blue-sky aspirations. Although some of the stories are deeply moving, Kinder isn't soliciting these confessions just for emotional value, he's trying to show how innocence and pain "get hooked together" in people's lives, not least when it comes to money. He tells the planners that they need to be open to nuance so they can hear the source of their clients' pain. He wants them to be able to sense when questions about money or anxieties over the Number are actually tied to things that might not have to do with money at all.

COMING OF AGE

Stage three is Knowledge. Here, Kinder observes, is where a person enters the realm of financial adulthood. Knowledge amounts to knowing, more or less, how saving and investing works. This doesn't mean that once you've acquired a bit of knowledge about money you're out of the woods—far from it. Knowledge is only the beginning of the beginning of a life plan. Here the planners are on terra firma: knowledge they've got, knowledge of bond ladders and dollar-cost averaging and all the rest. You may have some knowledge, too. If you don't, Kinder advises, you'd best find someone to help you acquire a bit of it. You don't need to know how to do your own taxes, or how to jawbone Fed policy at a cocktail party. You just need enough practical skill and awareness to know, as the song says, your right foot from your left, your hat from your glove, as far as personal finance is concerned.

The fourth stage: Understanding. Just because you may know how to ladder a bond portfolio doesn't mean you can now skip happily out of Number darkness into bright Number sunshine. At this point Kinder asks a couple of his assistants to come to the front of the room and take their places next to large pads mounted on easels. One of them is assigned to write down a list of words that describe how money can make us feel bad. The other writes down how we would feel if we liberated ourselves from feeling bad. The planners are invited to call out words, which the scribes dutifully record:

The Bad Pad	The Good Pad
Fear	Freedom
Guilt	Empowered
Anxiety	Relief
Jealousy	Resourceful
Shame	Pride
Panic	Happiness
Insecurity	Responsible
Hopelessness	Contentment
Trapped	Grateful
Confusion	Charitable

Through understanding, Kinder says, you can gradually move from the Bad Pad to the Good. This doesn't happen by epiphany; it's a process that occurs when you, and/or someone helping you, untangle the deeper knot of your money anxiety.

Stage five is Vigor, by which Kinder means the energy and commitment it takes to follow through on your financial goals once you've figured out what they are. His scribes resume their places by the easels. One lists commonly occurring obstacles, the other what it takes to overcome them:

The Bad Pad	The Good Pad
Too many choices	A workable timetable
Lifestyle entitlement	Physical energy/exercise
Debt	Elimination of dependency
Complacency	Support from others
Lack of encouragement	Clarity of purpose
Self-pity	Clear focus

Kinder tells an interesting story about how things can start to come together at this stage. He once had another client, also a doctor, only this time the doctor is male and makes a ton of money. His wife is a doctor, too, although she practices part-time. Their three daughters attend an expensive private high school. The family is extremely well off yet the doctor feels unfulfilled, a spiritual bagel. He says that what he wants most is to give up his practice and become a rabbi. (Kinder doesn't reveal what innocence or pain led to this particular desire, but one can only assume it was intense.) But the rabbi dream is unthinkable, the doctor says ruefully. The family would have to make major sacrifices. No more shopping? Fuhgeddaboutit. The doctor says it wouldn't be fair to put everyone through that. Kinder then asks him if he has discussed all this with his wife and daughters, and if not, why not? So the doctor goes home and the family has a heart-to-heart. It turns out that almost everyone is supportive. The doctor's wife says she'd be willing to increase her hours to bring in additional income. Two of the three daughters say they would be more than willing to transfer to a public school if it meant so much to their father. The third holds out. No way does she want to transfer out of the expensive private school.

Kinder and the doctor sit down and do a financial plan that shows that while an immediate career change isn't financially feasible, the family can certainly adjust its lifestyle over time, and in four or five years the doctor could leave his practice and enter a seminary. Would it be easy? No. But the family turns out to be vigorous enough to make it work.

ANDREW CARNEGIE MEETS ROBERTO CLEMENTE

Whenever I ask people what they're working so hard to achieve, they almost always answer in terms of beach houses and golf rounds and trips to wonderful places. Call these the level one aspirations. Level two aspirations, which fewer people express but you still hear a lot, have to do with unfulfilled passions: read the classics, open a bed-and-breakfast, grow grapes.

A third level comes up fairly often, but I get the sense it's shared by more people than let on. It has to do with what the doctor-turned-rabbi was looking for—giving something back, leaving a legacy, filling a void. Kinder's final two stages of money maturity have to do with this yearning, and here's where things might seem a little wispy.

Kinder maintains that a person doesn't fully reach money maturity until he or she attains what he calls Vision, the sixth stage, then Aloha, the seventh and last. The two are closely related. Vision, says Kinder, is a giveback to a community; Aloha is a giveback to another living person—regardless, he adds, of any financial difference that may exist between the two of you. Vision and Aloha are the two most profound reasons to live and work, Kinder contends. Indeed, it wouldn't surprise me if he were to say that Vision and Aloha were, metaphorically, the Number itself. To Kinder, Nelson Mandela is the exemplar of Vision. Andrew Carnegie and Roberto Clemente were also notable visionaries, no matter that they are two guys who have never before appeared in the same sentence. Each in his way left something important to his community and the planet.

You and I can be, should be, visionaries, too. What if, instead of taking a dollars-and-cents view of retirement—starting with beach houses, boat rides along the Alaska coastline, a flat in London—we looked at retirement through a giveback lens? What if we saw our retirement years as an opportunity to improve a neighborhood, a school, Mother Earth herself? Even in a tiny way, not just by sending money to worthy causes? To be a person of vision doesn't mean you can't also live on Baldy Island, play the great courses of Scotland, be the proprietor of a quaint inn on Penobscot Bay. What it means, says Kinder, is that you invest your effort in reclaiming a small park in a city that needs green space or, if you happen to be Harriet Case, open a medical clinic in Guatemala.

The final stage, Aloha, is a touch different. Aloha means one thing when you're lounging around your cabana at the Mauna Lani Bay Hotel and Bungalows, but something else in Kinder's lexicon. Kinder uses it the way the ancient Hawaiians used it: the passing of a blessing from one person to another, an act of kindness, generosity, or compassion. To achieve Aloha, you are not obliged to exchange your Harry Winston choker for a dendrobium lei. It can mean as little as a smile, a helping hand, an embrace.

Say you retire early, move to an incredibly beautiful house on a Kiawah Island marsh. You have the means, certainly the time, and most certainly the lust, to play golf every day at one of the resort's great courses. But you don't. You play golf only six days a week. On the seventh day you leave your clubs in the trunk of the Lexus and drive to Charleston, where instead of shopping on King Street and munching a salad at the Planters Inn, you go to a hospital or hospice. There you hold hands with a patient and listen quietly as she tells you details of a life she remembers, maybe her own, maybe a loved one's, maybe the life of a stranger who just crossed her path one day and vanished again. As she tells you that story, you notice how her eyes light up.

You have reached Aloha, the seventh and last stage of money maturity. You worked hard, planned right, and have it all: the beach house, the nice car, the titanium sticks, but best of all the blessing you passed along when you took that woman's hand and gave her a chance to remember.

THE THREE BIG ONES

George Kinder's signature exercise is to ask three questions. He knows that some of the planners have answered these questions in other training sessions or read about them in *Oprah* magazine. No matter—he would like them to answer them again here. Kinder claims that he asks himself the three big questions several times a year, as a way of staying focused on priorities. He instructs his audience to take out a piece of paper and write their answers down, not just think about them. Take out a piece of paper yourself right now. Pretend you're sitting in the horseshoe along with my man Shags and me and the others.

Kinder introduces question number one: "It's a fun question. Assume that you've got all the money you need—enough for the rest of your life. Maybe you're not as rich as Warren Buffett, but you never have to worry about money for any reason. The question is, what would you do with it? How would you live? Feel free to let your imagination roam. What would you do with it all? Think for a moment, then write down the answer." The planners sit tapping their pencils, staring into the middle distance. Then the room fills with the sound of scribbling.

Kinder moves on to the second question. "You go to the doctor. The doctor discovers you have a rare illness. He says that you're going to feel perfectly fine for the rest of your life. But, he says, the illness will prove fatal. The sorry outcome will occur sometime within five and ten years. It will be sudden. The question is, now that you know that your life will be over in five years, how would you live it? What would you do?" More scribbling.

Kinder goes to the third big question. "I really want your attention on this one," he says, "because it will sound a bit like the previous question, but it's different. It starts the same way. You go to the doctor. You're feeling perfectly healthy. And again the doctor says you have a serious illness. But then the doctor says, 'You only have twenty-four hours to live.' What I want to know is, *what did you miss?* Who did you not get to be? What did you not get to do?" Silence in the room.

When the scribbling comes to an end, Kinder asks if any of the planners would share their answers with the group. One woman says that there is very little difference in the answers she gave to questions one and two, that what she would do with unlimited time was pretty much what she would do if she had only five to ten years. After he compliments her on how articulate her comment was, Kinder says that a great many people reach the same conclusion.

A man in the back of the room mentions that he is struck, and rather dispirited, by how little he's doing on behalf of the goals on his list. Kinder replies that a good planner, a good life planner, would make that comment the focus of future sessions with a client—how could they make some of those things on that list happen, and by when?

Kinder has been asking these questions for years and he says there's a consistent pattern to the answers. The first two questions, he says, produce much longer lists than the third and concern material wants. The third, he says, is almost always about something qualitative. And it's here, Kinder says, in the answer to question three, that he zeroes in on what the Number is really for.

17

BOTTOM LINES

Kinder's three big questions and all the other exercises at his life-planning sessions are designed to convince us that money can be used as a mask. Take my own decision to move to Wisconsin and work at Lands' End. Did I really move my family halfway across the country, to an entirely foreign place, because of real estate and college costs and the possibility of a dreaded disease twenty years hence? Or were those just handy, who-could-argue-with-them excuses, elements of a cover story that sounded fairly convincing at the time? What if my little experiment with manifest destiny had less to do with laying claim to more property, with striking gold, and far more to do with expanding boundaries in a variety of directions—financially, yes, but also professionally and creatively? What if I was just too damn frisky—even at my age—to be semi-retired, coasting listlessly in the New York suburbs, working just a couple of days a week? What if I was mostly looking for a hill to climb? Or just feeling bored and useless, mired in a slump? The answers we give to Kinder's questions, to questions like those above, are ours alone—which is why there can be no universal truths about the Number and why, like snowflakes and fingerprints, no two Numbers can ever be the same.

But even if there are no universal truths about the Number, there are some bottom lines. A bottom line doesn't reach as far or as wide as a universal truth; think of it as a universal truth you get on sale.

BOTTOM LINE 1
Obsess all you want, but don't be a sicko.

There are many people who don't go in for a lot of mushy talk about life's true purpose. They don't blab about what it *feels like* to experience the rush of a second adolescence. They are men and women for whom the soft core just doesn't count. To them, it's not the meaning, it's the money, stupid. The Number is not about heart's desires, tender touches, and gentle smiles. It's not about passing blessings to people who won't know you passed them till after you're dead. It's getting credit for the Number you amassed. If you want examples, take a walking tour of the New York University campus and observe how the buildings got their names. The Bronfman Center. The Kervorkian Center. The Lillian Vernon Center for International Affairs. Tisch Hall.

But just because somebody is into hard core, or isn't ashamed of being rich, that doesn't make him a bad person.

One evening I'm sitting with a hard-core Number man in his midforties. He's in the investment game, traffics in money all day. Unwilling to piss off any of his investors, he asks that I not identify him by name. Let's call him Deep Pockets. Deep Pockets has a huge Number. He won't tell me how much, he won't tell you, his wife doesn't know. The reason nobody knows is that he is very cool about money. He doesn't throw it around in obnoxious ways. A devoted husband and father, he provides a comfortable but not flashy life for his well-adjusted brood. But he thinks about the Number all the time. Deep Pockets knows what his Number is right down to the last several hundred thousand dollars. Earlier in his career he knew it right down to the last ten thousand. Sometimes late at night, alone in his home office, he'll switch on his computer and bring up a spreadsheet that shows exactly where his Number stands. Now and then, while he's doing this, his wife will wander into the room. Deep Pockets doesn't frantically attempt to get the spreadsheet off the screen, as he might if she caught him leering at the other kind of hard core. He knows that his wife is aware of what he's looking at on the screen, but he also knows that she isn't at all curious about the details. They have more than enough, and that's enough for her. They never really talk about what's on the screen, although sometimes he'll shake his head at the wonder of it all, turn to her, and say, "It's just amazing, isn't it?"

When pressed, Deep Pockets admits that the Number has been a preoccupation all his adult life, ever since he began making a halfway decent salary. In time he became something of an amateur Number anthropologist. Margaret Mead had Samoa; Deep Pockets has New York's East Side and the eastern end of Long Island. In this role he observes colleagues, relatives, friends as they pick their way through the Number's minefields. He knows who's worried and who's not, and by exactly how much.

One night I arrange to meet with Deep Pockets and ask him to provide a snapshot of how he thinks the Number works its will among the people he knows. He reaches for a piece of paper and pulls out a pen. It's back-of-the-envelope time. But before he writes anything down, he tells me there are some caveats to get out on the table. He's not going to talk about people on the low end. For people on the low end, the Number is obviously irrelevant. Not only that, it's "repulsive" even to talk about the Number in the context of those just trying to scrape by, even if it's their own lack of discipline that got them into trouble. He says he's not going to get into people on the high end, either. For them, the Number is also irrelevant. It isn't that people with $100 million don't think about the Number—they do, obviously—it's just that they already have everything imaginable, which makes them anthropologically uninteresting.

No, he's just going to talk about colleagues, relatives, and friends who have enough money to think hard about the Number but not so much that they can easily *stop* thinking about it.

Deep Pockets sketches out the following:

If you're here . . .	. . . then you need . . .	. . . which means a Number of . . .
"COMFORTABLE"—lives in one place, eats/travels modestly, though better than most, etc.	$50,000–$100,000	$1–$2 million
"COMFORTABLE+"—likes occasional upgrade, mid-priced country club, maybe small second home, etc.	$175,000–$250,000	$2–$5 million
"KIND OF RICH"—likes finer things, eats/drinks/travels well, gives $ away, picks up checks, couple of nice houses, etc.	$350,000–$500,000	$7–$10 million
"RICH"—spends week/months abroad, exclusive gated golf communities, place for every season, fractional jets, sits on boards, etc.	> $1,000,000	> $20 million

Then he puts his pen away, crumples and tosses the paper. No muss, no fuss. Life is no more complicated than this. When I ask Deep Pockets about meaning, satisfaction, legacy, the other soft-core fetishes, he gives me a look as if to say, Hey, what the hell do I know? I'm just a guy who got lucky, who made more money than I ever thought possible and didn't get all that screwed up by it.

And it's true. He's fun to be around, down-to-earth, one of the sanest people I know—mostly because I sense he's not harboring any secret questions.

BOTTOM LINE 2
Those who say that this is either (a) the Apocalypse or (b) the Golden Age are both wrong.

Most experts who look into our financial future can be classified as hawks or doves. The hawks screech that the future is terrifying, worse than you think. The doves see mostly blue skies ahead. The hawks tend to write op-ed pieces and give talks on C-Span taking the nation and its citizens to task. We're all spendthrift sinners hanging by a hair above the hellfires of personal and national bankruptcy. Hawks tend to be éminences grises who use their impressive credentials and distinguished platforms in academia or the corporate world to scare the pants off us. Big-time economist Laurence J. Kotlikoff writes of the coming "generational storm." Not content with five pissant risks that threaten the Number, Dr. Kotlikoff says it's far worse than that: there's a demographic, economic, financial inferno ahead. Crushing tax rates. A puny dollar. Political chaos. Because Kotlikoff's warnings are a tad shrill, he doesn't frighten so much as give you a case of the willies.

Not so when Pete Peterson lets fly. By day Peterson is chairman of the Blackstone Group, a white-shoe private investment firm, as well as chairman of the Council on Foreign Relations. By night, however, when he sits down at his computer, he just may be the single scariest human being on the streets of midtown Manhattan, our own answer to George Orwell, Arthur Koestler, Franz Kafka, and Alfred Hitchcock. And I say this admiringly. The man is damn good at this, Stephen King with an advanced degree in finance.

Want a book to keep you up at night? Try Peterson's *Running on Empty* or his earlier one, *Gray Dawn*. A confessed lifelong Republican, Peterson charges that the current tax-cut ideology is faith driven, not fact driven, and is sending us straight over the economic cliff. The Democrats? A pox on them and their policies (or lack of policies), too their grip on fiscal and Social Security reform is no better than the GOP's, just dysfunctional in a different way. Peterson's diabolical strength is a Janus-like ability to speak in one voice but through two heads. One head belongs to a man who sits atop the economic Establishment, with easy access to the Bushes, Clinton, Rubin, Greenspan, so you figure he's more than a garden-variety alarmist when he limns how badly you, and we, have mortgaged our futures. The other head belongs to someone who might be mistaken for Wilford Brimley, a kindly, folksy grandfather who is desperately, deeply, sorrowfully concerned about the frightening mess we're making for his nine beloved grand-children, and your children, and my children, and—if things don't get turned around soon—even us!

The doves, for their part, offer a simple rebuttal to high-octane gloom and doom. Chill. Surrender. Iris Krasnow has now written three popular books telling us to surrender to marriage, surrender to mother-hood, surrender to ourselves. She says it's time to "excavate your pas-sions" (nod to Jung), to surrender to your inner goodness. "Spirituality is everything, and materialism is nothing," she says. "I'm glad the '80s and '90s are over. I'm an old hippie and proud of it. We're seeing a renais-sance of people who are trying to build a better world. And we are see-ing the soul seeds of a movement."

The doves believe that the future will bloom if we just provide water and sunshine for those soul seeds. They say we are blessed to be living at a time of boundless human potential. Who's afraid of a little interest rate spike? Not Dr. Gene D. Cohen, presumably. He directs the Center on Aging, Health and Humanities at George Washington University, where he's also a professor of psychiatry. In *The Creative Age* Cohen celebrates the arrival of *your* personal creative age, midlife and beyond, and *our* creative age. Those ages are *now,* a time when Jungian impulses will start cranking out life satisfaction in 77 million middle-aged souls. The boomers aren't just self-absorbed phonies, Cohen believes, they have a deep capacity to be sincere, empathetic, and generous of spirit. They are, he says, "the first major population group to grow up with pos-itive images of aging." They will be good and honorable old people, find-ing creative expression in art, politics, recreation, and public-spirited community activism. Thus shall they triumph over any petty, material shortfalls.

So who will it be, the hawks or the doves? If you can't pick the win-ner, then cover your bet: let your feelings be, as George Kinder says, but don't quit your current job.

BOTTOM LINE 3
Living in a college town is no panacea.

When asked what kind of life they want, a good number of people answer neither financially nor emotionally but geographically, especially if
they live in or around big cities where the Number doesn't stretch very
far, where they're surrounded by homes and cars and beautiful things
they can't afford, and where they're always asking themselves where the
hell *do* all those idiots get their goddamn money? These people say
there's got to be a simpler, more affordable, more honest way to live, a
place where there's culture, access to teaching hospitals, plenty of bike
trails, organic food stores, and where the townsfolk don't chatter only
about face-lifts, prostates, and real estate. If they could, they say, they'd
volunteer for the Number's answer to the witness protection program:
they'd go live in a college town.

That's what a successful periodontist tells me one day, his eyes
ablaze even as he stares into my mouth: "You live in Madison! Wow! I
love college towns! I went to school in Bloomington. Incredible. Beautiful. If I thought I could have the kind of practice there that I have
here, I'd move to a college town in a minute!"

A middle-aged writer who works for a magazine: "Oooh, Madison,
I've never been there, but I can't tell you how much I'd love to live in a
college town like Madison. Foreign movies. Good clubs and bars. I
could have a house with some decent space finally, get a big dog finally,
do a lot of stuff outside. I could live like a *real person* finally!"

College towns are disproportionately represented in all those best-
places-to-live surveys. One of them calls college towns "the new but
not the final frontier" for living a great Rest of Your Life. Amherst.
Williamstown. Ithaca. Athens. Oxford. Chapel Hill. Ann Arbor. Ames.
Norman. Tempe. Boulder. Provo. Eugene. Bellingham. Chico. Santa
Cruz. Are they what the Number is for?

Well, not really. College towns have their place, but they're hardly a

substitute for a more comprehensive life plan with dollars and cents at-
tached. I know, because I live in a college town and like it a great deal.
I like its values: people are decent, polite, and tolerant of diversity.
And the traffic, while getting worse every day, is squat compared to the
Long Island Expressway, the Kennedy in from O'Hare, the 5, the 10,
the 405.

Yet most college towns, thanks to all those best-places-to-live surveys, are now at best badly kept secrets. Housing prices have soared,
property taxes rival those of big-city suburbs. The restaurants, well, let's
just say you won't starve, especially if your palate can be kept amused
by lots of pizza, falafel, and fish fry. The shopping, well, nearly every college town has a Banana Republic. So while it's understandable that
people dream about downshifting to a college town, a college town is
not the complete answer—unless, of course, there's a college in the
Seventh Arrondissement.

BOTTOM LINE 4
Good financial advice rings true.

In a time when you can't turn on TV or open a newspaper without
somebody shoving investment advice in your face, how do you turn
down the noise and watch Larry David in peace, knowing that someone
of solid judgment is awake to keep an eye on your Number?

The best financial advisers, I've found after a year of listening to
them, are thoughtful and pragmatic, don't take themselves too seriously, and are confident enough in their knowledge that they need not
hyperventilate when issuing advice.

This is going to sound like the start of a joke, but it's not. There are
these two money managers in Chicago, partners in a money management firm. One is in his seventies, the other is twenty years younger. At
the close of an interview, the junior partner hands me a copy of a letter
he has just sent to a wealthy client in Florida, a man with a zaftig Number by anyone's standards. Like any self-respecting rich person, the

client is inclined to pit investment managers against one another, whereas you and I will rely on one at most, and that would be Bernie.

Instead of loading up on advisers, Number shrimps like us have a tendency to load up on six, eight, a dozen mutual funds, thinking we're covering our bases, spreading the risk, just like the magazines tell us. But too much mutual fund diversity, like too many cooks in a rich man's financial kitchen, only overcomplicates things. Which brings us to the junior partner's letter, a model of what good advice sounds like. Substitute "funds" for "managers" and the letter applies to you as well as to the man who is wealthy enough to have someone else read it to him and peel his grapes at the same time:

Dear [Your Name Here]:

I wanted to take a moment to outline a few thoughts and ideas before our meeting Friday morning. Some of this may seem old and redundant, but I would like to present this in the context of your upcoming asset allocation decisions.

1. Overdiversification—This is the single biggest mistake made in managing assets. Once you get beyond three or four managers, you might as well index the whole pool of your assets. If you have more than one bond manager and two or three equity managers you are not really doing much to increase your return expectations or diversification.

2. Value investing works better. Almost all great long-term investors are value investors. Growth investing in the public market works for moments in time but typically does not produce investment results that hold up over longer time periods (i.e., ten years).

3. Don't be afraid of volatility. If you get your mix between stocks and bonds right, you can use volatility as an opportunity—especially if you are a net buyer of stocks. Your fixed income al-

location should meet your cash flow needs and spending plans for the next five years in *any* environment. So, knowing that your lifestyle needs are met, you can operate as a long-term investor if you have a comfort level in your manager's investment style. That way you don't need to be concerned with volatility in the equity market in any given quarter or year.

4. Fees can kill you. In any given year an extra 1% in fees is no problem, but when you get into allocation of large amounts of money to fund low volatility products, arbitrage strategies, and other "alternative" asset class vehicles, you will be spending 2–4% of your expected return of 8–10% every year in order to achieve the "Holy Grail" of low volatility.

5. If you don't believe in the fundamentals of any given investment, don't invest in it. The quickest way to get in trouble is to be seduced by past returns. When you hit the first significant bump, you'll pack up and get out—this is not a good prescription for long-term investment success.

6. Low turnover is key. Almost no one has made a lot of money engaging in high turnover strategies. It may work for a year or two but the ability to actively trade your way to wealth is all but impossible. When you incorporate the impact of short-term tax rates into the equation, the mountain you need to climb to achieve successful results gets a lot higher. I would be hard pressed to ever hire an investment adviser (or buy a mutual fund) with an annual turnover rate north of 50%. (I make this comment knowing that the average fund manager has turnover in excess of 85% a year, according to the latest studies.)

I look forward to seeing you at 10:00 on Friday morning.

Sincerely,

[The Junior Partner]

When the older partner learns that the younger partner has shown me the foregoing copy of his letter, the senior partner decides he wants to add his own two cents, so he sends me an e mail. It is based, he says slyly, on many more years of experience. The tone is markedly different. Taken together, the documents illustrate that effective financial advice can be delivered in earnest form or smart-assed form. What you don't want is the third form: bullshit.

Lee:

[My younger partner] sent you his rules of investing. Mine are much better:

1. Only buy stocks that will go up. The others are a waste of time.

2. Give your broker a lot of business. By trading in and out he will become your best friend.

3. Pay attention to Wall Street research. The people who produce it are intelligent, honest, and really care about you.

4. Read the papers daily and listen to TV financial reporting. Do exactly what they tell you.

5. Be nice to your barber—he'll always have the best stock tips.

> Wishing you the best,
> [The Senior Partner]

BOTTOM LINE 5
Those who know better don't always do better.

This bottom line picks up where the previous one leaves off. Ordinary investors are notoriously undereducated, which sounds mean-spirited but is true. One day I came across an interesting piece of evidence published a while back in the *Journal of Financial Planning* The author,

planner Robert Markman, notes that the number of people who regularly read the *Wall Street Journal, Barron's, Money, Smart Money,* and
Kiplinger's are but a tiny, single-digit percentage of those who maintain
active portfolios. All this information doesn't make them smarter, it just
tends to make them overactive. Markman says that the surveys show investors overall are growing dumber, not smarter, year to year, presumably because more people are getting into the stock market through
retirement plans at work. But I also think it has to do with people acting
on fleeting advice picked up day to day in the media. Just as too many
competing tips can ruin your golf swing, too much on-the-fly counsel
can muck up an investment strategy. Markman passes along results of
an employee survey conducted by Morningstar, which provides comprehensive research and analysis of a broad range of investments, notably mutual funds. There's no better repository for this kind of market
data: past performance, levels of risk, expense fees, manager qualifications—Morningstar knows it all. Well, it turns out that Morningstar's
employees, even though they are awash in analytic tools and research
reports, have been known to manage their 401(k)s about as maladroitly
as the rest of us, falling victim to the same dopey mistakes: haphazard
allocation among funds, failure to rebalance from time to time.

Yo, ever heard of a simple life-cycle fund?

BOTTOM LINE 6
Younger people always undercall the Number.

This bottom line is so widely accepted that it may actually be a universal truth. The observation comes up time and again in conversations
with seasoned financial advisers. There's a golf analogy for this one, too,
the dictum about gripping the club as lightly as if you were holding a
live bird (the Ozzy Osbourne tip). Thirty-year-olds hold the Number
this way, too, and it's a mistake. To hold a Number, you need to squeeze
hard, lest savings and spending get away from you and fly right out the
window.

Younger people need a *much* firmer hold on how to think about the Number. A financial planner in the college town where I live says that they undercall their Numbers because they don't fully understand the relationship between net worth (invested assets plus home equity) and the lifestyle to which they assume they're entitled. In particular, they don't understand that real estate isn't, at least in practice, fungible. If you sell your house but don't downsize to something considerably less grand, chances are you'll replace it at equal or greater cost. You don't exactly require postgraduate economic skills to realize the consequences of this: you haven't gotten yourself anywhere. Sometimes people buy and sell houses several times over before they realize they're still living in the same old financial neighborhood.

Remember the lawyer we met earlier, the one who's hedging his longevity risk by eating rashers of bacon? He confesses it took him quite a few years to accept his status as a classic undercaller. Ten years ago he was convinced that his Number was $4 million, tops—which he assumed would throw off about 10 percent per year until the bacon finally kicked in. Eventually he came to see that (a) there are always going to be stocks like Qualcomm, and bear markets in general, to throw off the plan; and (b) a house is a fungible asset commensurate only with your willingness to trade down. And don't get him started on boats, cars, and planes. Grown-up toys neither appreciate nor generate income and cost a king's ransom to maintain.

BOTTOM LINE 7
The innocent get eaten.

Too many people are afraid of hurting a financial adviser's feelings. People are far more decisive hiring and firing haircutters than screening someone with whom to entrust their Number. Often as not, an investment adviser is a person who just fell into your lap. Then you let him sit there for years, in spite of nagging doubts and sagging results.

Sometimes all it takes is a cold call, and suddenly you're playing

Santa to some grinning, acquisitive financial consultant who's plopped on top of you like a toothy kid at Christmas. A woman I know has a friend, single and in her fifties, who headed up a division at a big New York entertainment company. One day the phone rings. It's an investment adviser at a big financial services company, only he works in a branch that's halfway across the country. Go figure. How he got her name, why he thought she was a prospect, who knows? The man gives good cold call. Charming and intelligent, he assures the woman that he specializes in clients of her professional standing. He's coming to New York on business and wonders whether it might be useful to meet and discuss how he could be of help to her. Since he's nice and he sounds perceptive, she agrees, and the two hit it off. She transfers her accounts; he tells her to do this, that, or another thing with her portfolio, none of which matters one way or another. However, one potential transaction goes unexamined. It turns out she's seriously overweighted in her own company's stock. She has enough stock options, if she exercises them wisely, to keep her secure for the rest of her life, and the stock price is at an all-time high. But he tells her to *hold*, not sell, the shares. He tells her not to exercise the options. Within months the stock drops 70 percent. (It's still at that level more than a few years later.) Worse, she and her company part ways soon thereafter. She now works part-time, when she can get it, at a fraction of the income she had before. Her nest is devoid of all things ovoid.

What she should have done was ask a few questions. The National Association of Personal Financial Advisors has posted a long questionnaire on its Web site that you can download and ask a prospective adviser to fill out and return to you. His answers will give you a good idea of what you're getting into. Asking him to fill it out has the added value of letting him know you mean business. If this process strikes you as pushy or paranoid, at least pluck out the most important questions and ask those:

How long have you been at this game? Could I talk to some of your former clients? Could I see some professional references? Will it be you who calls me or your twelve-year-old financial-consultant-in-training? How are you compensated? Please explain in full, including any incentives and other payoffs that might fall into the, well, "cute" category. And are you willing to sign a copy of the Fiduciary Oath, swearing that you shall at all times act in good faith and in my best interests, disclose conflicts of interest that may compromise your impartiality, and that you won't take a hidden cut if I choose to buy products from you, as I just happen to have a copy of that Oath on me.

BOTTOM LINE 8
It pays to play tricks on yourself.

It ought to be clear by now that there are forces beyond a mortal's control that can mess up the Number. That said, people are also their own worst enemies. If common sense, wise counsel, protection of loved ones, and the natural law of self-preservation aren't enough to rein in excessive spending, induce people to save, and work out a sensible plan, what is? Have you tried messing with your own brain? Or paying someone to mess with it for you?

You'll recall that adviser Don Haas likes to work up financial plans that carry his clients a good several years longer than the most generous life expectancy table would call for. This is but one of the many tricks that you, or your certified financial practical joker, can play in the hope that it makes a positive difference to your management of the Number.

Here's another trick, courtesy of an otherwise sober, straight-as-an-arrow local planner from Wisconsin, a man who wouldn't lie to an ear of corn. He uses it when people explain that they're so concerned about outliving their money that they fail to use the Number in ways that could bring them satisfaction, or benefit family members or charities, or just keep it out of the hands of the tax man. What he does is ask people to estimate what they think they need for the rest of their lives, and then he doubles that amount. If he's wrong, what's left over can be given away or used to splurge on life's greatest luxuries (besides health): peace of mind and fun.

BOTTOM LINE 9
Tricks or no tricks, almost everybody suffers from reference anxiety.

Reference anxiety is a form of mental distress closely aligned with Debt Warp, its psychological cousin. Diagnostic details may be found in a book called *The Progress Paradox* by Gregg Easterbrook. Reference anxiety in its simplest iteration, Easterbrook says, is the compulsion to keep up with the Joneses. They have new carpeting, yours is seven years old, so you need new carpeting. But Easterbrook points out that reference anxiety is more insidious than this. Research suggests that it isn't just the Joneses who set the bar for our imagined needs; we feel a great deal of pressure just to keep up with ourselves. Call it spiraling lifestyle entitlement. George Kinder would say reference anxiety stems from all those earnest dinner-table conversations when your parents told you to study hard so you could go to a good college so you could make a lot of money so you'll never have to worry about money the way they did. Still, one thing leads to another, doesn't it? When is good, good enough? Once upon a time, even though vodka is vodka, Gilbey's was good enough. But it wasn't good enough after you tasted Smirnoff, which was not good enough after Stoli came along, which was not good enough compared to Absolut, which was not good enough after Ketel One, which was not good enough after Wyborowa, which happens to come in a Frank Gehry–designed bottle described by the distiller as a "unique crystalline and prismatic expression [that] emulates the artistry" of what's inside. Thus does reference anxiety make you tipsy—okay, sloppy drunk—and cause you to spend money on what you don't really need, a vicious circle that makes you wind up with a Number that doesn't keep up with the Joneses, who are sinking their tootsies into a plush new Karastan while you're still scrubbing away at the spots Fluffy left while still a pup.

Although he's not specifically focused on the Number, Easterbrook provides abundant evidence that explains why the Number is so torturous to your mental health. We exist in a world of paradox gone wild, and a world like this can really mess with your brain:

The I'm Poor No Matter What I Have Paradox: In an era of unprecedented affluence we labor under the conviction that we don't have enough money.

The I Never Have a Free Moment Paradox: We say we don't have enough free time, either, but in fact we have more free time now—five hours more a week than in 1960—than at any point in history, according to recent studies.

The I'm Happy but I Shouldn't Be Paradox: Not only do we suffer from reference anxiety, we're also afflicted with a massive case of what Gregg Easterbrook calls collapse anxiety. This means that even if you have a fat, juicy Number in hand you feel threatened by global economic and political crises, environmental disasters, and terrorist attacks that can wipe us out in a heartbeat.

The What's That Twinge? Paradox: This comes from living in a time of extraordinary advances in medical science. The past century, the past *week,* have produced amazing drugs and procedures to lengthen lives and relieve suffering. So what do we do? We worry about every ache and spend countless hours and dollars making sure that twinge is nothing serious. And, in a related development, our company's benefits department just announced that health insurance premiums are going up again, and by a healthy margin, next year.

And then there's the all-consuming Nobody Is Happy theory, which is not exactly a paradox, but closer to a universal truth. Easterbrook reports on the work of one of the best-known leaders in the what-makes-people-happy discipline, Edward Diener at the University of Illinois. Diener finds that "lacking money causes unhappiness, but having money does not cause happiness." And that "millionaires as a group are no more happy than people of average income."

But let's move on—time is money. Check that. Time is meaning, too.

BOTTOM LINE 10
Practicing "financial correctness" is a huge waste of energy *and* time.

The idea that the Number is an enduring taboo is often advanced as a way of underscoring how sensitive and private, how impure if not altogether perverted, is this abiding longing for great gobs of moolah. Jung said it in his way, as did Jacob Needleman twenty-five years ago. George Kinder mentions it frequently in his workshops. I said it, too, thinking it was a more or less original insight, when I first discussed the idea for this book.

That so many people regard money as the Last Taboo is testament to how the Number mauls an exposed nerve. Positing that a person needs millions and millions to feel whole is sure to generate indictments ranging from crimes against the spirit to first-degree, premeditated elitism. Some people say they're morally outraged at the suggestion that it takes millions of dollars just to scrape by in this uncertain, way-too-expensive world.

Either way, getting incensed over who has what strikes me as a waste of psychic energy and a waste of time. Better to invest this valuable energy, and use that time, to come to terms with who you are, or, if it better pleases you, to make more money. Others can write books on how to die rich or how to die broke. How to die laughing, that's up to you.

THE NUMBER,
QUICK AND DIRTY

A good part of this book tries to explain why there are no easy formulas to arrive at the Number. While online calculators and magazine worksheets are freely available, most conventional aids are deaf
and dumb to what it takes to lift your spirits and make your heart sing
through old age. A financial plan without a meaning plan leads straight
to the thudding realization that—duh—all the money in the world
doesn't buy happiness.

Still, everyone clamors for a Number, however quick and dirty. A
friend of mine, for example, is relentless. He says all he really wants to
do is walk into a bookstore, pick up a book like this, and riffle straight to
the single page, the chart, the graph, the formula, the elusive ark that
will reveal precisely, and for him alone, how much money he needs to
gain release from his temple of financial doom. So I tried, really tried, to
come up with a quick and dirty way to give him what he wants, a *deus ex
Number* with which to end this saga. I called several financial advisers
and asked if they could devise a simple worksheet, an easy-to-use formula. Not surprisingly, every one of them warned that the Number was
not something a thoughtful person should do on the fly, certainly not

while standing in a bookstore with a cappuccino in one hand. They reaffirmed the need for diligence and access to at least one critical (if low-tech) tool: a shoebox. Into the shoebox would go a year's worth of bills and receipts that would yield a precise tabulation of your annual expenses, including how much pocket change you fritter away day to day; all current brokerage and cash management statements; a comprehensive net-worth statement; documents relating to how you plan to dispose of your assets upon your death; all durable powers of attorney, health care proxies; a complete file of insurance policies, including life, health, long-term-care, and liability. Thus stuffed, the shoebox is then emptied onto the desk of a qualified financial planner, who'll crunch the numbers until they reconstitute themselves into a responsible, conscientious Number. This is about as quick and dirty as planners can imagine, and who's to argue?

Undaunted, I then went to the man who, I assumed, would be least likely of all to have any patience whatsoever for a quick and dirty solution to the Number: George Kinder, the life-planning shaman. Kinder believes that to find meaning you need to probe deeply into the soul and/or retain an empathetic adviser to help you explore your psyche before you can aspire to a custom-made financial plan. This kind of spiritual mining can be dirty, but it's certainly not quick. Kinder, however, being generous of spirit, nonetheless proffered some helpful thoughts if you're determined to bypass a lot of soul cleansing to get at a quick and dirty Number.

Kinder's suggestions begin with the magic 4 percent idea discussed in Chapter 10—i.e., it's safe to withdraw around 4 percent annually from a reasonably well diversified portfolio. If you think you need, say, $100,000 to live on, simple multiplication tells you that your Number should be $2.5 million. (Remember, this is a rough calculation; tax-advantaged investments, such as munis, might allow for a somewhat smaller nest egg.) If you need $1 million, then your Number is $25 million. Nothing could be quicker or dirtier. Kinder, however, advises that you take at least a few more steps to refine matters:

A. Total up your invested assets (assuming they're well diversified, i.e., a 60/40 stocks-to-bond ratio): _____

B. Multiply A by .04, which tells you how much annual investment income you might reasonably withdraw each year: _____

C. Add in the annual value of any home equity you have (to do this, divide your total equity by the number of years you expect to live. For example, if your age is sixty, and you have $400,000 in home equity, and expect to live to be one hundred, the annual value of your real estate would be $10,000): _____

D. Add any income you expect from any inheritance (again, total inheritance divided by the number of years you expect to live): _____

E. Add the amount of Social Security you assume you're entitled to per year (for help, visit www.ssa.gov): _____

F. Add any expected annual pension benefits: _____

G. Add any remaining income you expect, such as from part-time work or other sources: _____.

H. Total B through G, and you arrive at how much you can safely spend each year to get through the rest of your life: _____.

But here's the rub: by relying on the above formula—which is all about income—you're probably doing yourself "a huge disservice," says Kinder. You're simply trapping yourself in a never-ending cycle of acquisition and you haven't even taken a stab at figuring out what it would cost to do what you really want. To do *this* you need to focus not on income but on expenses. You need to multiply H by what I'll call the Satisfaction Factor. Say you dream about a time when you can meditate every morning, then devote a few hours to writing the great American novel, and the rest of the day to do volunteer work in the community. This life, or some variation of it, will generally require significantly less money than what you spend now, not to mention the fact that you won't have commuting-to-work costs; you'll need to buy fewer spiffy suits and dressy shoes; and you probably won't have to shell out on things like maintaining a boat or on mortgages you'll have either paid off or gotten rid of by jettisoning excess real estate that isn't integral to the dream. What is a reasonable Satisfaction Factor? Eighty percent of your current expenses? Seventy percent? Sixty percent? You make the call.

The moral here is obvious: An unexamined life may or may not be worth living—but it's almost always more costly than an examined one.

ACKNOWLEDGMENTS

O ffloading your financial secrets is not easy, especially to a person holding a pen to your head, one who's intent on passing those intimacies along to anyone who'll listen. From the start I knew I had to offer grants of anonymity to those who were inclined to speak out. To the men and women who trusted me with confidences—you know who you are—thank you. That said, I am under no such obligation to shield those who were kind enough to lead me to wary if pliable sources, particularly Lesley Alderman, who provided a pathway to a number of hesitant talkers, and Paul Kleyman, editor of *Aging Today*, who no doubt doesn't remember me, let alone how much valuable assistance he provided. At the beginning of this project, Kleyman replied to an unsolicited e-mail with a thoughtful missive that directed me to a dozen people and organizations who found their way into passages throughout the book.

The financial planning community yielded numerous benefactors, even though none received so much as a minor tax deduction for their generous donations. In particular, I'd like to thank Tim Christen and Fred Broihahn of Virchow Krause in Madison; and especially Don Haas of Southfield, Michigan, who spent a good number of hours helping me

sort out the financial complexities of the Case family, offering unvar-
nished wisdom that comes with a half century of experience. The folks
at Fidelity Investments provided valuable assistance vis-à-vis the Cases
and other topics. Scott Beyerl, who coordinated interviews with various
Fidelity executives, and Peter Herlihy paved the way.

Thanks also to David Heller and Brien O'Brien at Advisory Research, Inc., in Chicago. Each shared intelligence about the art and
science of managing money and delivered it with wit and wisdom.
Paulette Koch of the Corcoran Group in Palm Beach was likewise
pleasant and enlightening; she spent the better part of a day showing
me houses she knew I had no intention of buying.

Flashback thanks go to Gary Comer, Dick Anderson, and Dave
Dyer, then the big cheeses at Lands' End, for luring me to Wisconsin in
the first place. Were it not for this unexpected detour there would have
been no prologue, let alone a book. While I'm at it, I'd like to say thanks
again to all of the Lands' Enders—from phone operators to copywriters
and art directors—who welcomed us warmly and put up with far too
many unfunny cracks about our family's decision to move to Badger-
land. Madison and Dodgeville turned out to be great places to live and
work.

For their hospitality and good cheer during return visits to New
York, I'm grateful to Betsy Carter and Gary Hoenig, Lisa Grunwald and
Stephen Adler, Glen Waggoner and Sharon McIntosh, Bruce and Polly
McCall, and also to Becky Okrent and Nancy Alderman, whose other
halves will be justly praised in a moment. I am grateful to Dane
Sorensen in Madison, and D. J. Stout at Pentagram in Austin—both
gifted graphics designers—for their friendship and contributions. And
in Knoxville, Tom and Melissa McAdams were a charming source of
help and, as always, extraordinary hosts. Thanks, too, to Cesar and
Dorothy Stair, for making available their guest cottage, which was offered up as a research base but was so comfortable and well stocked it
felt more like a vacation retreat.

Soon after I began work on the book, Jack Haire and John Huey at

Time Inc. offered encouragement and support, and I am grateful to them for getting things off to a good start.

While I alone am responsible for any errors of fact or judgment, I want to thank the following for reviewing the manuscript: John Nelson, who showed up serendipitously, then helped me in a dozen different ways; Dan Okrent, whose uncanny ability to bring a dinner party to life is matched only by his ability to bring a draft of a manuscript to greater life through challenges that are in equal measure nettlesome and invaluable; Chris Jerome, who made sure all the *i*'s were dotted and provided a wealth of editorial insights; and John Alderman, who proved to be a faithful sounding board and a font of good ideas about where to take this story, all unfailingly delivered with encouragement and good humor.

Everyone at Free Press was terrific: Carolyn Reidy, Martha Levin, Carisa Hays, and everyone on their fine staffs. Nicole Kalian was tireless on the publicity front, as was Sandi Mendelson of Hilsinger-Mendelson East. And there aren't enough stellar adjectives to assign to my editor, Bruce Nichols, who was from beginning to end steadfast, perceptive, and a truly good guy. Bruce, thank you.

The spark behind this book was Jim Gaines, a great magazine editor, a wonderful writer, and an interesting man. It was a couple of years ago that we looked at each other and said, more or less in unison, maybe there was a story in the Number. Esther Newberg, my agent at ICM, took it from there. Other clients who reach this point in their own interminable list of appreciated assets routinely describe Esther as "incomparable." "Incomparable" is hardly too strong a word for this woman. She is funny, smart, clever, and yes, even nurturing in her own incomparably direct way.

And throughout it all there was Linda, who put up with more than the usual craziness this past year. For this and many other things I am eternally and lovingly Debt Warped.

INDEX

ABOUT THE AUTHOR

Lee Eisenberg is the former editor in chief of *Esquire*, where he served for nearly twenty years. Under his stewardship *Esquire* won National Magazine Awards in a number of writing and design categories. Most recently he was executive vice president and creative director at Lands' End, the global direct merchant. He has written numerous articles and books, including *Breaking Eighty: A Journey Through the Nine Fairways of Hell*. He divides his time between Madison, Wisconsin, and Chicago.